The Faces of Local Food

CELEBRATING THE PEOPLE WHO FEED US

by **Charlotte Caldwell**

foreword by **Bill McKibben**

Dedicated to those people worldwide,
who feed us local food.

And to my husband, Jeffrey,
who is the "wind beneath my wings."

ISBN: 978-1-59152-200-3

Published by Locally Sourced, LLC

Photography and text © 2018 by Charlotte Caldwell

Edited by Shannyn Smith

You may order extra copies of this book by calling Farcountry Press toll free at (800) 821-3874.

sweetgrassbooks
an imprint of Farcountry Press
Produced by Sweetgrass Books.
PO Box 5630, Helena, MT 59604; (800) 821-3874; www.sweetgrassbooks.com.

The views expressed by the author/publisher in this book do not necessarily represent the views of, nor should be attributed to, Sweetgrass Books. Sweetgrass Books is not responsible for the content of the author/publisher's work.

Library of Congress Cataloging-in-Publication Data

Names: Caldwell, Charlotte, 1951- editor.
Title: The faces of local food : celebrating the people who feed us /
   [edited] by Charlotte Caldwell ; foreword by Bill McKibben.
Description: Helena, MT : Barn Board Press, [2018] | Includes
bibliographical
   references and index.
Identifiers: LCCN 2017039557 | ISBN 9781591522003 (pbk. : alk. paper)
Subjects: LCSH: Farmers--South Carolina--Interviews. |
Restaurateurs--South
   Carolina--Interviews. | Food industry and trade--South
   Carolina--Interviews. | Local foods--South Carolina.
Classification: LCC S415 .F25 2018 | DDC 630.92/2757--dc23
LC record available at https://lccn.loc.gov/2017039557

Produced and printed in the United States of America.

22   21   20   19   18   1   2   3   4   5

Table of Contents

Foreword
by Bill McKibben

It is fairly easy, at this moment in time, to grow dark and despondent. In a country divided, on a planet heating fast, there's seemingly less to pin one's hopes on. My, we're even thinking about nuclear wars again, which we haven't really done for decades.

And so it is a particular pleasure to be able to pick up a volume that undoes some of those divisions, turns down some of that heat, offers us a peaceful path forward. All of that may be too much to hang on local food—but food is the most important thing in the world. If we get it right, we'll get much else right as well.

And these are the powerful stories of the people who've gotten it right—who've done the hard work to grow, distribute, cook, preserve the bounty that this good and fertile land provides. I remember, not long ago, when there weren't so many of them: I taught what may have been the first modern course on local food production at any college in America, in 2000. We had no textbooks to turn to (only, of course, the writings of Wendell Berry), so instead we sought out the small band of farmers who were helping make Vermont a vanguard of this revolution. They were remarkable people and so many (including a few from that class) have followed in their wake. For the last fifteen years farmers markets have been the fastest growing part of our food economy. There is now—and to me, this is a seriously hopeful fact—hardly a town on this continent where you can't buy a delicious bottle of beer produced somewhere nearby.

There are a million good reasons to love local food: what it does to soil and pollinators, what it means for local economies and carbon footprints. But the best news of all is what it means about dinner. This book is deservedly a celebration!

BILL MCKIBBEN
SCHUMANN DISTINGUISHED SCHOLAR
MIDDLEBURY COLLEGE

Why Eat Local?

The Faces of Local Food champions farmers, fishermen, foragers, distributors, chefs, retailers, and consumers. Each plays an important role in creating a robust local food system. Through portraits and narratives, their stories reveal their history, perceptions, experiences, challenges, and insights. It is my intention and great hope that *The Faces of Local Food* will be a catalyst for a paradigm shift in the way we understand and value our food producers; it will encourage the creation of the local infrastructure necessary to successfully move food from family farms to our plates—effective crop planning, marketing, and distribution services; and it will inspire us to purchase locally sourced foods and support our local farmers.

The forgotten farmer next door

Most of the food we eat travels an average of 1,500 miles from its origin to our plates.[1] Accompanying these foods are the external costs associated with transporting them that distance—fossil fuel, carbon dioxide emissions, food safety, and the depletion of nutrients. But why do we purchase milk, eggs, grains, vegetables, fruits, meats, and seafood from across the country and around the world when we could be purchasing these items from local producers? The simple answers are price, convenience, and our desire to eat fruits and vegetables that are out of season.

After World War II, with the creation of the interstate transportation system and the industrialization of our food system, a cheap food mentality was created—one that displaced small family farmers. It is cheaper for dairy plants in South Carolina to import milk from across the country than pay local farmers like **Patrick Myers** to produce it. Large dairies and farms, because of their economies of scale, experience a significant cost advantage with regard to land, labor, and inputs. As a result, national and international agribusinesses are able to sell foods sourced from thousands of miles away for less than you and I can purchase them from the farmer or fisherman next door.

Chef Frank Lee observes that we Americans have come to expect and feel entitled to cheap food, partially because government subsidies have created an unequal playing field within which small farmers must compete. Local food is not cheap to produce, and local producers are pushed aside in favor of cheap subsidized food.

The price of local food is impacted by other factors. **Elliott Shuler** suggests that consumers pay close attention to their foods' country of origin. Farm laborers outside the United States may be getting paid less than a tenth of what Elliott pays his laborers, providing another reason why imported foods are cheap. Cheap food often means cheap labor.

Excessive regulations—federal, state, and local—impact the cost of local food. **Campbell Coxe, Jeff Massey,** and **Urbie West,** along with others, speak of the regulations that were originally created to control agribusiness practices. Many of these regulations now apply to small farmers. Being forced to compete on the same regulations playing field as agribusinesses is inequitable, and compliance comes with a significant cost in time, effort, and resources. Campbell, Jeff, and Urbie question who is lobbying for support for small local producers in the state capitals and Washington, D.C. And if small local producers are regulated out of business, then who benefits—rice producers from India and Asia? Shrimpers from China? Tomato growers in Mexico? And what kind of food safety and fair labor regulations do those foreign governments put on their food producers? Cheap food is cheap for a reason!

An investment of time and resources

Why do meats raised by local farmers cost more? **Marc and Annie Filion** raise their chickens and livestock humanely and without using antibiotics, steroids, or growth hormones. Because of the way they raise their animals, sixty percent more grow-out time is needed to produce their meat compared to a factory farm. Time is money, and Marc and Annie invest significantly more time, labor, and resources in each animal. When Marc breaks down his costs per bird, it becomes clear that he can't compete with

agribusiness giants using antibiotics, steroids, and growth hormones. If local farming is to be sustainable, he says the community must be dedicated to buying locally. Consumers need to look beyond the dollar cost of food and seek to understand the true costs behind the production of local food. Again, cheap food is cheap for a reason!

Farmland is a precious resource; nevertheless our fertile and productive farmland is rapidly being bulldozed away. According to The American Farmland Trust, whose motto is *No Farms No Food*®, we lose almost forty acres of farmland each day, and once it is gone, it is gone forever. Throughout these stories, one hears of the pressures to convert farmland into condos and shopping centers. But when consumers make a solid commitment to purchase local food, then farmers become financially more secure, public awareness and public support for local farms builds, the farming culture and rural communities strengthen, and farmers are less likely to sell their land to developers. Key to achieving this—growing food must be financially sustainable to the producer!

Accessibility and convenience

In 2011, according to South Carolina's Bureau of Labor Statistics, South Carolina residents purchased $11 billion of food, with over ninety percent sourced from outside the state. (Each state's Bureau of Labor Statistics can provide this information.) We consumers have the opportunity and power to change that imbalance. By purchasing locally grown food, we keep our dollars within our local community where they are invested and put to work. For every $100 spent locally, an average of $45 is reinvested in the local community, an amount three times greater than non-local item purchases.[2] Household consumers **Kate and Lindsay Nevin** state that "buying locally is a vote for sustainability and a vote for our community. It's more than just a purchase; it's an investment in this place and people, but especially in the future of our children."

Understanding which foods are in season and eating more seasonally will improve the success of local farmers. Transportation and refrigeration are ubiquitous, enabling anything we desire to eat to be shipped from halfway around the world, rendering regional growing seasons inconsequential. Many local foods—meats, milk, eggs, and grains—can be purchased year-round regardless of climate and season. **Chef Travis Grimes**, of world-renowned

Husk Restaurant, looks at the seasonal fruit and vegetable surpluses of local farmers as a way to build up his larder for the off-season. Travis' goal is to buy everything that a farmer has to sell, so he creates winter treasures by canning and pickling. Farmers like **Eric McClam and Brian Evans** are working to extend the local growing seasons by using greenhouses and other forms of controlled-environment agriculture. Their farms enable consumers to access fresh, local produce year-round.

According to the Harvard Medical School Center for Health and the Global Environment, food transported long distances does not maintain its nutritional value.[3] Locally harvested fruits and vegetables are more nutritious and taste much better. The flavor of a carrot pulled from the earth or a tomato picked from a vine is simply better, both nutritionally and in flavor, than a carrot or tomato that is harvested weeks before their natural ripeness and shipped over land and sea before ending up on our plates.

It is not always easy or convenient to find local food sources. Most grocery stores don't carry local eggs, milk, meats, and produce. Farmers markets, U-Picks, and farm stands are not necessarily held at convenient times or in convenient locations. However, as enlightened consumers, we must seek out local foods, get to know our farmers and strongly advocate that retail managers carry local foods. As retailers hear consumers' demand for local products, the supply and convenience will increase.

Making locally sourced foods more accessible is what **Sara Clow** does as general manager of GrowFood Carolina, a local food hub. She and her team work with local farmers throughout the state to market their products and distribute to local retailers, restaurants, and institutions. Paying the growers eighty percent of the sale price, GrowFood Carolina has helped boost farmer revenue and create a stronger rural economy by returning $2.8 million to local farmers in five short years—money that would have otherwise gone out of the state, and likely to agribusiness.

Patrick Kelly's venture, SILO (Sea Islands Local Outlet) provides an easy approach for household consumers to access and purchase local foods. SILO is an online food hub that provides sales opportunities for local food producers and gives household consumers access to a convenient online marketplace. Both SILO and GrowFood Carolina are models that can be replicated in other locations nationally.

Jamee Haley's story about Lowcountry Local First and its *Growing New Farmers* program sheds light on the astounding fact that, according to the

United States Department of Agriculture, nine out of ten farmers of small to medium-sized farms today are required to have off-farm jobs to sustain themselves. She tells about the national demographics of an aging population of farmers and the variety of ways Lowcountry Local First is providing skills to new farmers. Their *Growing New Farmers* program provides potential farmers with farming and business skills, tools, and support, and opens doors for creating relationships between local food producers and local chefs.

Institutional buyers—hospitals, corporate cafeterias, school systems, and universities—usually purchase from national distribution companies. **Ashlyn Spilis Hochschild and Abby Tennenbaum's** story tells how these two young women and their colleagues at the College of Charleston's Office of Sustainability, through vision and hard work, have fostered the relationship between the college's global food service corporation and GrowFood Carolina.

Does eating feel like an agricultural act?

American writer, environmental activist, and farmer Wendell Berry says, "Eating is an inescapable agricultural act."[4] Berry's statement begs the question: Does the average person, as they sit down to a meal, think about their connection to a farmer, to the dirt, and to the sweat and hard work required for producing the food on their plate? Maybe eating is an inescapable agricultural act, but it seems the connection frequently escapes our consciousness and stops abruptly in a grocery store.

The Faces of Local Food takes us out of the grocery store, as we step onto fishing boats and into fields to hear firsthand how the culture, techniques, regulations, and challenges have changed over the years. These vignettes lead the reader to develop an interest in knowing the person who milked **Casey Price's** goats, picked **David Anderson's** blueberries and **Pete Ambrose's** tomatoes, gathered **Brother John and Father Stan's** mushrooms, and cultivated **Frank Roberts'** oysters. The reader will become aware of their hard work, the time spent, and the love farmers have for producing nutritious food. Each story will inspire the reader to know and buy from their local farmers.

Kathee Dowis and Drew Harrison will

show how schools are introducing and connecting children to growing and eating healthy food in model programs that cultivate food, minds, and community. Through observation beehives, **Tami Enright** introduces students to honey bees, their behaviors, and the intrinsic value of all pollinators to our food system. **Germaine Jenkins** brings to light the reality of food insecurity and provides an understanding of what it is like to live in an urban food desert—miles away from any grocery store. She tells of the dream and vision to transform the vacant lot next door into a neighborhood farm and farm store and her willingness to share the blueprints of her success with others. And **Glenn Roberts,** an agricultural visionary, tells the story of heirloom seeds that were lost for generations being found, reproduced, and generously shared with regional farmers.

The Faces of Local Food also brings attention to innovations in food production. As the human population rapidly approaches nine billion, most of whom will live in or around urban areas, forward-thinking entrepreneurs like **Stefanie Swack-hamer and David Flynn** are converting forty-foot shipping containers into controlled-environment farms. With software, special lights, and very little space and water, these farms produce an annual equivalent to four acres of farmland.

We are what we eat

As Michael Pollan, author of *The Omnivore's Dilemma*, points out, we are more than the adage, "we are what we eat." We are also what we eat eats! So how did **Don and Susan Brant's** sweet tasting spinach grow? Did the nutrients and microorganisms in a healthy living soil feed the spinach or was the spinach fed petrochemicals while rooted in dead soil? Are **Del and Debra Ferguson's** spectacular tasting turkey, chicken, and eggs produced from birds that are free to wander around in the grass, scratching and pecking, or are they confined to a small, overcrowded pen and fed antibiotics to hasten their growth? Reasons to know your farmer!

How often do we cast aside an ear of corn because it is imperfect? Extension service scientist **Powell Smith** points out that consumers don't understand the impact they have when they reject food with minor levels of insect damage, discoloration, or slight imperfections. Those imperfections are not threatening from a food safety perspective, and it is actually safer to eat a food after a pest has been on it than after a chemical has been on it.

The farmers in this book cultivate healthy soils, use beneficial insects to control pests, and provide safe, healthy food. Nevertheless, many have chosen not to become organically certified because of the regulatory hassles. I came to realize that for me, it is far more important to know my farmer and fisherman and to put my dollars to work in the local community than to buy certified organic food grown and shipped from thousands of miles away. As a successful businessman entrepreneur and restaurateur, **Michael Shemtov** knows the farmers he buys from and visits their farms. Because he knows their growing practices, he has gotten over being overly concerned about whether or not they are organic in favor of procuring locally sourced foods.

Consumers' choices

Each of these narratives echoes a common theme—educated and responsible consumers are necessary for the sustainability of local producers. Many farmers say consumers speak of wanting to buy local food, but when it actually comes down to it,

consumers' purchasing priorities seem to be based on cost and convenience. How consumers make their purchases sends a clear message to both the local farmers and the factory farmers.

So many of these producers, like **Jimmy and Jo Livingston**, know that farming is an honorable career and are very proud of what they are growing. It is disheartening when customers walk away saying their produce is too expensive. Farmers are not getting rich, but they do want and deserve to sell their products for a fair price that will make them economically viable.

Local farmers want consumers to be more educated and thoughtful about the impact weather has on their crops. As **Babs Ambrose** points out, everyone understands the impact that a flood has on their basement or hot weather has on their electricity bill, but there is a lack of understanding about how weather events affect farms and farmers. People still expect to have food. They don't realize the weather has destroyed the crops, and the farmer has just lost a season's income, must replant, and start over.

Factory farms, labor issues, and labeling

There are certain subjects that I simply cannot delve into with this book. Anyone can read Michael Pollan to get a good idea about the conventional monocultures of the agribusiness system and its heavy use of chemicals, cheap labor, and the unsustainable depletion of energy, water, and soil.

Although it is mentioned frequently and is a problem almost across the board, these farmers recognize that farm labor is skilled labor, that immigrants are not taking jobs away from anyone, and that immigrant labor is critical if fruits and vegetables are going to make it from the field to our plates. Attaining a skilled and reliable labor source is a significant challenge. Unfortunately, stringent immigration policies are hampering farm labor and sometimes leading to entire crops being left unharvested in the fields.

I encourage readers to take the time to learn about the fallacies of food labeling. Terms like natural, cage-free, free-range, and grass-fed are often advertising and marketing ploys, which may be "technically" correct, but are not accurate based on what a consumer envisions and interprets. For example, all cows are grass-fed, but are they grass-finished or are they sent to a feedlot and fed grain? As we learn more, we become more discerning in our choices.

Gratitude!

The Faces of Local Food has taken me on quite a journey, meeting wonderful people, learning, and hearing both tough and inspirational stories. In the process, I have changed our family's purchasing and eating habits.

It is my greatest desire that these stories will inspire people to develop a deep understanding of and value for the producers of local foods; that communities will make local foods accessible to consumers by creating the necessary distribution infrastructure and services for small family farmers; and as better-educated consumers, we will champion change that will benefit small family farmers and the economy of an entire region.

Often we give thanks for our food, but how often do we give thanks for the producers of our food? Hopefully these stories will inspire us to be more in touch with the agricultural act of eating.

Is local food sustainable? I'm optimistic, but the answer to that question resides with each of us—in our values, choices and ultimately, our actions. Let's choose wisely. ❧

This book is intentionally and quintessentially local—and relevant everywhere! Throughout The Faces of Local Food, *I use one community, my greater neighborhood in the Lowcountry of South Carolina, as a case study to illustrate and share ideas and methods that can be replicated nationwide. We all can learn from each other.*

If the reader would like to follow up with any people featured in this book, to learn more about their experiences, insights, models, or methods, their contact information can be found on my website: www.CharlotteCaldwell.com

1   "Food, Fuel, and Freeways," the Leopold Center for Sustainable Agriculture in Iowa and WorldWatch Institute, Washington, DC.
2   Civic Economics, a Chicago research firm that provided data to Lowcountry Local First in 2013.
3   Greenwood, Beth, "How Do Fruits and Vegetables Lose Their Nutrients After Picking?" Livestrong.com, October 15, 2015.
4   Berry, Wendell, "The Pleasures of Eating," from *What are People For?* 1990.

Celeste and George Albers
Sea Island Jerseys

*C*eleste is a revered sustainable agriculture figure in the Lowcountry. She seizes the vicissitudes and challenges of farming, adapts, and creates new opportunities. Her tenacity is coupled with her enthusiasm and infectious joy. She and her husband, George, lease land at Rosebank Plantation from the Sinkler family for their dairy operation. Celeste allowed me to join her daily routine, starting with preparing bottles for feeding the calves and readying equipment for milking the cows. Celeste and George have a deep passion for their animals, the land, their livelihood, and each other.

A new concept—local food

Celeste: Hurricane Hugo slammed into the Low-country with a vengeance in 1989, wiping out farmers throughout coastal South Carolina. It devastated George's crops and commercial shrimping business. Like other farmers, he wasn't down for long, and he came back strong. He sold his fifteen acres of land on Johns Island, which he had already transitioned to organic farming, leased it back, and purchased another small shrimping boat and more farmland.

George and I met and started farming together in the early 1990s. We became the first certified organic farm and established the first CSA (Community Supported Agriculture) in Charleston County. Initially, I sold our shrimp and veggies at the roadside stand on our farm. With the success of the Charleston Farmers Market that opened in 1989, we quickly realized that we would reach many more customers selling there.

Chefs were not buying local food prior to Chef Frank Lee's arrival in Charleston in the early 1990s. Extolling the virtues of local and fresh ingredients, he started buying shrimp and produce from us at the farmers market. Soon, well-known chefs Glenn Roberts and Mike Lata also started coming to my booth at the farmers market and for visits out to our farm.

George and I farmed organically and were purchasing chicken manure to use as fertilizer until we figured we should just create our own. We got a flock of chickens and started experimenting with movable pens to allow the chickens to roam on pasture. Soon we added a free-range egg business, Sea Island Eggs, to our organic repertoire.

Chef Mike Lata initially said, "I don't know Celeste, eggs are cheap, and I can get all I want when I want. Why would anyone pay extra for local eggs?" Then he tasted one and became our biggest fan. The taste and quality of pastured eggs from good, healthy chickens are noticeably different from their inexpensive factory-raised counterparts. And eggs are one of the most affordable protein sources available.

The disappearance of labor

Farming has changed so much in the last twenty years. In the 1970s, 1980s, and 1990s, these sea islands were buzzing with commercial agriculture—hundreds of acres of tomatoes, squash, cucumbers, beans, okra, you name it. It was all shipped out-of-state. There were big packinghouses, migrant workers, and labor camps.

In those days, it was easy to hire labor for hoeing, planting, weeding, picking, washing, and packing from the surplus of migrant laborers. We had a labor crew of ten working our nearly fifty acres of veggies, while George shrimped from dawn to dusk and I planned, marketed, and sold the farm produce and shrimp.

In the late 1990s, the big farms started going out of business, and with them went the labor. There were a number of factors that contributed to the decline, but the primary reasons were that land values began to escalate as development boomed and South Carolina was squeezed out of the competitive market by neighboring states and faraway countries. In a short period of time, it all disappeared—industry, investments in agriculture, and labor.

Ironically, the demise of large farms made it harder for us to continue to make a living from our small farm. We lost our labor pool. Contrary to the general belief, farming actually is skilled labor. We tried to hire college students, but they couldn't do the work and wouldn't work for what we could pay. We also tried to hire some of the migrant workers who remained, but we didn't have enough work to pay year-round. It is very hard for a small farmer to pay employees a living wage year-round. So, after forty years of produce farming, we were no longer able to continue.

Encountering a perfect storm of high fuel and ice prices and low shrimp prices, we eventually had to scrap our shrimp business as well. In 2005, fuel escalated from $0.20 to more than $3 per gallon. The price of ice, which had been minimal, skyrocketed to several hundred dollars to fill the shrimp boat's hold. At the same time, the price for shrimp plummeted.

Further compounding the deflated labor force and the inflated operational expenses, the development boom made it prohibitive to keep land in agricultural production. The land we had been leasing since Hurricane Hugo was sold out from under us in 1997 and is now a high-end resort development. We continued to farm the thirty-five acres on Wadmalaw Island for the next nine years until our landlady died and that property was sold as well. That closed another chapter for us. We shut down Sea Island Eggs and started to explore our options.

Mobile pasture milking

I was involved in Acres U.S.A., an organization dedicated to educating farmers on organic and sustainable practices. I attended their conference in Minnesota, where the keynote speaker gave a presentation on raw grass-fed milk. It sounded like a good plan, and worth a try.

Our first cow, Dahlia, lived in our backyard. We hand milked her for our own consumption while we learned about caring for a cow and navigated the raw milk permitting process. Meanwhile, Dana Sinkler asked us to farm his family land, Rosebank Plantation, on Wadmalaw Island. Because of the loving support of the Sinkler family, we are able to raise Sea Island Jersey milk and beef cows. After Dahlia came Lilly, Mandy, and Jean. Every cow has a name. We have more than sixty cows now, only Jerseys. They provide an excellent quality of milk and delicious cream, have great dispositions, and fare well in the South Carolina heat.

George designed and built a mobile milking operation, or parlor, which allows two cows to be milked in the field simultaneously. We wanted a true pasture-based milking system, and furthermore, it doesn't make sense to build a permanent structure on land we don't own.

We milk in the mornings. The cows, ready to be milked, will often walk right to the parlor, which has a tarp cover providing shelter from sun and rain. However, there are times when they are not cooperative, and a time-consuming chase occurs. At those times, it is easy to understand why confinement dairies came about!

Spectacular tasting milk

George: At the moment, we are milking nineteen cows. Production is high, and we are getting more than fifty gallons per day. We have a single-bucket milking unit. A pulsator goes on top of the bucket, which attaches to the claw, which attaches to the cow. The pulsator regulates the vacuum so it gently squeezes, not pulls, the cow's teats.

One of the reasons our milk tastes as spectacular as it does has to do with the soil and plants growing in each paddock. Each paddock is a little over three acres and has a diversity of grasses, wildflowers, and plants that the cows like to eat. The fields are abundant with rye, coastal Bermuda, crabgrass, wild grasses, clover, vetch, native plants, primrose, feverfew, and herbs. I'm always building my seed inventory. I plant rye grass and clover in the fall, which will go to seed after the cows graze it down. Then, I'll bush hog the field. Right now, I have more grass than the cows can eat, which is why a lot of farmers make hay, but I don't have haying equipment. I plow it in and plant sorghum-sudangrass, a drought tolerant summer cover crop, which shades out weeds and amends the soil with organic matter.

Celeste: Between getting the milking equipment ready for George and bottling the milk, I head to the paddock to take care of our calves. We take the calves off their moms after receiving the colostrum and bottle-feed them three times a day for two weeks, after which we drop down to twice a day. It is a big job, but bottle-feeding ensures they are getting enough milk, and it makes them tamer and easier to handle. I bottle-feed them for three or four months.

After they finish their bottles, I release them from their individual hutches to run, play, and eat grass. While they are little, we overnight them in hutches to keep them safe from predators, like coyotes. As

> Whether local farming will be sustainable or not rests with consumers . . . Every time you purchase anything, you are voting with your dollars and each purchase makes the statement, "This is what I support."

they grow, we put them in a small fenced pasture, and at six months, they join the rest of the herd.

We breed our heifers when they are about fourteen months, and they have their first calf when they are two years old. We do raise some bulls, and all our steers are raised for grass-finished beef.

History of dairy processing

I fetch the full pails from George in the field and bring them back to the milk house to combine the milk and strain it into smaller pails. Blending the cows' milk provides uniformity, as the level of butter fat is a little different depending on each cow's age and stage of lactation. I fill the half-gallon bottles, label and date them, and put them in iced water. The milk goes from the cow to the bottle and into the chiller in a very short time, with no processing of any kind.

Voting with your dollars

Of course, the vicissitudes of weather, disease, and labor are always big challenges, but whether local farming will be sustainable or not rests with consumers. It is so important for consumers to know how their milk and all their food is produced. It is important for health reasons, and it is important to understand the value of what we farmers are providing. Producing milk in this humane and healthy manner is much more thoughtful, careful, and labor intensive.

My mantra to consumers is this: every time you purchase anything, you are voting with your dollars. Each purchase makes the statement, "This is what I support, and I am okay with everything they are doing to create it." You can't buy cheap, preservative-laced food and then say, "Oh, I hate the chemical companies," because your purchase is a vote supporting those chemical companies.

George and I just keep doing the best we can. We are trying to make enough of a living to keep going. Everything we make goes right back into our farm. We are also mentoring an egg farmer and a cheese maker, both of whom want to farm. We want to encourage them, and then we wonder if that is the right thing to do. The life of a farmer is difficult. Making a living at it is even harder. But there is so much joy in what we do and so much to be said for making your own life. I get such pleasure from being with our animals and working the land. As we work, we watch nature, the transition of different grasses in our fields, the budding leaves in the surrounding woods, the herons and egrets making their nests near the wetlands, and the alligators in the ponds. We have been blessed. ❧

Pete, Babs, and Barbara Ambrose
Ambrose Family Farm and
Stono Market & Tomato Shed Café

I met Babs and Barbara, the mother and daughter team, at the market-café where they entertained me for hours with family stories from childhood to the present. Ever the entrepreneur, Babs' goal with the Stono Market & Tomato Shed Café was to provide her husband Pete's fresh local produce to the community. Incorporated in 1991, it was truly a first in the now very popular farm-to-table movement in the Lowcountry. Fifteen minutes beyond the Stono Market, I came to Ambrose Farm. Pete demonstrated some of his new farming methods and told me that after forty years of farming, he is still learning to become an even better farmer.

Planting ourselves on a farm

Babs: Our farm, restaurant, market, and CSA (Community Supported Agriculture) members fulfill our dream of growing and selling our produce to our community. Our whole lives are vested in every seed we grow and the people who support us.

I was born on the Coburg Dairy and raised on James Island. Pete lived three houses away. We fell in love when I was thirteen, married right out of high school, and had five children.

When we were first married, Pete was introducing his father and brother to the shrimping industry. We picked up and moved to Rockville, where his dad started a boat repair yard and shrimp dock, and his brother bought a shrimp boat. Pete and his brother sailed off into the sunset and often were away for up to six months. Sometimes, after long stretches, our two oldest children didn't know who he was when he returned. So we decided to plant ourselves on a farm rather than adrift at sea. We bought our home farm, a sixty-acre piece of land on Wadmalaw Island in 1977. For the first two years, during shrimping's off-season, Pete worked with a neighbor who taught him to farm.

We named all our animals—cattle, rabbits, turkeys, geese, ducks, guinea hens, chickens, and peacocks. We had one milk cow, Rosey, and I made cheese from our goats' milk. We ate shrimp, beef, rabbit, chicken, and pork. I made our bread, butter, mayo, cheese, and much more. Our aim was to purchase nothing but gasoline. We did buy more than that, but very little. Then and now, I wake up every morning excited to greet the day.

Still learning and experimenting

Pete: We have two farms. Our oldest son, Petie, and youngest son, Sam, live on the original 60-acre home farm where we raised our kids. We have another 135 acres, and although the two farms are very close in proximity, one abuts a creek and is therefore three to four degrees warmer. The two microclimates allow us to grow different crops for different lengths of time and extend our harvest capabilities.

We are truly a family farm; each family member's involvement leads to our success. I do the ordering and coordinating; son Sam does about ninety-nine percent of the planting and harvesting; Sam's wife,

Billy Jo, is the sales coordinator to the restaurants; and Billy Jo's mother, April, does the CSA packing and manages the labor crews that pick. April also takes care of the U-Pick stand. Barbara manages the Stono Market and Tomato Shed Café, and Babs keeps the entire business running smoothly.

We grow just about everything possible on our combined 200 acres. We plant about forty different crops, which keeps us planting and harvesting year-round. I am always trying different plants to see if they will work. Citrus was grown here in the 1800s, so I planted seventy-five citrus trees a couple of years back, but we got an unheard-of freeze of 17°F for two days and lost every one of them.

We use organic farming practices, but we are not certified organic. Our prepaid CSA memberships provide us with up-front money to purchase seeds and equipment. Because our members invest in our produce in advance, we will use a synthetic product to save a crop if absolutely necessary, but it is very rare.

I started Ambrose Farms forty years ago, and I am still learning how I can become an even better farmer. Currently, I'm exploring polycropping by planting multiple crops in the same field at the same time in order to enhance the soil. The polycropping method of farming is new here, although it has been done in other parts of the world. I love researching stuff like this.

In one of my experimental polycropping plots, I started with sunn hemp, a fast-growing tropical cover crop, which shades out weeds, provides lots of organic matter, and makes nitrogen available in the soil. After mowing, I leave it on the beds and plant another two cover crops, Abruzzi rye and winter peas. Like the sunn hemp before it, the height of the rye provides the additional benefit of a windbreak for the tomatoes in the next row. The rye absorbs nitrogen from the previous crop of sunn hemp, and the peas fix more nitrogen. Then we turn them all into the top two to three inches of soil. In this way, we are not only improving our soil, but also creating more of it.

We have composted from the beginning, but we've evolved in our methods and have become much more efficient. In the past, we would gather the spent plants and tractor them over to the compost pile, which took man-hours, mechanical equipment, and fuel. Then we tried tilling them into the soil. The crops thrived from the organic matter, but so did the weeds. It required lots of labor for weeding.

Now, we are mowing our cover crops, leaving them on top of the beds, and planting through them. I use a machine called a coulter to drill seed through the blanket of mowed cover crop. The lettuce, for example, will bolt when the ground temperature reaches 85°F, but the layer of mowed cover crop has an insulating effect and keeps the ground cooler. It also reduces labor, because there are fewer weeds.

I am passionate about my earthworms and want everyone to know their value. On so many farms in the United States, you can't find an earthworm because synthetic chemicals have killed the healthy soil environment. Over the years, I have been naturally amending my soil to build the earthworm population. My goal was to reach down and pick up a handful of soil full of earthworms. Now, when we till the soil, we do so minimally to protect our earthworms. We also grow a variety of native plants to attract wild honey bees and bumble bees year-round. Bumble bees do double or triple the job of honey bees, and will work even when it is cloudy

▲ Barbara and Babs.

or misting rain. These hard-working pollinators are so important.

Labor is a real challenge for small farms. Our farm has been very fortunate; much of our crew has been with us for twenty-five years. When I was growing a hundred acres of labor-intensive tomatoes, I had a hundred laborers working for me. Those were the days when large commercial farming operations occupied the sea islands. They pulled out of this area in the mid-1990s, and with them went the labor force. Now that good and reliable farm labor is so difficult to find, we only have a team of fifteen who do the work of many more.

Harvesting vegetables and fruits properly is a skill. Our laborers are experienced and dedicated. Fortunately, our current Obama administration continues to give them amnesty. We provide housing on the farm and pay a fair salary. We really value their skill, loyalty, and hard work. No matter how many acres of production we have, if we don't have the labor to harvest it, we can't bring it to market.

We have a variety of different modes for distributing our produce. We sell in our Stono Market & Tomato Shed Café, have about 600 CSA members with thirty-five drop-off points each week, and deliver to thirty-five local restaurants three times per week. At the farm, we have a robust U-Pick business and a small farm stand. In the past, we attended local farmers markets, but became discouraged with some other farmers who, rather than sell their own produce, were purchasing produce from non-local venues and reselling it as their own.

Childhood on the farm

Barbara: I have such fond memories of my childhood. Some of my favorites are raising calves in the laundry room; my brother Petie's rooster, Patrick, who thought he was a member of the family and would sometimes sleep with Petie; and the time Dad proudly lassoed a cow and then was dragged around the barn—we all laughed so hard.

Often consumers profess to want organic, but will choose produce that looks perfect. The essential question is this: do you want invisible, harmful chemicals in your corn or an occasional worm on your corn?

We all understand the impact a flood has on our basement or hot weather has on the air conditioning bill, but there is a lack of understanding about how those weather events affect our farms and food.

Each year, when we were kids, Dad would give us an acre of land to plant, care for, harvest, and sell. With his help, we were responsible for the whole process. One year, we grew an acre of bell peppers. Sam and I were pretty little and could hardly manage to drag the buckets of harvested peppers to the truck. That year, the value of a box of bell peppers flew sky high to $35 per box. We kids earned enough money to buy a pool and a jet ski.

I came back from college to work for Mom when I was twenty-one. She sent me to a farming convention in Ohio for a week with a bunch of old-timer farmers. I thought it was going to be so boring and that I would be miserable. I was the youngest by at least two decades. I sat next to a man who designed and created corn mazes. I came home with a corn maze design for Ambrose Farm. We implemented the idea and got a local radio station to sponsor it. It was such a novel idea. Everyone loved it, and it brought hordes of people to the farm.

Along with the corn maze, we also have a pumpkin patch, a farm stand, and of course, we have our U-Pick. The U-Pick is important because it introduces Ambrose Farm and the practice of farming to people who don't know anything about farming or the source of their food.

Dad is full of ideas, but he is working so hard on the farm that he can lose track of the details. Mom's an incredible entrepreneur, she is the business brain that makes it all work. She jumps in and learns anything. She figured out and created our website.

Mom also decided she wanted to learn to fly airplanes. So when the youngest child left home, she got her pilot's license. She would fly us over the farm in a little Cessna plane so we could see the corn maze from above. Nothing stops her desire to learn and her enthusiasm for living a full life.

Farming's challenges

Babs: I wish consumers would develop a deeper knowledge and better understanding of where their food comes from, how it is grown, and what grows in our region. Also, I wish they were more aware of our climate and the impact that severe weather— flooding or drought, high temperatures or freezes— has on our farms and food. We all understand the impact a flood has on our basement or hot weather has on the air conditioning bill, but there is a lack of understanding about how those weather events affect our farms and food. If we lose one crop or ten due to weather, people still expect to have food. They don't realize the weather destroyed the crops, nor do they think about the farmer, who just lost a season's income and must start over by replanting, if there is still time, and wait at least forty-five days to grow replacement crops.

I wish consumers understood that local, organic foods are grown in soils without synthetic chemicals added to them, and so those foods will not be perfect like their unblemished supermarket counterparts. Because we don't use chemicals on our produce, it is more vulnerable to weather and pests. Buying organically must be more than a "feel-good" term. Often consumers profess to want organic, but will choose produce that looks perfect. The essential question is this: do you want invisible, harmful chemicals in your corn or an occasional worm on your corn?

There are up and down years with farming. There were times when we were stone-broke and probably should have filed for bankruptcy, but kept going. And there were times like 1991, a great year for tomatoes. That Christmas consisted of goggles, flippers, and snorkels, and nine of us traveling to Key Largo.

Pete and I love a challenge and trying new things. If it's shrimping or farming, a CSA or a café, polycropping or composting—we're willing to take measured risks. We do it because we love this lifestyle that has allowed us to raise free-range children and animals, seasonal vegetables and fruits. And now we have the joy of working with our adult children and extended family to continue reaching our goals of farming and providing great local food for our community. 🍃

Del and Debra Ferguson
Hunter Cattle Company

el and Debra delight in sharing their farming experiences with others—school groups, community events, or a farm stay in their renovated tobacco barn. They possess a generosity of heart that welcomes and embraces the hard work and talent of others, and is manifested in their farm store, where they sell the products of other local farmers. At one of their annual events, they invite local blacksmiths and other craftsmen to share the talents of their trade. During my second visit, I photographed Del and Debra in a pasture with their grandchildren, surrounded by cattle. One cow could not resist joining the fun.

Sharing the authentic farm experience

Debra: We raise, process, and sell grass-fed, grass-finished cattle, pastured-pork, and free-range chickens, but we like to think that we are in the education business. Most people are removed from farm and animal odors, sounds, and behaviors, so we focus on making connections and enabling visitors to see, hear, smell, and touch. We want to share this experience of farm life, humanely raised animals, sustainable agricultural practices, and healthy food.

Del and I moved to this farm in 2004. We quickly realized, by the number of guests who were stopping by each weekend, that people were yearning for that back-to-the-basics farm experience. Our first year, we hosted a Farm Day. Surprisingly, more than 600 people attended, with more than twice that number the following year. Five hundred students visited last week, ranging from elementary school age to college kids. Many have never seen a chicken. We try to meaningfully engage them to understand that food comes from a farm, not a grocery store.

From hobby to serious business

Del: Hunter Cattle Company started as a hobby, not a business. We owned a construction business and raised our kids along with various animals here and there, outside Savannah, Georgia. One day Debra said she wanted a cow, and so I started to look for a place with more land. Our plan was to raise enough beef to feed ourselves, to keep momma cows, and to sell calves once a year.

What started as a hobby with a couple cows rapidly became an occupation. At the time, our son Hunter was our only child left in the nest. Our construction business was named after Anthony, our eldest son, and since Hunter showed an interest in the cows, we became Hunter Cattle Company. In short order, we expanded, adding hogs, chickens, lambs, and turkeys, but we kept the original name.

Meat production is our main business. Grocery store labeling of beef as "grass-fed" can be misleading, because all cows eat grass for about the first year of their lives. "Grass-finished" means they have only eaten grass their entire lives. Most one-year-old cows are sent to a feedlot, where they are intensely fed and finished on grains. Grain is not a natural food source for cattle, so cows must be given antibiotics and hormones to keep them healthy. But the grain makes them reach butchering weight rapidly—eight to ten months sooner than our grass-finished cattle. When it takes less time to get the animal to the market, that translates into a cheaper product and more profit for the big-business producer. When consumers understand this, they will understand why food from local farms costs more. We raise our livestock differently—naturally and humanely.

Hunter Cattle are 100 percent grass-finished. Our breeding is natural and our calves stay with their momma for seven to eight months. We do the most humane form of weaning, a fence-to-fence weaning, so they can be close and touch noses, but not nurse. We have thirteen different pastures and practice an intensive form of grazing called mob-grazing, in which the cattle eat the grasses down, provide a healthy disturbance of the soil, and fertilize the pasture with manure. Then they are moved to another pasture, and the grazed land recovers quickly. At twenty-eight months the calves have reached a weight of 1,100 pounds and are ready to be butchered.

Lack of local infrastructure

The number of people farming the land and raising animals has decreased in the past fifty years, so too has the number of local butchers and processors. There used to be an abattoir in every town. Now slaughterhouses and processing plants have become centralized by the industrial food system, and large corporations are slaughtering and processing mass quantities of meat using nitrates as a preservative.

▼ The incubator.

Because our customers are informed and health conscious, they know there is a whole lot more to look for in the grocery store than price!

We raise, process, and package beef, pork, chickens, turkeys, and lamb. We had no intention of becoming a processor, but we chose to do so for our customers with health concerns who wanted meats without nitrates. The more we learned about nitrates, the more we wanted to find healthy alternatives for preserving meat. Salt and sugar are natural preservatives, and sea salt specifically has excellent qualities for preserving. The way we process may cost us more time and resources, but we are providing a different and much better end product.

Our son Anthony runs our processing facility. We thought doing it ourselves would save us a lot of money. It has not, but it has allowed us to be in control of our products. Without a local abattoir, we must transport pigs and cows to a USDA slaughterhouse a couple hours away on Mondays and pick them up on Fridays. Then we process and preserve the cuts exactly how our customers—individuals and restaurants—want them.

Incubating our own

Debra: We have a special room dedicated to incubating eggs, primarily chickens, but we also raise ducks and turkeys. In addition to collecting eggs to fill customer orders and sell in our store, we collect eggs to fill the incubator. To hatch chicks successfully, the eggs need to be incubated between 95°F and 100°F with the proper amount of humidity, and they need to be turned. Our incubator automatically rolls the eggs, simulating the turning a hen would do. We incubate close to 200 chickens every twelve to eighteen days. After they hatch, we can determine the sex at about one month by their appearance—shape, tail feathers, and comb. The hens become our layers, and the roosters become our meat birds that we slaughter and process at three months.

Our farm-fresh eggs sell for $5 per dozen. I am often asked why our eggs cost more than most grocery store eggs. Industrial-sized chicken operations raise literally thousands of birds confined in the same amount of space that our small flock roams. Even if their eggs are labeled "free-range," a term that is unregulated, those chickens are kept in deplorably crowded conditions and may never even journey outdoors. Those producers are providing cheap, cheap eggs.

Our eggs are more expensive because our chickens get to wander, peck in the grass, and eat insects, grass, and weeds. We also provide quality feed milled by a local Mennonite family. We raise worms and soldier fly larvae, which provide 100 percent protein. Raising chickens humanely takes a lot more time and resources, but we know it is worth it.

Supportive community and customers

We've developed close relationships with our customers since moving here fifteen years ago, and our customers have driven much of what Hunter Cattle Company has done. Customers' requests prompted the expansion of our production from beef to pastured-pork and free-range chickens. Customers wanted to be able to shop throughout the week, so we created a store. Customers wanted nitrate-free processing, so we started our own processing facility.

Customers drive from Atlanta, Jacksonville, and Charleston for our meats. We are very grateful to our community of regional neighbors; they have been very supportive. In fact, last night, we received a tourism partner award and a farm-to-table award from our local community. We have also won three state awards for our sausages and New York strip.

From farm store to farm stay

Hunter Cattle Company utilizes a variety of modes of distribution. Our MooMa's Farm Store is open Tuesday through Saturday from 9:00 a.m. to 5:00 p.m., and in support of other organic local farmers and producers, we sell their produce here at our store as well. We attend two farmers markets, which keep us in front of our customers. Many of them have become friends. We provide online ordering through our website. We sell to a number of small, retail stores that focus on local, organic, healthy foods and to some regional ones such as Whole Foods and Lucky's Market.

Agritourism is a great way to introduce people to farms, ranches, and agricultural ways of life. We host a Farm Heritage Day where we invite local vendors to share their talents and crafts like wool spinning, blacksmithing, homemade soaps, and other old trades that are dying out. We host farm-to-table dinners, bluegrass music events, and other family-friendly entertainment. One of our favorites is watching Del do his Elvis routine on stage. We call him "Delvis."

Realizing that many people are seeking authentic farm experiences, we built rooms in the loft of the old tobacco barn to provide a farm stay for up to ten people. Our guests can stay for one day or one week, and participate in the farm chores, fish, hike, and bike.

Del: Our three children each contribute to the success of the farm, and nine of our eleven grand-children are raised and home-schooled here. They also responsibly participate in daily farm chores.

We have a passion for farming and find it rewarding to provide wholesome food and farm experiences to children and adults, many of whom lack the most basic understanding of where our food comes from. It is important for consumers to know their farmer and the great dedication required to raise natural food. We are proud of the healthy, happy animals we raise, our chemical-free processing, and the quality products we sell. We have developed great relationships with our community and customers, and because our customers are informed and health conscious, they know there is a whole lot more to look for in the grocery store than price! If it weren't for good neighbors and the good Lord, we wouldn't be here today thoroughly enjoying this wonderful life. ❧

▼ Grandchildren and #211.

Frank Roberts
Lady's Island Oysters

O ysters are synonymous with the culture of the sea islands of South Carolina. High in protein and minerals, native peoples harvested them for thousands of years as evidenced by prehistoric oyster shell mounds throughout the coastal region. Early European settlers built homes and other structures from a mix of crushed oyster shells and lime, called tabby, a tradition—like oyster roasts—that continues today. When dining out, my husband and I always ask for the sources of the menu items, and we have delighted in Frank's oysters many times at various local restaurants. They are delicious—briny with a nice clean finish. If you want to experience these South Carolina oysters, you have to come for a visit. They are so good and in such demand, they never make it out of the state!

A delicate spiral of interconnectedness

Water and oysters flow through the veins of my life—first as a curious boy exploring the Chesapeake Bay surrounding my grandmother's farm, then when my dad was transferred to Long Island, New York. I built my first boat there at the age of twelve.

There is a delicate spiral of interconnectedness in marine ecosystems. When overharvested, the food chain breaks down leading to collapse.

Fertile estuaries and marshes surrounded me on Parris Island, South Carolina, when I was a recruit in the Marine Corps. After serving in Beirut, I focused my interests in mariculture and learned from Frank M. Flowers in Oyster Bay, Long Island. He was one of the first to recognize that unless we learned to cultivate oysters, we would quickly outstrip our resources. In 1998, I moved to an island not far from Parris Island and started a mariculture operation.

I cultivate and harvest oysters on state leases at the junction of McCawley Creek and the Whale Branch and Beaufort Rivers. The salt marshes and estuaries serve as a marine nursery, where all our indigenous species of fishes and crustaceans get their start—juvenile finfish, clams, oysters, crabs, and shrimp. Therefore, I tread lightly in this fragile system and maintain the smallest footprint possible.

There is a delicate spiral of interconnectedness in marine ecosystems. When overharvested, the food chain breaks down leading to collapse. Wild oysters are a limited natural resource with a survival rate of less than one percent. The Chesapeake Bay is a distressing example of how overharvesting of a marine animal can break the ecological balance and start a downward cascade of events.

Oysters filter the sediment and detritus in the water column. One mature oyster filters about fifty gallons of water each day, which benefits water quality and contributes to a healthy marine nursery habitat. Overharvesting leaves too few oysters and other shellfish to filter the water; water becomes murky and prevents the sun's penetration into the water column. Without sunlight, photosynthesis is inhibited, impacting the production of phytoplankton and zooplankton, the microscopic marine organisms that are the basis of the food web in marine ecology. The result—collapse.

The ongoing recovery of the Chesapeake is due primarily to private oystermen, who introduced large quantities of cultivated native oysters high in the water column. The more oysters, the more water was filtered. The cleaner the water, the more sunlight penetrated, generating growth of phytoplankton, zooplankton, and spartina marsh grass.

Hatchery, nursery, grow-out

The most responsible and sustainable way to harvest oysters is through cultivation. There are three primary stages to cultivating oysters—hatchery, nursery, and final grow-out in a river.

At Lady's Island Oysters, we begin the cultivation process by selecting 100 wild oysters with ideal features, like wide fans, deep cups, and good shapes. We put them in a tray filled with filtered seawater and raise the temperature to 80°F, which triggers them to spawn. During spawning, we identify the males from the females. Females open and close their shells and waffle up their eggs, while the males open and sperm emerges in a steady stream. We choose five females and one male and put them together for a couple hours. After the eggs have been fertilized, we wait an hour and check under the microscope for cell division. From a spawn of six oysters, we hope for 30 to 40 million larvae. A 300-gallon conical tank filled with filtered seawater serves as our hatchery habitat for the freshly spawned larvae. We add microalgae to the tank as a food source.

At first I grew the microalgae, but that was a full-time job in itself. Fortunately, I found a reputable microalgae producer in California. He figured out how to grow it densely, pasteurize it, and maintain its viability for up to three months. Using a microscope, we get a ballpark number of larvae so we can provide the correct amount of microalgae feed. About five quarts will feed 30 to 40 million oysters from the time of fertilization to when the oysters set and are moved to the nursery.

The hatchery tanks need to be drained and refilled with filtered seawater every two days. We run the water through a one-micron sieve (one micron is 1/1,000 of a millimeter or 1/25,000 of an inch) and then through an ultraviolet filter to kill microbes.

During the first twenty-one days in the hatchery stage, an oyster's life is the most precarious. Under the microscope, we vigilantly monitor samples of water. Occasionally we see competitors eating the microalgae and predators killing our larvae.

The larvae are very fragile, and nearly everything is a predator to the microalgae or the oyster larvae.

Oyster larvae have no shells and swim freely during this stage. They look like minuscule frisbees with a mustache. The mustache is their hair-like cilia, which allows them to catch and eat plankton. At day nineteen, the larvae develop an eye, which looks like an ink dot. If they were growing in the wild, they would have experienced a ninety-nine percent mortality rate by now.

At day twenty-one, we move the eye larvae into the nursery tank. Lured by natural pheromone attractors, they descend the water column and cement themselves to another oyster shell by dissolving an appendage called a foot. Then they start to create their own shell. After about four days, we check under the microscope, and once we see close to ninety percent setting, we begin adding filtered nutrient-rich water to the nursery tank. At this point, the larva's internal anatomy undergoes complete metamorphosis, and becomes spat. Utilizing calcium carbonate from the seawater, they put all their energy into the creation of their shells. The nursery phase lasts about forty-five days.

When large enough, the spat are transferred into one-quarter-inch mesh grow-out bags, put into floating cages, and set out in the salt marshes, where the flowing river provides them with all the nutrients they need. As they grow out, they are transferred first into half-inch and then three-quarter-inch mesh bags. The larger mesh allows more food to flow through.

Phytoplankton and zooplankton are oysters' main source of food, and are in the top portion of the water column. Oysters do well in our floating cages because they remain suspended in the best space for their food source. In the winter, when the pluff mud settles to the bottom of the river, the sunlight can penetrate as deep as six feet, yielding great plankton growth. November through April is the fastest-growing period for our oysters as long as the water stays above 50°F. If the water temperature falls below 50°F, they go into a temporary dormancy.

In the wild, oysters grow about an inch per year and become marketable-sized adults after three years. Our Lady's Island cultivated oysters grow twice as fast, with a life cycle from hatchery to market of twelve to fourteen months.

Oysters aren't harvested in the summer, because that is when native oysters are spawning. They are depleted from spawning and have a watery texture and little flavor. When the water gets cooler, they recover from spawning and rebuild their fats and tissues.

Our oysters also give off a big spawn, which contributes to the wild oyster population. Lady's Island Oysters is the only exclusive oyster hatchery in South Carolina and provides oyster seeds, or larvae, to most of the other oyster growers in the state. We grew 2.7 million oysters here last year and sold 1.2 million as seed. We kept 1.5 million to harvest ourselves.

Extensive regulations and certifications

This morning, we had a visit from the Department of Health and Environmental Control (DHEC) for an annual recertification inspection. As a live product that is consumed raw, the regulations for oysters are much, much stricter than other foods. Throughout oyster season, there are any number of unannounced food safety inspections. DHEC inspects our records, sanitary conditions, and the temperature of our coolers and back-up coolers. Refrigeration is required to be under 45°F, and we keep ours around 40°F. Everything we do is logged, checked, and double-checked.

When harvesting, we record the time from harvest to cooler. The amount of time to get the oysters under controlled temperatures is strictly regulated. In the winter, we have twenty hours. In the spring and fall, when the temperatures can get over 80°F, we only have three hours from the time the first oyster is harvested to get them in the cooler. The last thing we want is to have a bad oyster.

I am also required to get a stack of licenses for our leases. I'm permitted by the County of Beaufort, Department of Natural Resources, Department of Health and Environmental Control, Ocean and Coastal Resource Management, the Army Corps of Engineers, the National Oceanic and Atmospheric Administration, the Coast Guard . . . and on and on. The red tape and the countless jurisdictions can get rather onerous.

Ecological challenges

Some of the biggest challenges our oysters face are drought and flooding; both greatly impact the salinity of the water. Standard ocean salinity is 35 ppt (parts per thousand). Lady's Island Oysters are

naturally briny, because the salinity in South Carolina waters is 30 ppt. The Chesapeake Bay, Gulf of Mexico, Long Island Sound, and Great South Bay in New York are the biggest oyster producers on the East Coast, all with a salinity around 14 ppt. During a recent drought, which is always accompanied by lots of evaporation, our salinity reached 37 ppt in the small creeks. Too much salinity kills.

Likewise, the huge rains a couple of years ago killed a lot of our wild oysters. Salinity dropped from 30 ppt to 6 ppt. We had 30 million oyster larvae in our hatchery and had already carried them for eighteen days. We were very close to losing everything. Fortunately, someone working with me at the time came up with the enlightened recollection that PETCO carried an aquarium salt called "instant ocean" consisting of salt and the key minerals oysters need. We added "instant ocean" and monitored the hatchery water until we got it up to 18 ppt. Our hatchery larvae survived!

A new challenge, and one that we never expected, is a proposed jellyfish processing plant right in our backyard. A group out of China wants to catch and process the cannonball jellyfish to export. Apparently, it is a Chinese delicacy. The group wants to process 5 million pounds of jellyfish per week. That process would create jellyball "slime," a discharge that would pollute the Whale Branch River. Processing requires significant amounts of salt as well as tons of alum, ammonium aluminum sulfate, which has a pH of four! The negative impact on this pristine salt marsh would create a toxic cocktail. It would be devastating to our clean water, salt marsh nurseries, shellfish, sea turtles, commercial and recreational fishing, and tourism. We have been fighting the jellyfish plant for over a year, and we need all the help and support we can get.

Maintaining the integrity of the system

It is well established in the seafood industry that if the buyer knows the grower, they are much more assured of a fresher and better quality product.

For that reason, Lady's Island Oysters won't deal with a wholesaler, because they don't represent our product the way we want to be represented. I take the time to form relationships and really educate the restaurant chefs and owners. I invite them to go out on the boat to harvest with us, because I want each customer to know and value the way that we sustainably cultivate our oysters and add to the wild reserves. Lady's Island Oysters are responsible caretakers of our leases, and we are an asset to water quality and the ecology of coastal waters.

Restaurants and caterers are also recognizing their contribution to maintaining the full-cycle health of the marine ecosystem. The top and bottom plates of each oyster shell have live wild oyster seeds attached. Restaurateurs save and refrigerate the shells for us to pick up with our next delivery. In this way, they are participating in oyster shell recycling and restoration programs. We return the scrap shells to estuaries and salt marshes at specific locations, which establishes new oyster rakes, or reefs. Oyster rakes provide a habitat for new oysters while also preventing erosion of the salt marsh's critical spartina grass. Spartina grass is a valuable oxygenator for oysters, and it helps maintain the integrity of the system. One acre of spartina grass provides five tons of food for nursery finfish and shellfish. Keeping all the pieces of the puzzle intact and healthy is critical to the maintenance of these fragile ecosystems.

I've grown oysters up and down the East Coast, and without a doubt South Carolina has some of the best oysters in the country. We have pristine waters here and great growing conditions, but we can't take it for granted. Delicious oysters are predicated on working together to keep our marine ecology healthy. ❧

Germaine Jenkins
Fresh Future Farm and Market

ermaine is the founder and director of Fresh Future Farm. She is dedicated to growing accessible and affordable fresh and healthy foods. Her goal is to address food, health, economic, and environmental disparities in a food desert by establishing an urban farm and market. Her indomitable spirit and commitment to her community has made Fresh Future Farm a success and something to replicate in other urban food deserts.

The seeds were planted early

As a child growing up in Cleveland, Ohio, my daycare was across the street from an urban farm, where my brothers and I were allowed to harvest vegetables. That urban farm provided us with more than something to eat; it introduced me to growing and harvesting food. The seeds of vision for Fresh Future Farm were planted way back then.

In my late twenties, I was a single mom living in public housing with a four-year-old and an eighteen-month-old. My memories of the urban farm across the street from my daycare combined with my family's immediate need for food motivated me to enroll at Johnson & Wales University in Charleston to earn my culinary degree. I went from a full-time salary to being a full-time student and food stamp recipient. I promised my kids that when we got out of public housing, we were going to have a home with a garden.

After graduating from Johnson & Wales in 2002, I became the cook for the Kids' Café at the North

My neighborhood is an urban food desert. It is more than three miles from here to the closest grocery store, and many residents in this neighborhood don't own cars. Knowing this, it becomes understandable why kids get their meals from fast-food restaurants and convenience stores.

Charleston YMCA. The Kids' Café is a national after-school program for food-insecure children. It is a multilayered program that provides nutritious hot meals, a safe place to play, and an introduction to healthy cooking and eating.

Programs like Kids' Café are important, especially when considering the situation at home for many of the program's children. Many parents in urban, underserved neighborhoods work full-time in low-wage jobs, often two jobs, and come home exhausted. If they don't have a car and live in a food desert, it is very difficult to access a grocery store. They have to feed their kids, and much of their food comes from a neighborhood convenience store. I sympathize with these folks. They are doing what they can to keep their children fed, but convenience stores are expensive and do not carry fresh produce and other nutritional ingredients for meals.

A backyard garden in a food desert

When I got married, we chose our house because of its garden space. At that time, I was enrolled in the Tri-County Master Gardeners program through Clemson Extension. Most of my peers in the program were retired and had ample time and resources to apply the techniques we learned in class. Having limited resources, a friend told me about taking the base of veggies bought from the grocery store, like the roots from scallions, and planting them. That way, we could eat the scallion greens and replant the roots. I also searched online for techniques that people with limited resources can use to grow a bountiful garden, which led me to permaculture.

Permaculture is a method of agriculture that centers on care for the earth, care for people, and the reuse of materials. Essentially, I seek the least intrusive solutions, not only for growing food, but also for life in general. I grow in spaces nearby, use items that would otherwise be discarded, like cardboard boxes and wood chips, and try to reduce inputs and resources. Since 2008, I've been applying permaculture practices in my home garden. Every corner space on our property has something growing. We also have chickens. When I first started my garden, the neighborhood kids would walk past and ask if it was a farm. I hesitated, but then realized yes, indeed it was a tiny farm. We were able to manage the bills on our limited income, because we were efficiently growing our own vegetables and raising chickens.

My neighborhood is an urban food desert, which by definition is a place where residents must travel more than a mile to access fresh fruits, vegetables, and other healthy food. It is more than three miles from here to the closest grocery store, and many residents in this neighborhood don't own cars. So a trip to the grocery store becomes a six-mile round-trip walk, carrying groceries partway, often in hot, cold, or rainy weather. It is a very circuitous route to take a bus from here to a grocery store, and buses now limit the number of grocery bags riders are allowed because they need the space for passengers. Knowing this, it becomes understandable why kids get their meals from fast-food restaurants and convenience stores.

The challenges of obtaining fresh food got me wondering. If I could grow enough to feed my family for weeks, maybe I could also grow enough for my neighbors who are struggling to find healthy food. My ideas about an urban farm continued to germinate, which led me to Will Aiken and Growing Power.

Will Allen is an African American who started Growing Power, a nonprofit in downtown Milwaukee, Wisconsin, in 1993. His vision and message is that communities can build their own safe, affordable, healthy, and sustainable food systems. I wanted to learn more so I could make it a reality in my own neighborhood.

Transforming a vacant lot into a farm

I received $5,000 from SCACED (South Carolina Association of Community Economic Development) to attend Growing Power's Commercial Urban Agriculture and Aquaponics training program from January through June of 2014. Afterward, I started an edible landscaping business, helping my clients grow food in a way that doesn't require as much work as traditional gardening. Then I entered and won the South Carolina Community Loan Fund's Feeding Innovation competition. The competition was designed to support entrepreneurs interested in developing or expanding a business that provides access to healthy foods in underserved areas. I started to learn the business components that would be necessary to accompany my vision of an urban farm and market. Through these experiences, my ideas for a farm in an urban food desert expanded to include an entire community food operation with an on-site store to sell produce, along with other groceries and toiletries.

Finding the vacant lot for the urban farm was the easy part; there are many in our area. The zoning and approvals, however, were something else. I met with the mayor of North Charleston. He supported my idea and helped identify a space, but he couldn't make the decisions about leasing land without going through city council. I just about had to pitch a tent outside the city hall for several months to educate folks about what I wanted to do. I not only needed a five-year lease on the vacant lot, but I also needed to change the zoning from residential to business. That alone was a nine-month undertaking.

Fresh Future Farm—0.81 acre of a fenced, deserted school playground—was designed with the help of a permaculture expert. From the very beginning, creating this urban farm has been a group effort— family, neighborhood residents, parents, teachers, students, churches, the local business community, and area permaculture enthusiasts. Everyone came together, rolled up their sleeves, and transformed a vacant lot in a food desert into a working farm.

Without using any chemicals or heavy farming equipment, we eliminated the grass and built the soil using cardboard and wood chips. The cardboard from the Dollar Store around the corner went down first to inhibit grass and weed growth. On top of that went a layer of wood chips donated from local tree services, and then soil from Charleston County's

composting program. We "loved on" our soil in this embryonic stage by putting straw between the layers of compost and enhancing the soil's microbiotic activity with the addition of worms.

In November of 2014, we planted fruit trees and bushes, and in the winter of 2015, we planted vegetables. Now a year and a half after receiving our lease and zoning, our perimeter is full of blueberry and blackberry bushes and apple, pear, peach, plum, and banana trees. Our vegetable rows are thriving with a variety of seasonal vegetables and herbs. We have close to 30,000 honey bees hard at work in our observation beehive that the folks from a nonprofit, The Bee Cause, installed for us with a grant from the Whole Kids Foundation. And we recently finished building our chicken house.

Fresh Future Farm is divided into a production area and an educational area. The production area contributes to the economic sustainability of the farm, and the educational side has an outdoor classroom with crops that are historical to the Charleston region. Visitors learn about locally grown varieties of crops, how to save seeds, and how to grow and harvest a garden. People from the community can buy food from the store and take a stroll in the winding, wheelchair-accessible educational gardens.

A fresh future for all

Our next steps include getting GAP (Good Agricultural Practices) certification and building a commercial kitchen. We received a $50,000 Small Business Association Accelerator prize, and we are installing an incubator kitchen on-site so we can process, wash, chop, and freeze our produce to extend shelf life and create value-added products like sandwiches and salads to sell in the store. If the cleaning and chopping are already done, then those items become more convenient for parents to use when providing healthy meals for their families. When we're not using the kitchen, we plan on renting it to local food entrepreneurs.

Our store accepts SNAP (Supplemental Nutrition Assistance Program), also known as food stamps, which can also be used to buy seeds, fruit trees, and plants, so our customers can start a garden in their own yard. In addition to our fresh fruits, vegetables, and eggs, we sell chips, sweets, and soft drinks because we are not the food police. I want to develop relationships with members of our neighborhood, meet their needs, and reconnect customers with a taste for wholesome foods.

The bottom line is that Fresh Future Farm provides a fresh future for this neighborhood. We grow food to feed the community and grow relationships and community spirit through events, cooking demonstrations, and nutrition lessons. By growing food in our neighborhood, we are growing community. We are intentionally creating this farm as a destination that people want to visit—"placemaking," which will imbue our neighborhood with a sense of pride.

My hope is that Fresh Future Farm is the first of many urban farms built in the Lowcountry's many food deserts. I would like to help others develop agricultural spaces, as there is plenty of need. Fresh Future Farm and our market have become a reality. We provide affordable fresh and healthy foods to this community, and hope to be a model for other communities. We will always be a work in progress, but if I can do it here, then others can do it too. 🍂

Kathee Dowis
Charleston Collegiate School Garden, Manager
Hacker Burr
Charleston Collegiate Head of School

Kathee is full of joy, has a colorful and bountiful spirit, and provides a sense of welcoming peace into the creative space of Charleston Collegiate School garden. On numerous occasions, I watched the respectful interactions between her and students of all ages as they planted, weeded, harvested, and nibbled away at fresh garden treats.

Since the garden was built prior to Kathee's arrival, I interviewed the Head of School, Hacker Burr, who explained the philosophy and three primary goals behind the garden program.

And although I was unable to interview Brooke Haynie, Director of Outdoor Education, I did get a photograph of him with three young gardeners. Brooke's role in establishing the garden was formative. According to Hacker, Brooke and Kathee are to the students as the water, soil, and sun are to the garden.

Finding a sanctuary

Kathee: My love for farming was kindled at an early age. My grandfather was a farmer. As a child, I loved accompanying him to neighboring farms around Darlington, South Carolina. I grew up intimately connected to the farming culture; it became part of my vernacular. I learned about nematodes and soil microorganisms. I watched the weather and knew how it would impact my grandfather's yields, and I experienced the passing of the hat for donations when a fellow farmer suffered a crop loss. Times on the farm with my grandfather were formative.

After years of branching in different directions, I found myself in a Clemson University Master Gardener Program and volunteering in the greenhouses at a large local park. There, I got my hands back in the soil and experienced the serenity and productivity reminiscent of my childhood. When my son entered seventh grade at Charleston Collegiate School and his sports schedule increased, I found myself with lots of free time and searching for inspiration.

Upon learning about Lowcountry Local First's *Growing New Farmers* program, my urge to farm, dormant since childhood, began to surge. I jumped on the opportunity and enrolled. With three hours of class time complemented by three hours of hands-on field work each week for six months, I learned about soil conditions, seed collection, pest control, DHEC (Department of Health and Environmental Control) regulations, and the like. Soon I became a farmer's apprentice on James Island, and also volunteered in the garden at my son's school.

Fortunately, as my farm apprenticeship was wrapping up, I received a phone call from Hacker Burr, who asked if I would manage Charleston Collegiate School's garden. As soon as I started working, I discovered the garden's potential and richness and felt I had found my place of sanctuary and purpose. And now, here I am in this little slice of heaven!

An outdoor classroom

I help teachers coordinate their academic programs with garden experiences. Younger students visit me in the garden throughout the week, and the upper school's job crew spends two hours per week with me.

This is a hands-on, sensory place—a true outdoor classroom with endless opportunities for learning about soils, seed collection, nutrition, science, math, art, poetry, and journaling. Kids of all ages touch, smell, taste, rake, prune, and harvest. We explore all possibilities. Like our cantaloupes, which typically grow horizontally and require a lot of garden space, we grow them vertically up our fence. Spanish classes made labels to identify our herbs and vegetables. We grow and use gourds for music, art, and purple martin birdhouses. The photography class has been working on contrast and macro photography. And we watch the honey bees and butterflies as they pollinate our plants. There are endless ways to apply academic learning to garden experiences . . . and then there are times when the younger students come and just chase butterflies.

In one third grade project, each student chose a native plant, researched its history, learned about its growing conditions, preferred climate, soil, pests, and companion plants, and presented their findings to the lower school. The fourth graders made a garden bench to allow for meditation and contemplation. There is a lesson in just being outdoors—watching birds build their nests and feed their babies or listening to the crickets, frogs, insects, birds, and wind. This space

▼ Brooke Haynie, Evie, Alexandra, and Hadley.

▲ Hacker Burr and Hadley.

provides inspiration and serenity. Mother Nature has a way of quieting the soul.

Planting what we love to eat

Our school chef coordinates with us to grow specific vegetables and herbs, and the kids harvest, wash, dry, and deliver them to her in the cafeteria. One day we picked peas, and the next day we feasted on them. With our abundance of mint, one kindergarten student asked if the chef would make smoothies. The kids researched how to make them, and shared them with students, staff, and visitors. They were a huge hit.

In addition to planting what we love and eating what we plant, one of the most valuable aspects of the garden is that it provides a way to give back and share our bounty. One student showed his mother how to harvest cilantro and peppers, and then they took their harvest home to cook dinner together. Another student comes every Tuesday and Thursday to harvest and share vegetables with teachers throughout the school.

The day I started working in the school garden, I felt its potential and richness. I thought then, and I know now, that I found my place in the world.

I feel that I've gone back to my roots, to my grandfather's farm, a place where I first felt fulfilled. It is a joy, a privilege, and an honor to spend my time in this nourishing place with children of all ages, and to help them find inspiration, joy, and nutritious food.

This garden is a metaphor for our school

Hacker: Charleston Collegiate School's garden-to-table program evolved from an idea and vision about the educational value of school gardens. Being a project-based learning school, we are always looking for opportunities to get our students out of the classroom and let them apply textbook learning to real-world experiences. What started as an idea continues to grow and blossom, quite literally. Charleston Collegiate School's garden exemplifies our philosophy that the most effective way for students to learn and develop is by tying academics to meaningful real-world projects.

Brooke Haynie, our Director of Outdoor Education, championed the vision and oversaw the implementation of the garden from the beginning. Building the garden soil was the first step and an all-school

There are endless ways to apply academic learning
to garden experiences . . . and then there are times when
the younger students come and just chase butterflies.

project. Brooke engaged pre-kindergarten through twelfth grade students, teachers, administrators, and parents in the garden's creation. We created a vibrantly healthy seven-layer soil starting with a cardboard base followed by wood chips, manure, hay, more manure, hay, and compost. Together the lower and upper school students had their hands in the dirt, were pushing wheelbarrows, and were collaborating to find solutions to challenges along the way. High school math classes crunched numbers to calculate how much rainwater would run off the roof. Middle school science classes estimated annual rainfall and researched how best to collect and utilize the rainwater. Their findings were fundamental to our garden design and the creation of functional garden paths and trenches for water transfer. One beneficial result was the reduction in campus flooding after major rainstorms.

We cultivate multiple crops together in a method called polyculture. The compelling distinction of a polyculture farm versus monoculture is the important symbiotic relationships. By planting companion plants next to each other, they collaborate above and beneath the soil. One plant provides nitrogen to the soil, while another attracts pollinators, and another draws beneficial insects.

We explicitly speak of polyculture as a metaphor for the culture of our school—by valuing our diverse ethnic, racial, and economic backgrounds, we create a supportive, companionable, and cooperative environment. Polyculture cultivation is not only a launching pad for great discussions about the natural world, but also how we, with our different strengths, talents, and capabilities, can collaborate in logical, strategic, and beneficial ways. It is a model that encourages us to bring different strengths to the table to accomplish significant things.

Growing food, business skills, and community

Our garden has three primary purposes: to grow food, to develop business skills, and to engage in community service.

Growing food: Not all of our students receive three square meals per day at home. Our garden provides nutrition and the learning environment for creating a sustainable food source. What we harvest ends up in our cafeteria salad bar, unless of course it becomes a snack in the process of gathering it. During lunch, our school chef occasionally talks about what came from the garden that day and involves the students in the process of what to plant next. If kids complain about the salad bar selections, the chef suggests they solve the problem by planting what they want to eat.

We also create our own compost. All our utensils—paper plates, forks, and cups—may look like plastic, but are manufactured from vegetable matter and quickly degrade. We work with a composting company that collects our cafeteria waste each week. When we need more compost for the garden, they bring our food waste back to us in the form of soil.

The business of farming: At Charleston Collegiate School, we believe that financial literacy is one of the most important skills we can provide our students, and they start learning business dexterity at an early age. Through the garden they can incorporate business concepts in an easily accessible way. We have second and third graders working on marketing plans, branding products, collecting data, strategizing how to widen sales margins, and making adaptations to account for lagging sales. By the time the students enter our high school entrepreneurship class, they are familiar with cash flow and other business principles.

Community service: The nutritional benefits and the business experience gained from the garden dovetail into meaningful service learning. Students learn to be social entrepreneurs with the competency to do good for our community through sound business development. The model we are working toward is that first we feed our school, and on the third Friday of every month, we take our excess harvest to the local food bank. We won't just drop off the food or a donation check, but we will stay and volunteer and meet the clients to provide our kids with a greater perspective and appreciation for helping others.

Eventually, on the fourth Friday of every month,

Our garden has three primary purposes: to grow food, to develop business skills, and to engage in community service.

we plan to sell the excess harvest through a local farmers market or a local food distribution hub. We have not reached enough production to implement these goals, yet, but we are heading in that direction.

Cucumbers and a giving spirit

The garden provides multi-faceted learning experiences. My favorite example is our second graders' service-learning project. In the fall, through a local nonprofit they adopted a family in need with the goal of providing Christmas gifts on the children's wish list. Because the children slept in the same bed with their grandmother, the wish list included bunk beds and mattresses.

With minimal teacher management, the students figured out the cost of each item on the Christmas list. Then they decided to earn the necessary funds through our school garden and their entrepreneurship skills. They created a value-added product, which they called "quickles." They developed a brand, a logo, and a marketing plan. Cucumbers were grown specifically for this project, and using a quick process for pickling, they made quickles.

The students went to the farmers market on three occasions and sold their quickles along with two other products. They were the inventors, makers, and salespeople for each product. Along the way, they learned about goods and services and creating a budget, and developed the soft skills and customer service experiences needed to operate a business.

After discussing needs versus wants with their teacher, they decided to prioritize, first purchasing bunk beds, mattresses, sheets, and pillows and using the rest for Christmas toys.

Their teacher witnessed the development and learning that occurred during this process, but the students didn't even realize it. The garden became a vehicle allowing them to learn financial literacy experientially, to engage in service, and to nourish themselves and others in a sustainable manner.

The garden is a nurturing place. It provides us with an abundance of learning opportunities by connecting all levels of academics with meaningful real-world projects. Through it we are growing food, developing business experiences, and engaging and sharing with the broader community. The garden and our aspirations for it continue to grow. 🍃

▼ Hadley, Brooke Haynie, Alexandra, Madison, and Macy.

Jamee Haley
Lowcountry Local First

Lowcountry Local First's (LLF) founder and executive director, Jamee Haley, is a pioneer in the local movement, focusing on the important role local businesses play in Charleston's economic development. She is optimistic with a graceful, yet formidable determination to shine a light on the value that homegrown businesses bring to our community and quality of life. As a grassroots organization, LLF provides training opportunities, support, networking, and advocacy for local independent businesses, which include farmers. One of LLF's primary goals is to grow the supply of local food by growing the next crop of farmers, ensuring that the Lowcountry has a strong agricultural economy.

The path to inspiration

Twenty-three years ago, inspired by Nantucket's chefs who were incorporating local and regional cooking into their menus, my husband and I arrived in Charleston so I could attend the Culinary Arts School at Johnson & Wales University. After graduating, I ran an inn on a barrier island eleven miles north of Charleston, accessible only by private boat or ferry.

After my second child was born, I couldn't dedicate the time to the inn, so I created a line of hand-

Lowcountry Local First is endeavoring to encourage our community to buy local and eat local. Supporting family farms allows us to invest in what we value.

embroidered bedding and pillows. Initially just for friends, family, and acquaintances, my handiwork grew to the point where it needed to be outsourced. I shipped samples to Peking Handicraft in China. They replicated my embroidery pretty well, but I was shocked by their proposed pricing. There was no way the skilled workers doing this meticulous handwork were being paid fairly. I knew firsthand how much time was required to make just one of my items. Supporting horrible labor practices like that was completely counter to my morals, and so I was compelled to walk away from that opportunity. That experience was a turning point that led me to focus my attention on the economic impact of supporting local businesses.

Soon after my experience with Peking Handicraft, my husband and I were at a fundraising dinner where I was seated next to a man who had recently attended a meeting at the national organization of Business Alliance for Local Living Economies (BALLE). Throughout the evening, we shared our stories. I told him about my embroidery business experience and my interest in encouraging consumers to support local businesses that employed local people, paid local taxes, and added to our community's quality of life. My new friend was very interested in putting together a steering committee and getting people engaged to buy local and eat local in Charleston. Four months later, I was asked to launch a grassroots organization to do just that.

The principles I had as a business owner were very much encompassed in this newly forming organization's mission. Since its founding in 2007, leading Lowcountry Local First and supporting a strong local economy has been my passion.

In 2008, the South Carolina Department of

Agriculture (SCDA) approached LLF and another local nonprofit, the Coastal Conservation League, seeking our support of their *Fresh on the Menu* program, an initiative to generate agricultural commerce in the state by linking local farmers and chefs. Clemson University, Coastal Conservation League, Lowcountry Local First, and SCDA hosted a meeting for farmers and chefs. We expected thirty people and were caught totally off-guard when we had standing room only with over 130 participants. Clearly there was a deep hunger for creating these relationships and a local food culture.

That's when the light went on for me. So many people wanted to make this local connection and simply didn't know who to work with or where to find local food. The participating restaurants in the *Fresh on the Menu* program were asked to commit to using a minimum of twenty-five percent of their ingredients from certified South Carolina-grown producers. While on the surface that sounds like an easy commitment, several hurdles needed to be overcome to make that a reality—mainly the lack of supply.

Growing New Farmers

One glaring reality revealed during that first *Fresh on the Menu* meeting was that our farmers were aging out. Nationally, for every new farmer under the age of thirty-five there are seven over the age of sixty-five. We need to encourage and provide training to new young farmers. LLF addressed this need by establishing a *Growing New Farmers* program to provide the education, tools, and support necessary

▼ *Growing New Farmers* program.

to become a farmer, or in some cases, to become a food system leader who advocates for the farmer.

Growing New Farmers is a six-month program providing three hours of classroom curriculum training every Monday evening and hands-on learning in the field every Wednesday afternoon. We partner with the organic farm at the historical rice plantation, Middleton Place. The farm is now managed by one of our graduates. Wednesdays may also consist of field trips related to classroom curriculum. If students learn about soils on Monday evening, they will go composting on Wednesday. If they learn about marketing, they may visit a farmers market. If post-harvest handling was the topic, a visit to the GrowFood Carolina warehouse is in order. Students also have the option to apprentice with an established farmer, which provides them with much more experience with day-to-day farming.

The *Growing New Farmers* program trains farmers as business owners. Being a successful farmer is not just about growing delicious food, it's also about marketing and selling. Working the land to produce food is the passion for a farmer, and it is no small feat. But it also is important to understand the market and build a business plan accordingly. What do the

customers want? How should each crop be harvested, washed, and packaged? How does the product move safely to the consumer? How is the sale made? The classes and the field trips provide the opportunity for participants to learn the science of production, to understand the business of owning a farm, and to do the hard work of farming. Combined, this experience determines if farming is the right career choice.

To date, LLF has educated 150 participants through our program. Our participants are similar to the current national trend with the majority being women aged twenty to thirty with a college degree in a non-agricultural field. They are looking for a unique quality of life, want to work for themselves, and like to be outdoors. We also have a strong representation of retirees—people seeking a second career, who are also wanting a unique quality of life and are looking for the opportunity to be active in the outdoors.

Investing in what we value

I want consumers to realize the power of their dollars. According to the research group Civic Economics, three times more is reinvested in our community when we purchase locally. For every $100 spent locally, an average of $45 is reinvested in the community. With each purchase, consumers make a choice—between local, fresh, healthy produce or inexpensive, imported produce with lower nutritional value; or even worse—choosing unhealthy, highly processed foods. With every dollar, consumers have the opportunity to support and advocate for a farmer in their community. It's so important to buy local!

LLF encourages consumers to buy and eat local food through our annual *Eat Local Challenge* during the month of April. The challenge engages household consumers in a fun competition with the goal of shifting their purchasing behavior by ten percent per week. We've created a number of resources that help achieve this goal—a *Farm Fresh Food Guide*, which includes all the farms, what they sell, and where they sell it; information about farmers markets, wholesalers, and local purveyors; a ripe chart that illustrates what is in season by the month; and an app that maps out area farms.

The *Eat Local Challenge* culminates with our annual *Chef's Potluck*. Our goal is to introduce local farmers and fishermen to area chefs. We pair fifteen chefs with thirty producers—fishermen, farmers, and dairymen. Each chef-producer trio showcases two dishes made with all local products. It is a festive affair with farmers, chefs, local beer, local spirits, local music, local food, and local consumers. It creates awareness and great enthusiasm for local food in the community. Last year we raised nearly $60,000 during *Eat Local Month*, with proceeds benefiting our *Growing New Farmers* program.

There's enough pie for farmers, too

The industrialization of our food system in the 1940s and 1950s, which until then was primarily comprised of small family farms, created a cheap food mentality that supports large-scale agriculture. This forced many small farmers out of business and created a monoculture system—cultivating a single crop in one area—which depletes nutrients from the soil and increases the necessity for chemical fertilizers. This is the same system that subsidizes so many of the products that contribute to our country's health problems (e.g. corn—omnipresent as high fructose corn syrup).

Even though consumers are paying a fraction of the true cost for their food, they complain about their grocery bills. Sadly, only a very small part of their bill goes to the farmer. We have devalued our food system by expecting cheap food. Lowcountry Local First is endeavoring to encourage our community to buy local and eat local. We seek to emphasize the importance of reinvesting in our community, our health, and our environment. Every purchase we make is a vote with our dollars. Supporting family farms allows us to invest in what we value.

It's my goal, and the goal of Lowcountry Local First, to get to a point where the producers of our food make a living wage. Nationally, according to the USDA, nine out of ten farmers of small to medium-sized farms are required to have off-farm jobs in order to sustain themselves. It's all about supporting local community, knowing our neighbors, valuing local businesses, and putting a face on our food. There's enough pie for all! ❧

Don and Susan Brant
Brant Family Farm

Don's face beamed with pride as he held out his hands filled with the rich black soil he has so carefully cultivated. He contends that it's his soil that determines the delicious taste of his produce. Having frequently tasted Brant Family Farm's spinach and arugula, I can only say that something definitely sets it apart.

 After wandering through Don and Susan's vegetable beds and hoop house, we climbed in the truck for a ride around the farm. Their Belted Galloways came running out of the woods and into the grassy part of the paddock to say hello (actually to get a snack). The chickens were scratching away in their chicken tractors, and the hogs were lolling about in their comfortable habitat—a combination of woodlands and open pasture. I imagine it is the definition of hog heaven.

Don's retirement plan

Susan: I was a nurse and Donny was a chemical engineer, and now here we are—farmers! Neither of us grew up on a farm. Originally we purchased this land as a conservation area for wildlife and thought

We are convinced that the richness and flavor of our crops is a direct result of our soil.

we would use it as a retreat, but when we moved out here full-time, seven years ago, we decided to try growing food for our family and friends. Our small family garden evolved into larger-scale agriculture, and the next thing we knew, we had Black Angus and Belted Galloway cows, some Berkshire hogs, and chickens.

Don: After working as a chemical engineer for twenty-five years, I chose to "retire" early and return to our family and friends in the Lowcountry. Retirement is not exactly the right word since we have been involved in several ventures (or you might call them adventures) since leaving engineering and nursing. Farming requires every skill set—planning, growing, fencing, building, financing, marketing, and repairing equipment. I think it is the most challenging and yet rewarding profession of all. Farming is a serious business!

Learning to farm has been a journey; farming has a way of humbling a person. Our interest in farming started with a Google search, which quickly led us to farm stewardship conferences and organic growers workshops. We are fortunate to have an excellent Clemson extension agent, Zach Snipes, as well as our dear old-timey farmer next door. Recently he looked at our arugula and said, "What is that?" We seem to be good entertainment for these old farmers. Nevertheless, his guidance has been invaluable.

First, grow soil

Don: We are convinced that the richness and flavor of our crops is a direct result of our soil. We have about five acres under cultivation. The base soil is very sandy, which is good in this rainy climate. We have great drainage and are able to get into the fields faster after a big rain than farmers who don't have a sandy base.

Into that sandy base, we have increased our organic matter from under one percent to more than four percent and will continue to increase it. We amend our soil with organic matter through a variety of methods. Before we got our own cows and chickens, we brought in over 2,000 tons of chicken and cow manure to amend the soil. We added sifted sawdust, called fines, which consists of forty percent dirt, to increase organic matter.

We cover crop with crimson clover, blue lupine, Austrian winter peas, iron and clay peas, buckwheat, winter rye, and several legumes. We continue to learn about the best cover cropping techniques. Originally, I plowed our cover crops under before they flowered. However, Dr. Buz Kloot, a leading authority on cover crops in South Carolina, advised that rather than plow them under—which disturbs the soil's microorganisms, the soil structure, and the soil's web dynamics—it is best to mow and leave the cover crops on the soil as a temperature insulator and weed suppressor. With this no-till technique, we plant through the mowed crops.

Buckwheat and other cover crops are also very good for attracting beneficial insects, like bees and ladybugs. Bees are pollinators, and ladybugs prey upon insect pests. We plant bok choy in another part of the garden as an attractor for detrimental insects. We call it a sacrificial plant, because when it is hosting a high concentration of insect pests we harvest and dispose of the plant and insects.

We avoid soil-borne diseases and maintain our soil's health by rotating crops. Our garden is sectioned into seven zones from which we take soil samples regularly to check the soil's health. We grow kale, collards, broccoli, spinach, lettuces, arugula, carrots, peppers, onions, asparagus, tomatoes, and about six varieties of potatoes. We also have a fruit orchard with several species of apples, pears, figs, and plums. Last year, we had delicious fruit and made jams and preserves. We also freeze berries for winter desserts and smoothies. Next season, we will be attempting to grow upland rice as well.

Farming, a humbling but rewarding profession

Susan: Farming is a humbling endeavor. We were so proud of our beautiful tomatoes last year and planned on harvesting them through January. However, in November, we had two atypical nights that dropped well below freezing, and that sunk our aspirations of January tomatoes. We've tried to adapt to adverse weather situations by adding a hoop house. This extends our growing season by a couple of weeks on each end, and we can get a two- to three-week jump on the market while demand is high and supply is low.

Don: In addition to weather, we've also been humbled by deer. We've had to install a permanent eight-foot deer fence, some of which is electric, around all the fields to prevent their nightly foraging and destruction. However, on the upside, I like to hunt. So we also harvest free-range, organic deer for the family!

Pollination is one of the keys to a farm's success. We have five beehives. Our thirteen-year-old grandson oversees the bee operation. Today he is off trying to collect a wild swarm. Most of our hives have been created by splitting colonies when they get too large. To have healthy bee populations, we need to have multiple sources of pollen or nectar for our bees throughout the year. We have flowering fruit trees and bushes, cover crops of crimson clover, blue lupine, and buckwheat, and wildflowers growing in the woods, and we let some of our herbs and brassicas go to seed to provide food through the winter months.

We have four cow-calf pairs and rotate their grazing on four four-acre paddocks. Two paddocks have the added benefit of having trees on their periphery, which provides wonderful shade. When the time comes, we will sell two of the calves and keep two. We recently installed beautiful paddock fencing,

built to NRCS (Natural Resource Conservation Services) specifications by our thirteen- and eleven- year-old grandsons and a seventeen-year-old friend. This farm is a learning opportunity for every member of our family.

Susan: We raise chickens for meat and eggs. Right now, we have week-old chicks. Rather than incubate our own, we purchase and receive them when they are two days old. It was very cold last night, so I kept them under the lights with the heater on to keep them warm. Around four weeks, when our Freedom Ranger meat chickens are big enough, we will put them in movable chicken tractors so they can safely roam on the paddocks with the cows. We have five breeds of layers, producing an assortment of egg colors—brown, white, speckled, and a bluish-green—which our customers love! We keep the layers in a different spacious area. In addition to being free-range, all our chickens are fed a very expensive non-GMO feed.

We process our chickens when they weigh about five pounds. We are legally allowed to process and sell up to 1,000 per year, but we have never gone above 300 in a year. I remember my mother telling me to never learn to clean a bird or a fish, and for the longest time I let men do that job. But now that I'm a farmer, things sure have changed. Thank goodness for our automatic chicken-plucker!

Don: We have one boar and two sows. They

are registered Berkshires, which is a popular breed with the chefs. We have twelve acres for the pigs to roam, and before they start rooting to the point that they will potentially injure the trees, we rotate them between three paddocks. Unfortunately, our 300 pound boar needs to be put down because of an injured leg. He is too injured to breed, but he will provide many a good meal!

Brant Family Farm has always operated using organic practices, but we have chosen not to get an organic certification. The degree of record keeping required would add much stress to our lives. We have always encouraged people to know your farmer and his or her practices. We make sure our customers understand the quality and care we put into our fields and animals.

Raising future farmers

Susan: To be most productive in our sales, it's important to have multiple revenue streams. We have five modes of distribution. We sell to the Sea Islands Local Outlet (SILO), an online local food distributor; to restaurants in Beaufort; to GrowFood Carolina, a local food distribution hub; through direct email orders; and at local farmers markets. I attend four farmers markets each week, one of which is a year-round market. Our farmers market customers are very loyal, interested in and curious about their food. Our oldest grandchildren, all home-schooled, like manning the market booths with me. They are responsible for giving customers the proper change and have been known to instruct customers how to cook specific items.

We have been blessed in so many ways here on the farm, but especially with generous and willing labor. Since we are too small to have full-time help, we have relied upon a combination of interns and part-time employees. Three of our previous employees are about to graduate from college, and have echoed each other with the comment that college has been a piece of cake in comparison to working at the Brant Family Farm! All of our helpers over the years have become lifelong friends and continue to call us, asking if they can come help out.

Now, we are literally growing Brant Family Farmers for the future, as our grandchildren love being a part of the day-to-day farm challenges and opportunities. The four oldest (ages nine to thirteen) can each drive the tractor; the two nine-year-olds plant, weed, collect eggs, and do odd jobs; the eleven- and thirteen-year-olds can do anything from fencing to beekeeping, planting, pruning, collecting cow manure, harvesting, and processing chickens. It is exciting to watch them as they study, work, and play hard in such a natural, healthy environment. It will be fun when the infants and toddler can participate too.

We love this new life—living and farming as a multi-generational family. It is indeed a blessing to be surrounded by nature as we raise our animals and produce, and share the fruits of our labors! ◂

Sara Clow
GrowFood Carolina

T he food found in most grocery stores travels an average of 1,500 miles, according to the Worldwatch Institute. In an attempt to combat that statistic, Sara Clow, general manager of GrowFood Carolina, and her team are bridging the gap between local farmers, local retailers, and local consumers.

As a nonprofit food hub, GrowFood Carolina provides the infrastructure small farmers lack, and it manages sales, marketing, and wholesale distribution. It has played a key role aligning supply and demand by developing close relationships with and understanding the needs of retailers and chefs, and in turn, facilitating farmers' abilities to meet those needs by engaging in production planning. GrowFood Carolina enables farmers to focus on what they do best—growing fresh, healthy, and delicious food for our community.

Conserving land and creating healthy communities

GrowFood Carolina, a program of the nonprofit Coastal Conservation League, recruited me from Pacific Organic Produce in San Francisco in June of 2011. At that time, Pacific Organic Produce was the largest organic tree fruit marketer in the country.

I worked with more than 200 organic tree fruit growers and marketed their products to major retailers and other large-scale wholesalers.

I was also volunteering with the Marin County Agricultural Land Trust (MALT). As the first agricultural land trust in the country, MALT was visionary in understanding the environmental and cultural value of keeping farmland productive. Now I have the good fortune to be connected to another visionary organization.

For two decades, the Coastal Conservation League worked to protect land and wildlife habitat along South Carolina's coast by influencing land-use and infrastructure planning, promoting stronger zoning, and securing public funding for land conservation. While this work yielded great success, rural farmers and their lands were still at risk. The Coastal Conservation League envisioned and implemented a solution. If farmers could become financially sustainable, they would be less likely to sell their land to developers, and the farming culture and rural communities would strengthen. After many questions and much research, a local food distribution hub was the answer.

In early 2011, a longtime supporter of the Coastal Conservation League provided a grant to purchase a building. A 6,500-square-foot warehouse was found in an excellent location near two main Charleston thoroughfares. It was easy for growers to deliver produce and a short distance to retailers and restaurants. The building was upfitted to meet LEED specifications.

I will never forget opening day at the GrowFood Carolina warehouse in October 2011. I was sweating, partially because the warehouse had no air conditioning, but mostly because I was nervous about the first farm deliveries. The two farmers that delivered that day were also nervous. This was a new way to sell their produce—the name of their farm would be on the boxes, would hopefully show up on restaurant menus, and would be displayed in the grocery stores. They trusted me to market their produce. I emailed the harvest availability list to a handful of potential customers late in the afternoon and anxiously waited. At 1:45 a.m., Travis Grimes from Husk Restaurant texted me his order. Then came orders from Mike Lata of FIG and Frank Lee of Slightly North of Broad. These orders were cause for celebration! Now GrowFood had to deliver. And we did—that day and the next and the next.

At first it was just two part-time employees and myself, five growers cultivating thirty-two acres

If we invest now in sustainably and locally produced food, we will make local farmers economically viable and we will create healthier communities and lands for the future.

within a 120-mile radius of Charleston, a handful of restaurant customers, and two retailers. Five years later GrowFood has a passionate team of nine staff members, works with more than eighty producers who represent close to 2,000 acres of productive farmland in South Carolina, and distributes to more than 200 chefs, retail customers, and institutions.

We pay the growers eighty percent of the sales price, which is much higher than they would receive in a typical wholesale relationship. In the first five years, we returned $2.8 million to local farmers. This is money that would otherwise go to farmers in California, Peru, and Mexico, but now stays with our local farmers and communities.

Less than ten percent of what we eat in South Carolina is grown in our state, and we eat $11 billion worth of food each year. This statistic alone explains the real potential of a robust local food system. It's not only about the dollars; it's about conserving healthy lands and creating healthy communities. Food and farming can be the driver.

expanded our supply radius and partnered with more producers, we added new items with the caveat that they must serve our value-based supply chain. We have augmented our portfolio with grains, dairy, eggs, salt, non-GMO canola oil, and honey. These ever expanding opportunities build upon our established foundation. Product diversification will help us achieve our financial goals, serve more producers, and conserve more vital, productive landscapes.

Many small and mid-sized farmers face specific challenges regarding new food safety requirements: namely GAP (Good Agricultural Practices) and the 2011 FSMA (Food Safety Modernization Act). Many of the FSMA requirements make it more challenging for small, diversified farms to comply, leaving them out of wholesale opportunities. GrowFood Carolina is committing time and resources toward working closely with each of our farmers to obtain the necessary food safety certifications. We want 100 percent of our farmer partners to have 100 percent access to the market. This is a crucial step in stabilizing these farms, so they can grow and prosper.

Supporting producers

GrowFood Carolina focuses on creating a value-based supply chain. Our system values the producer, values the land, values the earth's resources, and values the health of our communities. We provide farmers with resources, information, and advocacy. We create effective production planning systems to help farmers expand and diversify their acreage. By aligning supply and demand, the farmers have new opportunities and, in some cases, have expanded their acreage or are now growing year-round and doubling their income.

When we started GrowFood Carolina, we focused only on fruits and vegetables. We were building the systems, building the customer base, and building the team. As we

Another priority is advocating for more resources for small, diversified farms from Clemson University (South Carolina's land grant university), the Farm Bureau, and the South Carolina Department of Agriculture. Oftentimes, the smaller farms don't have the same voice as the larger, industrialized farms simply because their value does not compare. However, when we combine the potential economic and community impact of all South Carolina's small, diversified farms, we have an important sector that needs attention and is worthy of support.

The critical link—
household consumers

Chefs were the first to recognize the value of local foods—the freshness, the flavor, the quality, and the impact that purchasing locally had on their community. Chefs provide a unique culinary experience based on taste, and they understand that the flavors of seasonally and locally grown foods are superior. While they have driven the local food movement in Charleston, they can only influence so much.

For local farmers to become financially sustainable, household consumers must change their purchasing habits and prioritize local food. They must insist that their grocery stores carry seasonal local products, their schools' cafeterias serve local fruits and vegetables, and their favorite restaurants use local ingredients.

If we invest now in sustainably and locally produced food, we will make local farmers economically viable and we will create healthier communities and lands for the future. 🍂

▼ Back row: Jackson Cauthen, Nate Toth, Jake Sadler, Benton Montgomery
  Front row: Alison Pierce, Sara Clow, Jessica Diaz, Nina Foy

Travis Grimes
Husk Restaurant, Executive Chef

*S*pending time with Travis at Husk was an experience in the authenticity of procuring, preserving, and preparing food. Upon entering the circa 1893 home converted to a restaurant, there is a large chalkboard listing the featured local producers. At the top of the stairs is a glass cupboard showcasing jars of pickled fruits and vegetables for use during the winter months. And on each table, in lieu of flowers, are mason jars filled with layers of heirloom seeds.

Behind the restaurant is a courtyard bustling with activity. Not unlike the configuration of Charleston homes generations ago, the prep kitchen and larder are located in outbuildings behind the restaurant. There is a covered area stacked with wood for the wood-fired oven and smoker, and local purveyors unloading their goods. Here authentic cooking methods of the past intersect with culinary challenges of today.

As we walked down the path toward the larder, Travis pinched, rubbed, smelled, and tasted different herbs from the garden beds, mulling over which menu items they would enhance later in the day. Husk is truly an experience in Southern culinary heritage.

Mustards & Kale	Ambrose Farms	MicroGreens	Dirthugger Farms /Meg Moore
Heirloom Grains & Field Peas	Anson Mills	Flounder	Crosby's Seafood
Kentucky aki & Smoked Salt	Bourbon Barrel foods, KY	GRITS, Tomatoes & Cornmeal	Greg Johnsman Geechie Boy Mill,SC
Beef	Southeast Family Farms	Greens, Radises, Courgettes	Grow Food Carolina
Triggerfish	Mark Marhefka	Trout	Sunburst Farms,NC
Bacon	Allan Benton	catfish	Rob Mayo,NC
Green Peanuts & Baked Benne Oil	Clay Oliver,GA	Eggs	Fili-West Farms
Oyster Mushrooms	Mepkin Abbey	Country Ham & Sausage	Edwards Family Surry, VA
Baby Carrots	Ambrose Farms	Manchego Cheese	Sean Sears
Benne	David Shields,SC	Quail	manchester Farms,SC
Bread	Butcher & Bee	Little Neck Clams & Oysters	ClammerDave

From Betty Crocker to Sean Brock

Until I was eleven years old, I didn't even know where to find the saltshaker in our kitchen. But then I started baking cookies to fill my after-school hours while my parents were still at work. Through Betty Crocker cookbooks and Julia Child shows, I developed a passion for cooking.

I attended Johnson & Wales University in Charleston, graduating with a culinary degree in 2000. I worked in several kitchens until I landed at McCrady's Restaurant, where I eventually became sous chef, first under Chef Michael Kramer and then under Chef Sean Brock.

Working for Sean was transformative. He grew up in rural Virginia eating food his family grew and preserved. As a chef, he became an ardent champion of local farmers, local food, sustainability, heirloom seeds and grains, and authentic Southern preparations. Seeking out indigenous foods and traditions of South Carolina's Lowcountry, Sean and I built relationships with local farmers, started a small farm, and raised pigs.

Sean opened Husk in 2010. I joined him as his chef de cuisine, and in 2015, I was promoted to executive chef. Husk is all about authenticity of ingredients, recipes, and cooking methods.

We cook everything from cornbread to pork chops in the wood-fired oven, which runs at about 800°F to 900°F from late morning to late night each day, using a variety of woods—white oak, hickory, pecan, or bourbon barrel staves—for additional creativity and flavor. Our woodpile and mobile smoker are also behind the restaurant and across the yard from the prep kitchen and larder. Adhering to the authenticity of food preparation in the past can be a challenge, but it's worth it.

Ingredient-driven menus

Food crosses barriers and draws into communion those who grow it, those who prepare it, and those who eat it. Sean and I have been advocates of the locavore movement in Charleston since 2006. We develop relationships with farmers and fishermen; we depend on and benefit from each other. Due in

At Husk we are championing local farmers, local food, sustainability, heirloom seeds and grains, and Southern culinary heritage by providing unforgettable experiences that we hope will change the perspectives of each and every one of our diners.

large part to the entire community of chefs in this town, who purchase from local growers, there are now more acres farmed, more local farmers, and a generation of younger people growing traditional and indigenous crops.

At Husk we want to inspire our patrons to develop a close connection with the people and culture of the South. Everything on our menu is Southern, and each of our items are sourced locally. We have a menu board listing the provenance of each ingredient, so our diners know what they are eating and where it came from.

Throughout the day, farmers pull into the courtyard behind the restaurant with deliveries of vegetables, fruits, mushrooms, fish, and meats. Today our larder and prep kitchen are packed with pigs from

Carolina Heritage Farms, large amberjack fish from Mark Marhefka, Storey Farm eggs, Geechie Boy grits, Pete Ambrose's cucumbers—some of which we are pickling, and other vegetables and fruits from the many farmers working with the local food hub, GrowFood Carolina.

Each morning, the first thing I do is grab yesterday's menu and I determine what's still available in the walk-in, assess other ingredients on hand, check the orders, and decide what more we need. Then I start creating recipes. It is a puzzle and challenge that adds to the fun of creating interesting cuisine every day.

Sometimes farmers will unexpectedly stop by and show me something unusual. If I decide to take it, I write a new recipe inspired by that ingredient.

Today farmer Pete Ambrose is delivering shishito peppers, which I love. I'm still trying to figure out what I will create with them.

Twice daily we create menus based on what is available in the larder and what farmers deliver. Justin Cherry, my chef de cuisine, has been with Sean and me for six years and is such an outstanding charcuterer that we give him free reign to create whatever he dreams up. Justin handles the lunch menu, and I create the dinner menu. Once we've finally made up our minds, both menus are printed upstairs in the office, where my wife, Meg, is the office manager.

From summer surpluses to winter treasures

During the peak of harvests, farmers often have surpluses. I believe it is our responsibility as chefs to purchase everything that we can from them. We must fully support our local farmers. And, because Husk only uses locally grown foods, we look at the farmers' surplus as a way to build up our larder for the off-season. The more we preserve and store, the

more we will have to work with in the winter, and the richer and more exciting our menus will be.

We build our larder just like my great-grandmother did when I was a child. One of my favorites is rhubarb, which I can only get once a year from a farmer in Tennessee. I use it to provide unusual and creative flavors during the bleaker months of the year. Today, we are preserving ramps (wild onions), peaches, and jalapeños. A forager in southern Appalachia brought us 100 pounds of ramps last week, and he is delivering another 100 pounds today. Every part of the ramp is edible. We are canning the bulbs and will use the tops in something—I've not decided what yet.

I just bought six cases of delicious South Carolina peaches to preserve. I let the peaches sit for five or six days, and today I will throw them in the smoker until they are so soft we can pull the stems and pits out. I'll simmer them with vinegar, brown sugar, and spices and then puree them, pass them through a sieve, boil, and put them in jars—and with that, we will have Husk's one-year supply of peach barbeque sauce.

We are also making a red jalapeño hot sauce today.

First, the jalapeños are salted and fermented for at least one month. Then we add white vinegar and simply enough, we've made hot sauce. We make several batches of hot sauce each year, each one a little different based on the chile peppers we get.

Seed saving

Husk has a one-acre farm on a nearby island, where we grow some unusual heritage plants like choppee okra, rattlesnake beans, and whippoorwill peas. The Husk Farm is dedicated to saving heirloom seeds. Sean and I have been some of the fortunate beneficiaries of heirloom seeds from Glenn Roberts and the Carolina Gold Rice Foundation. Each year we increase our seed banks by growing the seeds to full maturity, collecting the next generation of seeds, saving, sharing, and replanting. There's a culture around seed saving, which implies sharing. We share heirloom seeds with ten friends; they grow and collect them, and share with ten more friends. And on it goes—seed saving.

Because we focus on farmers, their farms and our farm, and seed saving, it seems only appropriate that the centerpiece on each table is a mason jar layered with beautiful, colorful heirloom seeds—Jimmy red corn, Sea Island cow peas, hickory king corn, indigo blue popping corn, and indigenous choppee okra. Our seed centerpieces fit with the relevance of Husk and our philosophy. We planted, harvested, and stored these seeds; they speak to our culinary authenticity and who we are.

Reconnecting

It is a shame that we even have to bring awareness to such a fundamentally obvious thing as where our food comes from. In just a couple generations, people in this country have become detached from food, a source of communion and pleasure, not to mention a source of our very survival. Many events in the past 100 years—from processing and refrigeration to supermarkets—have slowly led to the demise of our connections to the earth and the sources of our food.

I'm very hopeful that people will reconnect to their local community and return to the wholesomeness of seasonal food. It's not the easiest of transitions amid a convenience and fast-food culture, which is so embedded in the American mindset. But I'm seeing it happen with the numbers of people who are frequenting farmers markets and making a real effort to connect with their farmers. The local food movement is not a fad; it is about knowing and supporting the people behind local farms and businesses, purchasing and cooking responsibly, and recognizing that doing so benefits our health and our environment and puts money into the economy of the local community.

Since the Lowcountry region is such a desirable place to live and visit, one of my biggest fears is that new development will pave over our beautiful and productive farmland. It is happening, and as it does, we lose farmland forever and the ability to source food locally. It's up to all of us to advocate for protecting the places that need to remain rural farmland, and understand that there are certain places appropriate for development and others that are inappropriate for development.

Farmland protection is not something you'd think a chef would think about, but it's directly related to what we are doing here at Husk. We are championing local farmers, local food, sustainability, heirloom seeds and grains, and Southern culinary heritage by providing unforgettable experiences that we hope will change the perspectives of each and every one of our diners. ✍

David Anderson
Black Pearl Farms

The first time I visited Black Pearl, my husband and I sat with David and his daughter, Katherine, on the screened porch as the pelting rain saturated the sandy soil and clung to the early flowering blueberries. During the second visit a couple of months later, the farm was bustling with a flurry of activity—berries were being harvested in the fields and quickly transported to the shed to be dried, culled, packaged, and rolled into the refrigerator to await distribution. David's entire family was busy at work alongside their trusty laborers.

Natural productivity

When my wife, Suzette, and I bought Black Pearl Farms eight years ago, it was primarily a loblolly pine forest. My interest in planting blueberries was sparked by my walks through the woods, where I saw native sparkleberry, huckleberry, and rabbiteye bushes, as well as wild blueberry, growing prolifically.

▲ Above photo: Katherine, David, and Suzette.

I wanted to grow indigenous crops and allow the farm to be productive in its most natural way. I educated myself on all things blueberry, and I visited several veteran blueberry farmers. Then I ran the numbers; I'm good at math. The numbers added up, and that's how I decided to grow blueberries.

We started five years ago with 1,000 blueberry plants on half an acre. Each year we plant another three acres, and currently we have slightly more than a tenth of our 189 acres in production.

It is important to understand the lengths a farmer must go to in order to produce quality food on a small local farm. That understanding will lead to recognition of not only why local food costs more, but why it is worth every penny!

We plan to add another twenty to thirty acres of blueberries. Across the river we have another sixty acres sitting fallow on which we will grow organically certified vegetables.

A porous soil is the key for cultivating fruits and vegetables. We can get a lot of rain, so I want a sandy soil for good drainage as my base. Since sand does not contain organic matter, we are constantly upgrading our soil with compost, soil amendments, and beneficial micronutrients—copper, calcium, magnesium, and boron. Blueberries have been growing wild on this land for fifty years, but those wild bushes are growing in inadequate soil and won't even produce two pounds of berries. Our bushes are producing seven or eight pounds per bush. We take good care of the soil, because it is the root of our quality and productivity.

Currently we are the only certified organic, GAP (Good Agricultural Practices)-certified blueberry farm in South Carolina. Everything I add to the soil or plants is organic-certification approved. We use no chemicals, and we pull weeds by hand. We added eleven tractor-trailer loads of pine bark and organic fertilizers to the first 1,000 blueberry bushes. In the second field, we planted cover crops of buckwheat to build up organic matter, along with adding two tons of compost per acre. Fortunately, we have the invaluable guidance of a University of Georgia consultant who comes to the farm four times a year. Black Pearl Farms is most productive due in part to his analysis and recommendations.

Extra effort yields top quality

Each year around the third week of February, we start fertilizing, and will continue to do so every six weeks. Rather than use broadcast or drip irrigation for fertilizing, we carefully apply a measured amount of slow-release organic fertilizer to both sides of each plant. That way I know exactly how much each individual bush is receiving and can analyze each field's ratio of fertilizer to productivity. Although the fertilizer and labor are expensive, the benefits of hand fertilizing are well worth it. At four years, the bushes are mature and producing seven or eight pounds of blueberries each. They will remain productive for another quarter century.

The first two years, we bought blueberry seedlings, but if we didn't pull the weeds almost daily, the seedlings couldn't compete with the intense competition from the weeds. Now we purchase three- to four-year-old plants from North Carolina.

We grow five different varieties of blueberries at Black Pearl Farms. Our early and late varieties spread the harvest over seven weeks. The whole world seems to have blueberries coming in around June 10th, and of course, that is when the price plummets. It is not cost effective to compete against the larger North Carolina market at those times. So we plan to hit the market before the competition. Our early varieties, Stars and Emeralds, are cultured plants with patents. Legacies are our rock star. We have 15,000 Legacy bushes. They start coming in in early June and are prolific. We also have O'Neil's, the mother of Southern Highbush blueberries, and Duke's, a true Northern Highbush that normally struggles in our South Carolina heat.

Every flower creates five blueberries. Once the blueberry bushes have blossomed, they are in jeopardy of frost. Our greatest expense is frost protection. We have an overhead watering system with thermostats that automatically turn the system on when the temperature reaches 37°F. The coldest part of the night is around 5:00 a.m. When there's a frost, we make sure all the bushes are covered with water before 5:00 a.m. and continue to run the water all day. Normally blueberries start blooming in March. However, it was so unseasonably warm last January that some of the varieties started blooming months early. With our normal cold snaps that followed, we needed to frost protect seven times.

Wild bees, bumble bees, and wasps are important pollinators. We augment the wild species with thirty honey bee hives in six different locations to ensure everything is pollinated. The boxes are in different fields, all facing east so the bees wake up with the sun.

Once ready to harvest, we work seven days a week. We pick the same bush every three or four days. Even though the bushes may look ready, the individual ripeness of each berry is spread out on the bush. We only pick the ones that are blue. It takes longer when we have to pick through the cluster like this, and the cost of labor goes up, but we are going for the best quality product. Our blueberries are proof of our extra effort.

We could add mechanization, but we won't. We would need about seventy-five acres in production to make mechanization worthwhile, and our operation will top out between forty and fifty acres. A picking machine costs about $250,000, and it damages the berries. To be profitable, we would need to be able to process the damaged berries to sell to the fresh or frozen juice markets.

Labor and immigration

We are a family farm. The entire family has an interest in making our farm work. My wife, daughter, son, nephew, and brother-in-law are all here working today. We also have a big crew of local help, Hondurans, who are naturalized citizens. We have been doubling our production each year, and will probably hire thirty to forty pickers this year during the height of the harvest. They are seasonal workers. I pay $10 per hour, but I pay my star pickers by the pound, so they can earn more. We built a beautiful cedar shelter for the crew in the field as a place to escape the sun and rest with a sitting area, restrooms, a refrigerator, and a place to cook.

If the United States wants to continue to have family farms, it is imperative it does something about labor and immigration issues. Our workers have been here for thirty years. One has served in the U.S. Army; some have kids who are serving in the Army now. They all started as immigrants and have earned their citizenship. People think that California's big issue is water, but bigger than that are the regulations, the paperwork, and the onerous red tape that is interfering with and discouraging good, hardworking, non-naturalized labor—this is a problem everywhere.

From field to fridge

From the moment the berries are picked to when they are packaged and rolled into the refrigerator totals less than two hours. After they are picked, they are carefully poured into heavy-duty totes, called lugs, and placed in the back of the gator, an industrial-strength vehicle the size of a golf cart, and driven to a packing shed, which is kept at 69°F. We weigh each lug when it comes in, keeping meticulous records throughout the entire process. An inordinate amount of paperwork is required for organic produce to meet certification standards. The process is so time consuming and onerous for small farmers that many are choosing not to become certified, even though they are growing their crops using organic methods.

Once in the packing shed, the berries are loaded onto metal racks with fans blowing to remove the moisture. After the berries are cooled and dried, they are put on a conveyor belt that takes them up to a large fan, which blows away leaves, twigs, stems, and other debris. They move down the inspection belt where four or five people cull the berries that have bruises, cuts, or imperfections. Then they are batched into clamshells with the Black Pearl Farms logo, stamped with date and field of origin, packed into flats with seventy-two to a pallet, and rolled into the cooler at 37°F.

The cooler can hold six pallets, and we also have a refrigerated truck that I lease for overflow. In addition to fresh berries during the season, last year we froze 4,000 pounds of berries and will freeze 10,000 pounds this year to sell through GrowFood Carolina, the local food hub in Charleston.

Demand is high for local organic berries. We distribute all our blueberries through GrowFood Carolina, but will eventually outgrow their ability to distribute them all. I'm looking at other markets around the state and am hopeful that the GrowFood model will be replicated elsewhere.

Looking toward the future of Black Pearl Farms, in addition to our blueberries, we will start growing certified organic sweet potatoes, carrots, bell peppers, and onions in the field across the river. I'd like to get into processing, so we could make blueberry jam, vegetable dishes, and other items to sell year-round. We are open to new ideas and opportunities.

Lending a helping hand

I'm interested in helping other farmers in the state. We have a number of rural food deserts, where families have to drive more than twenty miles just to purchase food. By not having fresh produce more easily accessible, many people must resort to processed food, junk food, and fast food for the majority of their meals. There are many problems associated with that, including obesity, heart disease, and other health issues.

I would also like to help farmers learn how to improve the health of their soil, to conserve water, and to attain organic certification. Furthermore, if we could help farmers with major infrastructure issues, farming may become more accessible to those who want to farm. For example, I'd like to see programs developed for local farmers to share tractors or refrigerated trucks.

I am encouraged that more people are passionate about eating locally and organically; however, it is important to understand the lengths a farmer must go to in order to produce quality food on a small local farm. That understanding will lead to recognition of not only why local food costs more, but why it is worth every penny! ❧

Michael Shemtov
Butcher & Bee

An ambitious entrepreneur-restaurateur, Michael opened a Mellow Mushroom pizza franchise in downtown Charleston with two partners when he was just twenty-two. Ten years later, Michael opened his own restaurant, Butcher & Bee. Since this interview eighteen months ago, Butcher & Bee has expanded into a new, larger space. Michael has also opened a Butcher & Bee in Nashville, The Daily (an upscale bodega coffee shop and juice bar) in Charleston, and two more Mellow Mushroom franchises in the greater Charleston area. In Michael's current project, a fancy food court called Workshop, he is providing the space and opportunity for a number of incubator restaurants to thrive without the risks associated with the expense and commitment of brick and mortar.

A young entrepreneur

I moved from my birthplace, Israel, to Atlanta when I was ten years old. Around that time, I developed an interest and curiosity for business, and when I was thirteen, I started reading the *Wall Street Journal*. I read the Marketing and Strategy section every day and loved learning about start-ups and their strategies.

I started my first business when I was sixteen, selling loyalty cards door-to-door for neighborhood restaurants.

I came to the College of Charleston on a business scholarship in 1996 and graduated with a degree in business administration in 2000. Throughout school, I worked for a local restaurant and often applied my business education to my experiences on the job. I thought a lot about what was missing in the Charleston restaurant market. I felt the city lacked places to get great quality, but moderately priced, food—not fast food and not high-end—but something in the $15 range. I spent my senior year doing an independent study and writing a business plan for my own restaurant. My best friend, Johnny Hudgins, moved to Charleston that year, and we became business partners.

Growing up in Atlanta, I was familiar with the restaurant Mellow Mushroom, which got its start there in 1974. While I was doing market analysis and business planning, I discovered that Mellow Mushroom had started franchising, and Johnny and I could open one in Charleston.

In January of 2001, we opened Charleston's first Mellow Mushroom on King Street. As a franchisee, we were connected by name and mission "to create the most delicious craveable slice of pizza on the planet," but otherwise we could be a totally independent restaurant.

From management to leadership

After more than a year of spending every single night at the Mellow Mushroom, I noticed two of my employees taking the initiative, providing excellent customer service, answering questions, and generally handling things independently. I was amazed by the passion, enthusiasm, and freshness they brought to the job. Rather than being threatened by these employees' talents, I decided to focus on inspiring and training them. One of them, Josh Broome, worked his way up through every position, and soon after he graduated, he became our third partner.

These two employees were the catalyst for a new dedication to and interest in our people. I started to hone my skills to transition from a manager to a leader. I love food, business, strategy, marketing, and branding, but I realized that what I liked the most was mentoring our people. In the restaurant business, we tend to employ young people who are green and sometimes a bit lost. Mellow Mushroom provided an opportunity to anchor them and give them direction.

I had an awesome eight-year run working at Mellow Mushroom, but I needed to stretch, grow, and explore. My partner Johnny and I went back to Atlanta for two years and worked in the marketing and operations department of the franchise parent company, leaving Josh to manage the restaurant. We

I started thinking about locally sourced foods versus eating organic foods that were grown in Peru and shipped thousands of miles . . . I have stopped getting hung up on the word organic.

strategized about how to improve service across the board in all the Mellow Mushroom restaurants, and I did a deep dive into what makes great service in both a retail and restaurant setting.

Birth of Butcher & Bee

I returned to Charleston and decided to start something that could be all my own. I opened Butcher & Bee (B&B) in 2011 with the mission of "serving honest-to-goodness sandwiches made with flavor combinations and food quality usually reserved for fine dining." I wanted to be a benevolent dictator in my own restaurant, where I could encourage sustainable practices, make smart environmental decisions, and set procurement guidelines.

Reading Michael Pollan's *The Omnivores Dilemma* was a seminal moment, changing my thoughts on both eating and business. I started thinking a lot about eating locally sourced foods versus eating organic foods that were grown in Peru and shipped thousands of miles. I started to focus more on pastured meat, buying produce in season, and procuring food located as near as possible. I stopped getting hung up on the word organic.

I made connections with B&B's local purveyors. I went to the docks to meet fishermen, the farms to meet produce growers, and the pastures to meet beef providers. I wanted to get to know them and see each of their operations. What I heard over and over again was that while they grew organically, they weren't certified, because if they were faced with losing an entire crop worth tens of thousands of dollars or spraying, they would spray. As a businessman, I understood.

We do our best to source locally. B&B makes no claims to be all local or all organic. During the spring and fall, there is an abundance of local foods, but there are six weeks in the middle of summer and winter when the only local items available are microgreens and a few greenhouse items.

Another challenge we must address is the hard reality of price points in certain products like fish and pastured poultry. We serve magnificent sandwiches with unusual combinations of ingredients, but we are realistic about what people will pay. We've had to leave some items off the menu entirely, because the value proposition wasn't there for the guest, and we aren't willing to sacrifice quality and sustainability to get to a better price point.

Our culture and philosophy

I started B&B to provide healthy, natural, delicious food and also cultivate a philosophy and culture that I care about. I care about sourcing locally, reducing waste, recycling, and saving energy. I also care about my employees. B&B employees tend to be a bit older with more experience than my employees at Mellow Mushroom. You'll often hear the kitchen staff listening to NPR's *Fresh Air* each morning, and some are graduates from Columbia University and other prestigious schools. They are in different places in their lives, and therefore most approach their jobs as careers.

About thirty-five percent of the staff here are on salary, which is very rare in the restaurant business. We have nearly fifty employees, and we're still growing. I have a lot of managers. I'll take a restaurant full of managers, because the more people want to learn and manage, the more responsibility we can give them.

B&B offers a group medical insurance plan, and I recently introduced a retirement savings plan. A retirement plan is a novel concept for many of my employees, but I illustrate the importance of saving for retirement, and I try to incentivize employee contributions with up to a three percent match. Once they understand the benefits and do the math, they start saving.

I've had an interest and drive in business, marketing, and strategy since I started reading the *Wall Street Journal* as a young teenager. I love providing superb dining experiences at affordable prices, and I love mentoring and encouraging my employees. My approach to eating has evolved, and my philosophy has matured. I've developed a sense of responsibility, and I know how important it is to support the community around us. That community begins with our staff, extends to our purveyors, and includes the neighborhoods around us. 🐝

Mark and Kerry Marhefka
Abundant Seafood

Mark and Kerry, the husband and wife team behind Abundant Seafood, provide fresh, sustainably caught local seafood to the finest restaurants in the Charleston, Columbia, and Greenville areas and to local residents through their Community Supported Fisheries (CSF) program. Captain Mark fishes in the snapper grouper fishery, which includes seventy-two species of reef fishes—snappers, groupers, grunts, jacks, and sea bass. He also has permits to catch shark, mahi mahi, and king mackerel.

Kerry was a fisheries biologist with the federal government. She and Mark have been involved with fisheries management and are dedicated to improving the health of the resource and the viability of the industry. They are willing to take unpopular stances for the future of their fishery, they are vocal and influential in the fight against offshore drilling and seismic testing, and they are concerned about fish susceptibility as climate impacts the chemical composition and temperature of seawater.

Mark and Kerry are providing more than fresh, sustainably caught seafood, they are advocating for our coastal resources and their industry.

An untapped resource

Mark: I am not your romanticized version of a fisherman—with saltwater running in my veins, a passion for catching fish, and in love with the sea. What drove me to become a fisherman was a desire to work hard and be my own boss. I could have been a truck driver or the owner of a HVAC repair company. But I became a commercial fisherman.

After the Vietnam War, the federal government supported the creation of commercial fisheries as a means of stimulating job growth for returning veterans. In 1976, the Magnuson-Stevens Act was created to regulate fisheries in the United States. It extended the international fishing grounds from twelve miles offshore to 200 nautical miles, and it created the Bureau of Fisheries to develop commercial fisheries. After forty years, the Magnuson-Stevens Act has evolved. It is now the Fisheries and Conservation Management Act, and it fosters sustainable fisheries through regulations to prevent overfishing and to rebuild overfished stocks.

When my dad retired from the Air Force after Vietnam, he started commercial fishing. It was just Dad and my older brother. I wanted to fish too, but there literally was not any room for me on my dad's small boat. So the summer I was sixteen, I took a bus from Jacksonville, Florida, to Charleston, South Carolina, and found my way to the docks on Shem Creek. I was young and in a strange town, and I slept on the dock that night, waiting for the boats to come in.

I easily found work. This was a time when offshore fishing was a new thing, and there were huge numbers of fish. We caught the same species then as we catch now, but the fishery was an untapped resource. Everyone was bandit fishing, using big spool hook-and-line reels that are mounted to the side of the boat and baited with cigar minnows, mackerel, and squid.

After that summer on Shem Creek, my dad died while fishing. A year later, I graduated from high school and fished with my brother for a year. Then I decided to strike out on my own. One of the largest fishing companies asked me drive their delivery truck, and for the next three years I drove fish from Florida to New York's Fulton Fish Market. I became the face of the company and built relationships, which later proved to be a great advantage.

After three years, I saved enough to purchase my first boat, and I began fishing commercially from Southport, North Carolina. A few years later, I bought the boat I have now, the *Amy Marie*. She was built in 1985, more than thirty years ago. We've taken waves that have broken windows and cracked the cabin away from the fiberglass hull, but she is still reliable. Of course, I've gone through many engines.

In 2000, I moved to Charleston, a nice halfway point between my fishing jaunts from North Carolina to Florida, and continued to sell my catch to the plethora of fish houses up and down the coast. When those fish houses started to disappear—they were sold to developers due to the exorbitant value of waterfront property—Kerry and I decided to start our own business, Abundant Seafood.

Fishery conservation and management

Kerry: I grew up on the coast of Maine and landed in Charleston as a fisheries biologist in 1992. The Magnuson-Stevens Act established eight regional fishery management areas in the United States (New England, Mid-Atlantic, South Atlantic, Caribbean, Gulf of Mexico, Pacific, North Pacific, and Alaska), and I was the staff biologist for our South Atlantic Fishery Management (SAFM) area—from the Outer Banks of North Carolina to Key West, Florida. The role of each fishery management council is to oversee and protect the economic and biological sustainability of our federal waters, a jurisdiction that extends from 3 miles, where state management ends, to 200 miles offshore.

I gathered and analyzed scientific information, held public meetings, wrote fishery management plans, and helped develop fishing regulations. I provided the SAFM members with scientific information in order to vote on fishing regulations, which were ultimately sent to the Secretary of Commerce for approval.

My primary responsibility was to develop marine protected areas off the coast in order to protect the snapper grouper species on the reefs. Creating marine protected areas is usually very controversial and strongly opposed by many fishermen. Mark and I met when he was serving on one of the advisory panels. He arrived with his fishing charts ready to do serious work. Mark and I worked together well, because we both feel strongly about protecting the health and viability of the fisheries.

The Magnuson-Stevens Act is reauthorized every

six years. If any species is determined to be over-fished, then catching that species must be ceased immediately and a plan introduced for rebuilding it. Overfished species must be rebuilt for designated amounts of time. Because of the conservation aspects of the Act, the federal waters in the South Atlantic are actually doing very well. Fishermen in the United States are tightly regulated and fish responsibly.

I resigned as a fisheries biologist in 2007 and started helping Mark with the management of Abundant Seafood; nevertheless, we remain involved and very vocal advocates for conservation and managing sustainable fishing for the future.

A commercial fisherman's life

Mark: Weather rules our life. I have five different apps on my phone to check out the weather at a variety of locations—water and air temperature and wind speed and direction. Wind equals waves. A twenty-five-mile-per-hour wind can cause seven-foot seas. Right now there are twelve-foot seas, but I think it looks fairly good for tomorrow, so I'm heading out early in the morning. Because the trip is a short one—six or seven days—I want to have a man on each reel, so I will have a crew of two in addition to myself. I always go out with at least one crew member for safety, because without a moment's notice, things can get very dicey with the ocean or the boat.

I'll leave the house at 5:00 a.m. tomorrow for the Geechie Dock on Shem Creek where the *Amy Marie* is moored. I have a 175-horsepower engine with a cruising speed of seven knots, and I will motor about sixty miles offshore. We'll stay inside the Gulf Stream, because the current is too swift for bottom fishing in the Gulf Stream. It will take seven hours to get to my chosen spot tomorrow. It's winter, so it will be dark by 5:30 p.m. However, there's a full moon. If the weather is clear, we could catch vermillion snapper tomorrow night and triggerfish during the day. Each day, we will move around somewhere off the coast of Georgia and North or South Carolina.

The *Amy Marie* will return during a high tide, because we don't want to be lifting 150-pound boxes of fish eight feet up like we would have to if we got in at low tide. That means we will dock and unload around 2:00 a.m. I'll stick around doing chores until breakfast and go home to see the family. But I'll have to be back down to the dock to get the orders up for the restaurants. Before we sell, each fish needs to be weighed and recorded to provide details about our catch to the state and federal government.

The snapper grouper fishery is not seasonal, so I'm able to fish year-round, but there are regulations that limit which species can be caught at which times of the year. The regulations protect the species based on spawning season, size, and trip limits. The regulations may also require the use of different gear, hooks, monofilaments, and bait at that time. If we catch something we can't keep, we release it and generally move on to another spot. Throughout the year my catch may consist of vermilion snapper, black sea bass, triggerfish, pink snapper, amberjack, red grouper, mahi mahi, little tunny, snowy grouper, scamp grouper, white grunt, jolthead, or porgy. There is always something delectable!

Quality fish for the consumer begins once the catch is on the boat. I do a gut down immediately after the catch, which enables my fish to hold their firmness and freshness a lot longer than most.

Quality starts on the boat, not in the water

On the *Amy Marie* we have four electric bandit reels mounted onto the stern's deck, each with two hooks. Quality fish for the consumer begins once the catch is on the boat. Some fishermen will catch fish all day and throw them on ice. To gut and clean them at the end of the day, they must bring them off the ice and onto the deck, where it is much warmer. They will break the rigor mortis out of the fish to gut it, use lukewarm water to clean it, and then throw it back into the ice hole. Because the temperature of the fish has fluctuated significantly, it will never get the desired firmness of rigor mortis again. The fish will remain loose and limp. The meat is okay, but the quality has been compromised.

I want to provide the best quality fish at the best price, so I do a gut down immediately after the catch. I have someone on the back deck helping me gut, clean, and pack the fish on ice. This process enables my fish to hold their firmness and freshness a lot longer than most. Chefs know that, and appreciate it.

Tested by the mighty sea

I've had some scares at sea. They actually may be scarier for Kerry, on land waiting to hear if we are okay. We have a satellite phone on the boat, not for conversations, but to check in and for emergencies.

One night, we had anchored up because the current was going one way and the twelve-foot seas were going another. While we slept, the *Amy Marie* yawed back and forth and was sided-to in the sea when a rogue wave crested and nailed the wheelhouse window. The glass shattered, and we took on water. We couldn't take another hit like that, and we needed to get the anchor up and tethered behind us. We pulled on our boots full of shattered glass. I called Kerry and gave her our coordinates. She called the Coast Guard. We took the bin boards out of the fish hole and nailed them to the wheelhouse window frame for makeshift protection. We stopped taking on water, but our electrical system was compromised.

The next morning, soaked and cold, we were able to get underway and make our way home.

But the most memorable scare was when we were fishing in the Georgetown Hole. It was 4:00 a.m. and slick calm. We had set individual hooks out for Mako sharks, when all of a sudden I felt the thirty-nine foot *Amy Marie* lurch. I slowly brought in the line. The reflection of the stars glistened on the water; the blue-green light of the phosphorous glowed. All of a sudden from underneath the boat came a massive Mako, and then it receded into the depths. It took us four hours to get that fish up. We gutted and dressed it, and had to remove its head, tail, and fins to get it into the hole. We fished throughout the next day until the weather started deteriorating. Heading home, the wind was on our stern with fifteen- to twenty-foot seas. We were in the shipping lane and could only see the smokestacks and antennas of the big container ships when we were at the top of the swells. We started surfing the waves at about twelve knots. But the *Amy Marie* is not a surfboard! Suddenly a wave leapt out from beneath us, and we were heading straight down, bow first, and almost pitchpoled—when the stern pitches over the bow. I figured this is it, and we are going down because we have this beast in the boat. The karma is not good; the sea is testing us and is going to make us pay for this catch. I told the crew to put on survival suits. Somehow, I don't know how, we survived. We throttle jockeyed the last seventeen miles home. When we weighed the Mako back at the dock—headless, tailess, and gutted—it weighed more than the dock scale could register, over 550 pounds.

Releasing our catch—to consumers

Traditionally fishermen sell their catch to fish houses. That has its advantages, because they are an easy one-stop buyer, and the fish house will front you money if your boat breaks down. However, I realized that each time someone touched the fish, each of those middlemen tallied another cost to the consumer. When I sold our catch to a fish house in Murrells Inlet, they sold the catch to a distributor in

Atlanta, who sold it back to chefs literally down the street from our dock. I realized I could just sell to the chefs down the street. Furthermore, I didn't want my fish comingled with other fishermen's fish, because the quality of my catch is better. I wanted to raise the standards. In 2007, Kerry and I shifted our business model and started direct sales.

I got involved with the Sustainable Seafood Initiative at the South Carolina Aquarium. They connected me with Charleston restaurants, and I started selling directly to local chefs. The chefs were the genesis of the local food movement, and their initial focus was on farm to table, but quickly expanded to the sea. When I first started direct sales, chefs would come down to the dock to inspect my catch. Now, because they trust my consistent quality, I deliver to their restaurants.

In January 2010, Kerry and I started a Community Supported Fishery (CSF) as a way to sell directly to the consumer. We got the idea of a CSF from our farmer friends who ran CSAs (Community Supported Agriculture). The idea is that communities are brought closer by sharing the risks and rewards with their local fishermen. Our consumers get the highest quality product, and I get the assurance of having a market for my fish. And because CSF members pay upfront, it allows me to make repairs and invest in equipment for the boat.

When I come in from being out at sea and have 3,000 pounds of fish, I want to sell it as quickly as possible and get right back out to sea. Kerry emails each of our CSF participants informing them that the boat is in and the kinds of fish we have. Our clients come to the Geechie Dock to select what they want. We sell the whole fish, but if our customers prefer it to be filleted, we will do so at no cost. Each CSF period runs on a twelve-week cycle, and we offer half shares of fifteen pounds or full shares of thirty pounds.

We have never needed to advertise. The *New York Times Sunday Magazine* did an article on Chef Sean Brock and his Husk Restaurant recipe for triggerfish, but the article focused a lot on Abundant Seafood. The *Post and Courier* also did a big piece on us when we were starting our CSF, and the phone started ringing off the hook. It hasn't stopped.

Life after commercial fishing

I'm in my mid-fifties and don't want to be on the boat when I'm sixty. Abundant Seafood is doing well with our direct sales clients. Eventually, I'd like to have a brick and mortar retail shop.

Kerry and I also want to remain actively involved in the sustainability of state and federal fisheries. With ocean acidification and water temperature and salinity changing, we are seeing a shift in baitfish. They are moving north, and with them go the predator fish. Another threat is seismic testing and offshore drilling. We want to champion the health and viability of the fisheries and protect spawning grounds. There's much work to do.

And of course, I'd also like to be able to attend my children's sporting and school events. My eldest is approaching the same age I was when I took that bus to Shem Creek and began my life of fishing. 🐚

Kate and Lindsay Nevin
Household Consumers

Household consumers ultimately hold the key to success for local producers. I have pro-filed the following types of consumers—chefs, restaurateurs, distillers, retailers, and institutions. The Nevins are representative of you and me, individual and family consumers. What started with the priority to provide their children with the healthiest, freshest, and most delicious foods, broadened into a comprehensive way of life impacting all their purchasing habits. Kate and Lindsay recognize the impact they can have on their community as consumers. Whenever possible, they support not only local growers of food, but also local creators of goods and wares, as well as local service providers.

Nutritional value and incomparable taste

Kate: Eating local, seasonal food is now a core value for our family. When I first moved to Charleston in 2002, I got involved with the grassroots organization Slow Food Charleston. Slow Food International is a movement that started in Rome, Italy, in 1986 from one man's reaction to a McDonald's opening in an ancient piazza near the Spanish Steps. It has grown into an international organization with chapters all over the world. Slow Food focuses on regional seeds, plants, and food, and it celebrates local farmers and culinary traditions. It deplores fast food, industrial agriculture, and factory farms. Through Slow Food, I met local farmers who were planting and harvesting, and chefs who were celebrating local food by creating traditional cuisine. I learned about the increased nutritional value of local foods and came to understand the impact my purchasing habits have on farmers, their land, and the local economy.

People think that connecting with farmers is hard and purchasing locally is inconvenient. But once you learn why local food should be eaten, seeking it out becomes more meaningful and less of a challenge. Because local food is so fresh, its nutritional value is much higher and the taste is incomparable. Anyone can taste the difference between a local, seasonal food item and that same food item from a grocery store. Try it. A fresh, local carrot tastes rich and sweet, and a store-bought carrot, even if organically grown, seems tasteless. Once the health and flavor benefits are understood, we become empowered consumers and can make better decisions.

When Lindsay and I first started purchasing local food ten years ago, the choices were far fewer than they are today. We walked to the farmers market every Saturday and joined a CSA (Community Supported Agriculture). Rita Bachmann, whom I first met at the Charleston Farmers Market, leased land at a local farm nearby and sold her fresh produce through a CSA. Our front porch became the drop-off area for her downtown customers. Each week, our CSA basket was a surprise, and sometimes we had no clue what a certain vegetable was or how to prepare it. It was fun and interesting to try new things, and soon Rita added recipes to help with the mystery veggies.

When we heard about Mark Marhefka's Abundant Seafood CSF (Community Supported Fishery), we joined immediately. Following the same principle as a CSA, we pay in advance for our share of fish. All of the members' advance payments add up to an investment in Mark, his company, and his mission of sustainable fishing to support a healthy fishery. When Mark's wife, Kerry, emails us that his boat has returned after a week or so at sea, we head to the dock to choose our share of the catch. The kids especially love going with us; it is like a field trip. Mark shows us the products of his hard work—whether grouper, tilefish, red snapper, or porgy—and the kids are enthralled as he scales, fillets, and tosses guts to the seagulls.

A family commitment

Lindsay and I have schedules that can be quite busy. Between work, nonprofit commitments, and the varied schools and activities of our three kids, we still make it a priority to sit down together for a family dinner. I come home from work and go straight to the kitchen; dinner preparation becomes a communal time with everyone sharing and helping. If the kids are finished with homework, then I have some fine sous chefs. Our home-cooked meal is predominantly local meat or fish, local produce, and whatever we might pull out of the garden that day. Sometimes it feels like a three-ring circus, and many nights we may not sit down to eat until

▼ Lindsay purchasing fish from Mark and Kerry Marhefka.

Kate and I spend more on our food than we would if we purchased it at a grocery store, but we understand the value of farmers' hard work, and we feel that it's important to put the freshest and healthiest foods on our family's plates.

8:00 p.m., but our family dinner table is a sacred place. It allows us to pause, connect, and be grateful.

Fortunately, we have an online farmers market called SILO (Sea Islands Local Outlet), which has greatly simplified our lives since it launched in 2011. Local farmers within about a 150-mile radius of Beaufort, South Carolina, post available products each week and set their own prices. We go online, see what is available that week, and plan our meals accordingly. The kids enjoy being involved in this process too. SILO provides produce, meats, seafood, dairy, eggs, baked goods, grains, nuts, honey, and more. Orders are picked up once a week at a central location. SILO is a no-brainer because it makes purchasing from local farmers easy and convenient. We visit the Saturday farmers market to supplement our order and because we enjoy the personal contact with our farmers.

We also have a garden, which we share with our neighbors. My friend Rita, the farmer of our first CSA years ago, is my garden guru. I would not have this beautiful and robust garden without her help. My daughter, Grace, loves to plan and plant, my oldest son, Huck, is our weeder and harvester, and Hardy, the youngest, plays in the dirt. We are fortunate that we can crab and shrimp off our dock. Lindsay and Huck will shoot a few turkeys and hopefully a deer each year. We are all duck hunters. Grace is learning about honey hives, and we are preparing to get our own hives at home this spring. We are also ready to add chickens to our little homestead.

We mainly use the grocery store for staples—cereals and pantry items. Bananas are not on our list (unless the kids beg for banana bread), because we try to only eat local, seasonal fruits like peaches, kiwis, and the wide variety of berries.

Local—food, goods, and services

Lindsay: What this is all about is changing the way we think of our role as consumers. Ordering local food through SILO takes a whole lot less effort than shopping at a grocery store. Kate and I spend more on our food than we would if we purchased it at a grocery store, but we understand the value of farmers' hard work, and we feel that it's important to put the freshest and healthiest foods on our family's plates. Meats are more expensive, but by knowing the farmer, we know how the animals are raised and what they are fed. We also know who is growing our produce, how they have augmented the soil, and, in particular, what has not been added to the soil or sprayed on the plants. We are putting our money where our mouth is.

Our perceptions as consumers have changed. We reimagined how we eat, how we shop, and how we think about the source and seasonality of our food. It is not just about food. It is also about where all of our "stuff" comes from. Slow Food started a consumer movement by focusing on local seasonal foods and cultural culinary traditions, but it has evolved into a greater movement and moved into different sectors. It is now about supporting and purchasing from local vendors across the board—home goods, clothing, local service providers, and other local businesses.

We are fortunate to have the nonprofit organization Lowcountry Local First (LLF), which is a huge proponent of local farmers and local businesses. Through LLF, we learned the value of our spending choices and the impact that purchasing locally has on this community. For every $100 we spend supporting local farmers, artisans, businesses, and vendors, forty-five percent remains in the community. When we purchase non-locally and from big-box and chain stores, only fourteen percent of our dollars remain in the community. Keeping money in our community makes this a better place to live.

Kate: Lindsay and I have learned that shifts both large and small in our choices as consumers make a major impact. We feel empowered through our purchasing choices and recognize that buying locally is a vote for sustainability and a vote for our community. It's more than just a purchase; it's an investment in this place and people, but especially in the future of our children. ❧

Stefanie Swackhamer and David Flynn
Tiger Corner Farms and Boxcar Central

I met Stefanie and David in downtown Summerville for a totally different farm experience—aeroponic farming in shipping containers. Stefanie and her dad, Don Taylor, purchase and remanufacture shipping containers into self-contained farms. David and the Boxcar team develop the software to run aeroponic operations in the repurposed containers. This is a revolutionary and sustainable way of growing food that holds great potential for farming in urban areas, food deserts, or locations lacking arable land.

Stepping inside the ordinary looking shipping container, I felt like Alice in Lewis Carroll's Adventures in Wonderland, *falling down the rabbit hole and emerging in a world of a future reality. I picked a bag of greens from the vertical panels—collards, Bibb, kale, and spinach—tasting everything as I went along. Even the raw collards were sweet and tender!*

High-tech farming

Stefanie: Despite being an entrepreneurial and technological venture, the evolution of Tiger Corner Farms and its affiliate Boxcar Central has been very organic. Tiger Corner Farms started when my dad, a retired chief technology officer, became intrigued with aeroponic farming. His research led him to aeroponic greenhouses in Amish country, and then to Nevada, where Indoor Farms of America was creating farms in shipping containers. Next, "he bought the farm"—the shipping container farm—which arrived in our hometown of Summerville six months ago.

I was a high school Latin teacher and had recently decided to stay at home with my two young kids. The initial plan was that I would work part-time growing vegetables in the new container farm to sell to the local food hub, GrowFood Carolina. However, so much interest was immediately generated around the container farm itself that my dad and I decided to switch gears. Rather than producing food from one farm, we decided to think bigger and manufacture shipping container farms. We signed on some more investors and a chief engineer, and founded our affiliate software company, Boxcar Central. Now we are improving upon the software and mechanics of the original farm and manufacturing additional

farms for sale. Dad is the managing partner of both Tiger Corner Farms and Boxcar Central. His retirement hobby has quickly become another career.

The farm's structure is a forty-foot oceangoing refrigerated container with three inches of insulation between the interior and exterior steel walls to maintain the desired temperature and moisture levels for growing food. The entrance of the farm has a special feature, an air curtain. When the door opens, a strong blast of air creates a barrier and prevents any insects or particles from getting into the farm.

Currently we are growing collards, Bibb lettuce, spinach, kale, and bok choy in this totally controlled environment. The seeds germinate in an organic rock wool. The germination racks are two feet wide, two feet deep, and four feet high, stacked on horizontal flats that are lit with LED bulbs from the flat above. The germination lights remain on all day and have a lower intensity and bluer spectrum than the grow-out

▼ Inside the shipping container farm. Panels with seedlings and with ready-to-harvest produce.

Exploring the potential for new and efficient food systems is urgently compelling. The world's population is expected to reach 9 billion by 2050, with the majority of people living in or around urban areas—areas where our current food systems are incapable of sustaining them.

lights. After about ten days in the germination trays, the plants are transferred to one of fourteen vertical floor-to-ceiling aeroponic panels. On both sides of the panels are indented spaces called grow cups that each hold a plant plug. The capacity of the panels enables us to grow 4,500 plants at a time.

Inside each enclosed panel (purchased from Indoor Farms of America) are the plants' roots and water misters, which turn on every half hour for eight seconds. We only need a total of eighty gallons of water to run this farm. The water is pumped back into the water tank where the pH and nutrients are adjusted according to a computer-generated analysis before the misting cycle begins again. On average, we replenish the system with about ten gallons of water each day. In the summer, we use less water, because the system creates water from the ambient humidity.

The nutrient-rich mist along with the special lighting enable the plants to grow. Studies reveal that the sunshine in New Zealand provides the best intensity and spectrum of light for growing plants, so we try to mimic that range and intensity using blue and white LED lights. The grow lights are on seventeen hours per day. Our energy use is not terrible (about $500 per month), but we would like to reduce it. Down the road, we will pursue solar and wind energy alternatives, but at the moment we are focused on growing nutritious, quality crops.

David: The first shipping container farm that Tiger Corner Farms received became Boxcar Central's research and design lab. We improved on the existing software and created new software to operate it more effectively. We also learned more about the needs of each crop, then collected and analyzed data, and built software accordingly. With each successive farm we build in partnership with Tiger Corner Farms, we learn more and improve more.

Each plant has different needs. Our software monitors a plant's growth through probes that collect and analyze data on carbon dioxide (CO_2) levels, nutrient conductivity, pH, humidity, air and water temperature, and the spectrum of light from the LED bulbs. Our system incorporates cameras so day to day we are able to compare the visual results recorded by the cameras with the analytical data collected from the probes. This scientific information, from seed to harvest, allows us to improve and create the best container farms with the most effective software for efficiently growing delicious and nutritious food.

Currently, we are analyzing the amount of dissolved oxygen the plants are getting. In hydroponics, the roots are always in water and need dissolved oxygen. Because our system is aeroponic, the plant roots are not in water; rather, they are regularly sprayed with the nutrient water mist. We think the plants are getting enough dissolved oxygen from the air, but we don't know how much of the mist is staying on the roots and whether that is preventing them from getting enough dissolved oxygen. Our probes and software are monitoring this for further analysis.

The farm's entire system fits on one small desk, and its monitor collects, analyzes, and displays the data. It is the farm's brain. For example, the farm's CO_2 reading when we walked in was 393 ppm. The earth's average is 400 ppm. Three of us have been in the farm for five minutes, breathing oxygen and exhaling CO_2. By refreshing the computer, we can see that in that short time, we raised the CO_2 level to 411 ppm. It will continue to increase as long as we are in here. This is important information, because CO_2 has a significant impact on a plant's growth.

With the monitoring system, the farmer can observe and manage everything—at the farm or from a remote location—required to grow healthy, nutritious, and flavorful food. In addition, the software allows the farmer to manage the inventory and production schedule, and integrate the information with budgeting, sales, and accounting.

Stefanie and I take turns managing the farm each week. This is my week, and five days into it, I probably have spent no more than five hours total.

▲ An opened panel showing the plants' roots.

I seeded plants, adjusted the pH and nutrients, and will harvest for less than an hour this afternoon. Otherwise, I have just generally kept my eye on the monitors.

Stefanie: Estimating a year's yield with ten to twelve growing seasons, this forty-foot container farm can produce an equivalent amount of food to four acres of land. Currently our crops take from four to six weeks from seed to harvest. We are on our fourth harvest since we started six months ago, and we believe we can get it down to four weeks. The quality and nutrition of our vegetables are most important, not speed. So our focus is on quality now.

We are still in the experimental stage and not yet ready to commit to selling our produce, so we donate it to a nearby nonprofit group working to fight hunger. If what we harvest isn't in the best condition, we give it to the South Carolina Aquarium for their sea turtle program. We try not to generate any waste.

Point-of-consumption food production

David: Exploring the potential for new and efficient food systems is urgently compelling. The world's population is expected to reach 9 billion by 2050, with the majority of people living in or around urban areas—areas where our current food systems are incapable of sustaining them. And, as water scarcity increases and available arable land decreases globally, agricultural systems that currently use seventy percent of the world's fresh water will face potentially catastrophic consequences.

It is Boxcar Central's mission, in conjunction with Tiger Corner Farms, to manufacture sustainable commercial-size farms that produce fresh, nutritious food that will be abundant and available year-round at point-of-consumption. Our farms will not use pesticides or chemicals, and they will not be susceptible to weather conditions like drought, flooding, or hurricanes—like Hurricane Matthew that blew through here last week. Growing aeroponically at point-of-consumption eliminates high transportation costs, eradicates soil-borne diseases, significantly reduces the carbon footprint of agriculture, and uses ninety-five percent less water.

From growing food to growing farms

Stefanie: My passion is twofold. I want to feed people, and I want to provide the tools so people can feed themselves in a sustainable way. Food scarcity and hunger are everywhere, but we have our own set of challenges here in the Charleston area. So, at the moment, we are going to stay focused and stay local. Just imagine the impact on health and nutrition if these farms were in rural and urban food deserts!

One of our farms, depending on the model, will cost around $65,000—an expense that will decrease over time. Our first contract is with The Citadel, the local military college. The school plans to add a minor degree in sustainability and to grow produce for the school cafeteria. The cadets are learning how to operate our farm, while also helping us with the construction of their farm. This is the first farm we are building, and it will take about six weeks to complete. Subsequent farms should take four weeks or less to build. We are currently in conversations to manufacture farms for a culinary school, a couple of high schools, some people who are interested in urban farming, and even a local brewery.

Dad and I started Tiger Corner Farms with the intention of working our own farm within a shipping container. It quickly grew into something bigger, and now we are in the business of manufacturing shipping container farms with our affiliate Boxcar Central. We are creating farms and software packages in a way that is totally turnkey, allowing anyone to use it. It is revolutionary and a technological breakthrough for farming. ✿

▲ Two shipping container farms.

David A. Williams and Cassandra Williams Rush
Williams Muscadine Vineyard & Farm

David A. Williams and his daughter, Cassandra Williams Rush, manage Williams Muscadine Vineyard & Farm. At eighty-nine years of age, Mr. Williams still farms daily. The Williamsburg Hometown Chamber named him Agriculturalist of the Year in 2010. Cassandra manages the vineyard, and like her dad, she has boundless energy and multiple interests. She is engaged in numerous civic, health, historical, and educational activities. She has a passion for environmental justice, and when Williamsburg County received an EPA Brownfields Grant, she worked as a consultant for the project. She consults with beginning farmers on various projects and conservation easements, works on Rosenwald School and other African American historical projects, and owns a gallery and the Museum of African American Arts and Culture.

In addition to producing delicious, nutritious muscadine grapes, the Williams Muscadine Vineyard & Farm is an educational and cultural experience. The South Carolina African American Heritage Commission honored the vineyard with the 2009 Preserving Our Place in History Award. It is a remarkable place where visitors step back in time to get a glimpse of what farm life was like for African Americans in the rural South during the early twentieth century.

We have the opportunity for our farm to be more than a vineyard—it is a classroom revealing the history of what life was like for a rural black family in the 1930s through the 1950s.

The $400 misunderstanding

David: As kids, we walked up and down these unpaved roads and passed these wild muscadine vines, but the only reason a vineyard is here today is due to a misunderstanding three decades ago. It happened like this. At the age of sixty-seven, with a degree in Vocational Agriculture and undergraduate minors in biology and chemistry, I retired from thirty-seven years of teaching high school agriculture and the sciences. As a substitute teacher in another school, I met a man who told me about selling $6,000 worth of muscadine grapes the year before. I casually said that sounded interesting, and maybe I should give it a try. I evaluated my farm, where my dad had grown tobacco, cotton, and corn many years earlier, and determined the soil could be perfect for growing muscadines. But I left it at that and didn't think much more about it.

One year later, that man called me up and said he had rooted fifty vines for me in one-gallon containers. They looked like inconsequential little pieces of straw, but chagrined, I felt obligated to buy them. I almost fainted when he said I owed him $500. I got him to knock $100 off the price, but still, I wasn't planning on this. I came home with my "investment" and couldn't tell a soul about why or how I was starting a muscadine vineyard. My wife would have killed me for spending that kind of money! It wasn't until six or seven years later, when I was selling grapes successfully, that I revealed the real story. That 1987 vineyard and I are still going strong.

Growing muscadines

When I first started the vineyard, I went to the county extension agent for direction. No one seemed to know much about growing muscadines, but the county agent told me that muscadines in our area would grow for four or five years and then mysteriously start dying. Sure enough, mine started dying after seven years. I was about to go fishing on the Okeechobee in Florida and stopped by the field before leaving for my trip when I saw they were starting to die. I felt a soft bulge at the base of each stalk, so I stuck a screwdriver into the bark, and juice started running out. Under the bark some microscopic insects were cutting the cambium and interfering with the phloem and xylem, so water and nutrients couldn't flow to the vine. I started doctoring my vines by soaking the base of each with pesticides, and I nursed them back to health.

All of my muscadines are hybrids. I propagate them by burying a vine from the parent plant until it grows roots. After the new vines emerge from the parent plant, I dig them up and plant new plants. I've done this every year since 1987 and now have about five acres of muscadine vines.

The leaves emerge in March, followed by white and pink flowers, which are pollinated by the wind and wild bees. By the second week in April, we start to see a few grapes. Harvest starts in mid-August, and we harvest for about two months.

Around the end of November, we start pruning. Every vine that bore fruit needs to be hand-clipped before they will come back as new shoots and grow a new crop. As they re-emerge, I train the vines on wire and rake the vine clippings to be reused for wreath and baskets; some chefs use them for smoking. I then disk the field for aeration and rainwater saturation. That is my only form of irrigation. Each plant has a deep-growing taproot and feeder roots that spread outward about six inches below the soil. Disking the soil improves the roots' growth.

I put a cup of 10-10-10 fertilizer (10% nitrogen, 10% phosphorous, and 10% potassium) at the base of each vine. The biggest problems are the insects, specifically fire ants, which seem to like the muscadines as much as we do. Fire ants will climb up the stalks to suck the muscadine juices. Each grape they touch will fall to the ground. I have to spray for these pests every two weeks, which is the most time consuming and expensive part of the process.

Health and nutritional benefits

Cassandra: Daddy works the farm every day, and most times with the assistance of a part-time worker. As my brothers retire, they are becoming more actively involved with assisting Daddy with the labor-intensive responsibilities that the vineyard demands. About eleven years ago, when Daddy was seventy-eight, I realized it was too much for him to be harvesting all these muscadines each week. So we started an annual Williams Muscadine Festival, which now occurs every Labor Day weekend. That gives us the opportunity to showcase our farm and also bring as many people as possible to help pick muscadines. People come from all over. Muscadines are addictively delicious, and we make it a fun experience. One woman traveled by train all the way from Washington, D.C., just to pick muscadines for the day.

The latest research shows that muscadines have amazing health and nutritional benefits. They are high in antioxidants and possess anti-inflammatory and anti-aging properties. The bulk of the nutrients are in the seeds and skin. After extracting the juice for wine, jelly, syrup, and juice, some manufacturers are grinding the residual seeds, skin, and pulp and producing capsules as a health supplement.

David: We have a U-Pick. School groups, families, and seniors come daily, even after church on Sundays. We weigh their buckets, and of course they are allowed to eat what they can along the way. That is part of the experience. The U-Pick and festival are great forms of agritourism. Once we get people to the farm, they tend to also purchase our muscadine jelly, cider, and syrup. We also sell our grapes through the local food hub, GrowFood Carolina, and the IGA grocery stores. A number of health food stores are realizing the health benefits of muscadines, so they want them, too.

A rich African American rural history

Cassandra: I was born in this house and have come full circle, now spending time back on the family farm. My grandfather, the Reverend Gabriel Williams, bought this property in 1924, at a time when it was a huge accomplishment for a black man to buy and own property. He farmed tobacco, cotton, and corn crops on this land where the vineyard is now. Our family was totally self-sustaining with hogs, chickens, a cow, and a vegetable garden. After

▼ Great-grandson Tremayne, David, and Cassandra.

building the house, he allowed the sharecroppers, who were helping him with the land, live in it for a couple years.

My dad moved into the house when he was seven years old. He is the twenty-third child of two combined families. His father's first wife, Hester, died and left him with twelve children. He then married a widow, Mary, who had ten children. In 1927, at the age of forty-five, she gave birth to my dad.

There is a lot to learn here beyond muscadines. Today, we have the opportunity for our farm to be more than a vineyard—it is a classroom revealing the history of what life was like for a rural black family in the 1930s through the 1950s. We have barnyard animals wandering about, historical farm implements, kitchen utensils, and household demonstrations using butter churns, washboards with lye soap, and more. We also share what education was like for rural black children. In the early twentieth century, philanthropist Julius Rosenwald collaborated with Booker T. Washington to establish one-room schools to educate black children. My

dad and I both went to one of the ten Rosenwald Schools in Williamsburg County, and we feel it is important to share that history and culture with our community and farm visitors.

An inspiring legacy

David: I have more than 1,000 plants now, and continue to learn about the science and the art of growing muscadines. Several years ago, I spent some time at Tuskegee University in Alabama where I gleaned new growing tricks that will allow me to get an unheard-of second harvest from my vines this year. This will double my yield. Who says an old dog can't learn new tricks!

Twenty-nine years ago, I started with fifty pitiful, feeble-looking plants that I didn't even want. They are now going strong, and will live to be 100 years old if taken care of properly. The proud legacy of my father's farm continues, and I hope its history and current operations will inspire visitors for many more years to come. ❧

Frank Lee
A Local Food Movement Chef-Pioneer

*C*hef Frank Lee is widely known as the pioneer of the Lowcountry's local and sustainable food movement. He set the bar for Charleston's culinary renaissance before sourcing locally was fashionable, and he trained many top chefs who continue to advance the local food movement. His extensive training took him from his hometown of Columbia, South Carolina, to France, Chicago, and Washington, D.C. Ending up in Charleston as the executive chef for Slightly North of Broad and the Maverick Southern Kitchen Group, he combined his French culinary techniques with Lowcountry culinary heritage. Local farmers regard him as their champion; he was the first chef to source meats and produce directly from the growers. Many chefs credit Chef Lee as their mentor. In the small amount of time I spent with him, I found Chef Lee to be passionate, poetic, and philosophical—a great combination for an artist of culinary bliss.

A counterculture chef

I did not grow up on my grandmother's farm with my hands in the dirt. Nor did I grow up in the south of France. I was not passionate about cooking in any way, shape, or form. What got me into cooking was pure chance.

Three chums and I, right out of high school, were

American consumers are hardwired with expectations that food should be cheap. Fresh, nutritious local food should NOT be cheap; it certainly is not cheap to produce!

interested in meditation, Eastern religions, and vegetarianism. This was 1972. We were very counterculture. Embracing vegetarianism meant taking a political position in those days. It was becoming a movement across the country—the idea that diet not only contributed to health and wellness but also had a greater societal impact. After group meditations, we would cook together and share meals.

On a lark and with an investment of $5,000, we started a vegetarian restaurant. We figured that we were just taking one year off before going to college. Our restaurant, 221 Pickens Street in Columbia, was positioned between a down and dirty college bar and a liquor store that catered to patrons preferring Mad Dog 20/20.

At the start, we literally did not know how to boil beans. Our first meal was boiled pinto beans, boiled cabbage, and sautéed squash with soy sauce. It was a pretty bland beginning. Our motto was, "food for people, not for profit." We did not use any sugar, refined flour, or cheese containing rennet. Only once a week would we use eggs to make pasta. We hardly used any dairy. We sprouted grains, seeds, and sunflowers and made our own breads. We made tofu, and juiced carrots, apples, and beets.

We took over the storefront next to us and added a natural food store and co-op. Each night, we served a different ethnic food—Indian, Chinese, Mexican, and Italian—making everything from scratch. We even had a macrobiotic night.

The State Farmers Market was nearby, and twice a week I would shop there using my 1961 seat-less VW van to transport a restaurant's worth of ingredients. Determined not to miss out on the crème de la crème, I was certain to arrive at four or five o'clock in the morning. I looked like a hippy back then, weighing about 120 pounds with bushy Afro hair, so it took a while to garner the respect of the

local farmers. Eventually, they learned I was sincere. This is when I became dialed into the seasonality of food and committed to sourcing locally.

It was a seductively exciting time. My business partners and I felt like we were part of a movement, that we were the hammers in the hands. We wanted to change the world through vegetarianism.

Our restaurant and co-op lasted seven years, until 1979. During that time, I learned a lot about taking care of people and making them feel good. Seven years after high school, many of my friends were on their way to becoming doctors, lawyers, and leaders within the community, and I realized, "Well hey, I guess I'm a chef!" It was time for me to move beyond our little restaurant and co-op.

Revolutionary cuisine

I began taking an interest in the culinary revolution going on in France with Chefs Michel Guerard, Paul Bocuse, and Roger Vergé, who were cutting against the grain of cuisine classique, the heavier, traditional French cuisine. They introduced an innovative approach of lighter dishes with fresh local ingredients, which came to be known as nouvelle cuisine. I wanted to learn more about this cooking and petitioned Columbia Chef Malcolm Hudson for a job. He was doing the real thing—making his own sauces, butchering his meats, and sourcing locally and seasonally. He was adamant that he would not consider taking me on until I started eating meat.

He asserted, "If you are going to cook it for others, you need to be willing to eat it yourself." I became a carnivore, and he became my mentor.

In January of 1981, after working for Chef Hudson for one year, he arranged a trip through France, joined by his maître d' Tommy Moore and me. The three of us rented a camper van and toured France. We went on a truffle hunt in Provence, experienced the foie gras and truffle markets in Sarlat, and ate with famous chefs like Bocuse, Guerard, Vergé, and others.

The experience opened my eyes. I realized that I could have a viable future as a chef. These guys were superstars; they were artists and making a pot load of money. They welcomed us into their guild, were interested and enthusiastic, and willing to share their techniques. It was apparent that everything we ate was local. The delicious rabbit was from the butcher shop down the street; the produce was grown in home gardens and nearby small farms; the wine and cheese was produced in the region. They showcased their cuisine and were most proud of the characteristics that defined a specific place. When I asked what advice Chef Bocuse had for a young American cook, he said, "Develop your own technique, and apply it to your region and your heritage. Do not copy what we are doing." It's advice I've carried with me throughout my career.

I returned to Columbia, met my wife at Hudson's—a restaurant romance—and we moved to Chicago. I started working for Chef Jovan Trboyevic at

Le Perroquet. There we would break down the entire animal, keeping and using the head and every other part. Emphasis was on fresh and seasonal. After heading to Washington, D.C., and working at Le Pavillon under Chef Yannick Cam for a few years, I relocated to Charleston in the early 1990s and soon became executive chef for Slightly North of Broad.

Initiating a local movement

Twenty years earlier in Columbia, I was committed to finding local meats and produce from the State Farmers Market. In Charleston, I had to struggle to find local. There was not a scene or rhythm happening for local foods in the early 1990s. I spent a lot of time reaching out, researching, talking to people, putting boots on the ground, and getting tips about local farmers and then chasing them down. Eventually, farmers started seeking me out. Sometimes I told them, "I will buy whatever you have and create the menu around that."

Then, like now, farmlands on Johns and James Islands were under siege by developers and golf course designers. Recognizing the threat and the potential loss, Chefs Glenn Roberts of Anson, Mike Lata of FIG, and I were major advocates for local and would buy whatever the farmers were harvesting. Fortunately, the interest in local produce, meats, and fish started growing. Other chefs, like Sean Brock of McCrady's, took an increased interest in purchasing from local farmers and fishermen, and the idea morphed into what is now a serious local foods movement in Charleston.

Local food is not cheap

My concern today is how farmers, young and old, will be able to make a living on a small- to medium-size farm. It must be financially sustainable for them. American consumers are hardwired with expectations that food should be cheap. That's an entitlement that started with Earl Butz, head of the USDA under the Nixon administration. He did some great things, but he paved the way for mega-farms with their economies of scale and subsidies, which resulted in cheap food, among other problems. Fresh, nutritious local food should NOT be cheap; it certainly is not cheap to produce!

We need to expose the information about the amount of resources and labor that go into growing our food. The local food movement is only sustainable if the producers, farmers, and fishermen can make a decent living. Chefs have been advocates for a long time, and farmers markets have expanded in size and popularity, which helps. And, although we chefs have been the spark helping to make local popular, it's really the consumers who must demand local—from grocery stores and restaurants—by going to farmers markets and by advocating for farmers.

People must recognize the many benefits of local food—the increased nutritional value, the positive environmental impact, and the boost to the local economy. And they must recognize their responsibility and the power their purchasing habits have. They send a message that has either a positive or negative impact on the viability of the farmers in their community.

To be sustainable, we need to change our paradigm of growing. We can and must find a way to be more efficient with our use of water, energy, pesticides, and chemical fertilizers. We must also find a way to raise animals for protein in a more humane manner.

To be sustainable, we need to change our paradigm of eating. We need to pay attention to what we eat, and eat seasonally. We have been inundated with processed foods, sugars, and corn syrup. There is no escaping the direct link between the food we eat and our health. Finally, the dots are being connected between health, local farms, and the local economy.

The real question is how can we change our current broken food model and health system to promote sustainability. There are different ways that local, state, and federal governments can promote small- and medium-size family farms through things as small as reducing charges for a booth at the local farmers market or as large as changing the federal government's subsidies. If we can use taxpayer money to subsidize corn, soybeans, cotton, oil, and coal, it's important to level the playing field to benefit small farmers too.

The local food movement is only sustainable if people can make a decent living as a small farmer. The bottom line is this for consumers: Put your money where your mouth is. Support your local farmers by purchasing food from farmers markets, joining a CSA, or demanding and buying only local food from your grocery store manager.

Consumers can make a real impact. Our pocketbooks hold the power! ❧

Jimmy Hagood
Lavington Farms

fter a successful career as an insurance advisor, Jimmy began his second profession as a barbeque pitmaster. He created Food for the Southern Soul, a specialty food and catering company. Jimmy has placed in several World Barbeque Championships and dozens more championships in the southeastern United States. As a member of an extended family with ownership in a historical rice plantation, Lavington, one of his primary concerns is to ensure that the family's land is managed responsibly and sustainably for future generations.

History and stewardship of Lavington

The Ashepoo River oxbows around Lavington's fertile rice and cornfields, where over the centuries, the riverbed deposited up to twelve feet of alluvium and created a uniquely productive soil. My great-grandfather bought this property at the turn of the last century. It was part of the King's Grants, land in the Carolinas that Charles II, King of England, granted to eight lord proprietors in the mid–1600s.

The land was originally a cypress tupelo swamp, and because the property is situated far enough from the coast and has primarily freshwater tides, it was perfect for clearing and putting into rice production. By the early 1700s, Carolina Gold rice was being grown here and shipped around the world. The Civil War crippled rice production, but with the hurricanes of 1910 and 1911 the seed reserves were decimated. With no seeds to replant, the rice culture in the Carolinas was eliminated. Without rice production, Lavington slowly reverted to its natural state as a cypress tupelo swamp.

Historically, the two economic drivers for Lavington were rice and timber. My grandfather planted pine trees over his lifetime, and our family continues to actively manage timber. We also manage 100 acres of wetlands for rice, corn, and wildlife.

Diverse activities provide sources of revenue to help sustain the maintenance of our buildings, ditches, roads, canals, and fields. Our families' dedication to steward this gift from our great-grandfather drives how we handle the land. We placed a conservation easement on Lavington, which encourages traditional land uses while also preserving the natural landscape, resources, and wildlife habitat. It would be a travesty not to have this land in production, or protected in perpetuity.

Lavington's survival and sustainability has always been a primary focus for me. I attended the University of the South in Sewanee, Tennessee, to attain a degree in forestry and glean a better understanding for stewarding Lavington. Afterward, I worked in our family's flooring business, but decided I wanted to enter the insurance business. My mentor, who loved cooking, taught me many grilling techniques and shared his recipes. I entered some contests and brought home some trophies. I started bottling my barbeque sauces, cooking for charitable causes, friends, and family, and soon created a catering business.

In March of 2002, I took off my coat and tie and donned my apron. I gave up my day job for a day and night job! Food products from my company, *Food for the Southern Soul*, are distributed in 50 local grocery stores and more than 300 stores nationally. When asked, I tell people that I'm in the exporting business—exporting Southern food to the rest of the United States.

No matter how busy I am, my mind is never far from the business of Lavington. We have re-created markets for the historical uses of the land. Today, Lavington is cultivating heirloom specialty grains—Charleston Gold rice and Jimmy Red corn—along with Blue Ribbon sugarcane and corn for wildlife.

▼ Rice before hulling.

Reviving historical rice fields

In 2010, I met Glenn Roberts of Anson Mills, the "resurrector" of local heirloom grains. I encouraged Glenn, internationally renowned rice scientist Dr. Merle Shepard, and historian David Shields, all board members of the Carolina Gold Rice Foundation (CGRF), to visit Lavington's fields. The foundation was looking for people and farms to cultivate Carolina Gold and Charleston Gold rice. They thought Lavington would be ideal. In 2011, we planted three experimental acres of Charleston Gold rice. In successive years, it became five, nine, and thirteen acres. This year Lavington has fifteen acres in production. We are indebted to CGRF for initially providing us with pure starter seed free of charge.

As a historical rice plantation, Lavington has an infrastructure of canals, dikes, and rice trunks. The canal, filled with backwater—water from an inland swamp next to the Ashepoo River—is separated from the adjacent rice fields by an earthen embankment called a dike. Using a rice trunk, the historical sluice gate system, we flood the fields to suppress weed growth. The trunk, originally made from cypress tree trunks, has a huge flapper on the end. Water pressure keeps the flapper closed, and by setting the horizontal boards at different heights and sliding the gates open or closed, we can determine the level of water released into the fields. Flooding drowns and eliminates competition from weeds, while the rice, an aquatic grass, can survive being submerged for a limited amount of time. We recently received a North American Wetlands Conservation Act Grant to restore our dikes and canals so we can flood and drain the fields properly.

In the early spring, we disk the fields, and by the end of April, we start planting the rice in rows. By early summer, the rice will be about ten inches high and will have split into six stalks, or shoots. It will grow five feet tall, and by late September, the rice matures from a sea of green to a field of gold. We harvest it when the moisture content of the individual grains is low enough to harvest with a combine.

▼ A paddy of Charleston Gold.

Our families' dedication to steward this gift from our great-grandfather drives how we handle the land. It would be a travesty not to have this land in production, or protected in perpetuity.

Harvesting, milling, and selling

During the first three years of experimenting to determine the feasibility of this new rice venture, we borrowed harvesting equipment. It seemed like a great idea, but timing is everything. When the rice is ready, it must be harvested before it dries up or the birds descend and feast upon it. Once we decided to continue our rice endeavor, we knew we needed our own combine harvester to control our harvest timing. We found a combine with a header for rice and wheat and a separate header for corn. With our own equipment, we can increase our acreage and productivity. Last year we harvested nine acres, which produced an amazing amount of rice. After milling, it yielded more than 12,000 pounds.

We haul it to Campbell Coxe's mill in Darlington, South Carolina. It takes a full day to haul the rice up there to be milled and another day to bring it back. The next closest rice mill is a thousand miles away in Arkansas. Our goal is to build a mill here at Lavington, which would be the first in the Charleston area in over 100 years. It will be a feasible business endeavor if we, and other rice growers in the vicinity, expand production to at least eighty acres total.

After milling, we freeze the Charleston Gold rice to preserve its aromatic flavor. GrowFood Carolina, the local food distribution hub, buys about eighty percent of our rice and sells it to local restaurants. We sell the remaining portion directly to local grocery stores and through our website. Cultivating rice would not be a successful business venture without our partner, GrowFood.

Ventures with a local distillery

We've had great success growing wildlife corn, and recently engaged in another opportunity with a very different kind of corn. The heirloom seed for James Island Red corn, fondly known as Jimmy Red, was rediscovered by a farmer in 2009. The farmer shared some seeds with Glenn Roberts, who along with

Scott Blackwell, the owner of High Wire Distilling Company in Charleston, contracted Clemson University's Coastal Research and Education Center to reproduce the original seed. Glenn shared the grain with farmer-chef Sean Brock of Husk Restaurant, some other local farmers, and with Lavington. Since our rice combine will also harvest corn, we have formed a partnership with High Wire Distilling. We planted a twenty-acre field of Jimmy Red corn in early May. It's about waist high now and should be ready for harvest by the first of August. Scott will mill the corn, pulverize it into mash, and barrel it for his specialty corn whiskey.

We are also growing Blue Ribbon sugarcane for Scott's rhum agricole. Sugarcane, like rice, is a grass. David Shields and Glenn Roberts are working to recover the original Purple Ribbon cane from Sapelo Island, Georgia. Historically, sugarcane was cut with a machete, and a mule walked in circles powering a mill to squeeze the juice out of the stalks. Today, we use a tractor to power our hundred-year-old mill to squeeze many stalks at a time. A full pickup-truckload of cut cane stalks will only produce eighty gallons of cane juice. We put that in our cast-iron pot to boil and reduce it down to eight gallons of syrup. Clearly it is labor intensive with a low yield, but my uncle started making cane syrup as a hobby ten years ago, and we all enjoy it. And now we have a buyer. This year, Scott will use our Blue Ribbon cane to make his limited-edition rhum agricole.

Yes, there is an excitement and a bit of nostalgia to these new ventures, but foremost there is the potential financial component. We started growing Charleston Gold rice and Jimmy Red corn at Lavington as experiments, and Blue Ribbon sugarcane as a hobby, but each has grown into a commercial enterprise. Everything we do here at Lavington has the ultimate goal of sustaining the economic viability of this vibrant and historical property. Filled with gratitude for this gift from our forebears, and modeling responsibility for future generations, we are stewarding Lavington's land and resources with thoughtfulness, ingenuity, and respect. ❧

Scott Blackwell and Ann Marshall
High Wire Distilling Co.

I n 2013, Scott and Ann launched High Wire Distilling Co. in downtown Charleston. When it comes to making great food or libation into a great business, serial entrepreneur Scott Blackwell has tasted success.

As a child, he learned a secret from his great-grandmother—always use fresh local ingredients. This was no great mystery before World War II, as that was largely all there was. However, by the 1980s, it was a novel idea to use fresh, natural, and local ingredients. Somewhere along the way in the annals of agricultural "progress," flavor and taste were sacrificed for quantity and convenience. Through hard work, innovation, and a commitment to quality, Scott and his wife, Ann, have created another delectable business. High Wire Distilling Co. creates small batches of unique artisan spirits from heirloom seeds, grasses, and grains.

Fresh ingredients equal best taste

Scott: My great-grandmother was a scratch baker, and we would make cupcakes, cookies, and pies using fresh ingredients every weekend during my childhood. At sixteen, I worked in a commercial kitchen at a fried food place, first washing dishes and bussing tables, then making creations for spicing up fried chicken, and eventually baking desserts. I attended The Citadel, the Military College of South Carolina, on a tennis scholarship, but I wasn't allowed to have a job while playing on the team. After two years of being broke, I decided to go to a school in my hometown of Greenville and work in a restaurant. My neighbor was an eighty-year-old woman who took it upon herself to coach me in life. Among other things, she taught me how to use a sewing machine. And knowing that I baked pies, she asked me to make a pie for her bridge group. They judged it and insisted I start a business.

Soon I was making about 250 icebox pies per week from my apartment. This was the 1980s. My emphasis was on taste and quality, and that required using fresh ingredients. Food distributors were selling pies made with Cool Whip and Oreos; it was all about convenience, shelf life, and quantity over quality. I was interested in creating something authentic with a "to-die-for" taste. I used real key limes, real butter, real heavy cream, and real oranges. And I never said no when I was asked if I knew how to make another kind of pie. I was a frequent visitor to the library. A business idea was starting to percolate. I was nineteen.

Serial achiever

After graduating from Furman University, I got a certificate in baking from the Culinary Institute of America. I needed a job and interviewed for the assistant manager position at a couple of chain restaurants, but knew that was not what I wanted to do. I thought maybe my little pie business was the way to go instead. I rented a commercial kitchen and bought some used equipment and my first car. Believe it or not, I learned a lot from watching television shows. One was a PBS show called *Growing a Business* based on a book written by Paul Hawken, who started Smith & Hawken. Then I watched a show about some guys named Ben and Jerry, who started an ice cream company in Vermont. They had just hooked up with a distributor in Atlanta, so I met with their distributor, who offered to carry my pies. I also became a Ben & Jerry's distributor in North and South Carolina. I was twenty-one.

Three years later, I decided to stop traveling and move to Columbia. A friend asked me to start making muffins and coffee for her office and clients. That evolved into sandwiches and pasta. Eventually other people started asking me if I could make lunches for their offices. I had been doing all of my cooking from my apartment and needed more space. I went to the bank to borrow $5,000, but the bank wouldn't give me a loan. So I made it work without the loan. I found a commercial building, rented it, gutted it, and worked on the space at night while preparing meals during the day. Two months later, I opened my restaurant Immaculate Consumption. I was twenty-four.

Immaculate Consumption started as a restaurant serving only lunch. I quickly added breakfast. Then, I opened a bakery. Customers were also purchasing my cookies in large quantities, so I started making frozen cookie dough, and then refrigerated dough—all made with organic and natural ingredients.

I wanted to provide great quality coffee in my restaurant and bakery (a novelty in those days), so I flew to Seattle for a coffee show and came home with a roaster. I became the first micro-roaster in South Carolina and sold wholesale coffee.

I kept the restaurant, bakery, coffee company, and frozen and refrigerated cookie dough companies as separate entities. I worked hard. My ideas were original, but soon enterprises started springing up and imitating me. When the competition started to grow and reduce my margins, I realized it was time to cut the cord while I was ahead. I started selling the individual businesses. The last to go was Immaculate Baking Company, which I sold to General Mills in 2012.

The taste will be different, because the *terroir*—the flavor imparted from the soil, air, and the microclimate—is different.

Now what?

My wife and business partner, Ann Marshall, and I were trying to figure out what we were going to do next. We decided to move to Charleston, and although we had no idea what our next venture would be, we signed a lease to rent an 8,000-square foot warehouse the month we sold the bakery. We were coming up with business ideas daily. Maybe we'd start a natural and organic candy company. We

were brewing beer at home; maybe we could open a brewery. Ann said beer was a crowded market and suggested we try spirits. While doing a brewery feasibility study, a distributor agreed with Ann and suggested we look into spirits. My biggest hesitation stemmed from stereotypes in my mind—liquor felt seedy, beer seemed friendlier, and wine was romantic.

Ann and I started visiting distilleries around the country. I was concerned that there might not be a lucrative business in craft spirits. Would there be enough bandwidth? This is not a hobby. I'm not interested in fooling around with a half-million-dollar business. One of the most difficult aspects about craft spirits is that it is so new, which is precisely what is so exciting. So we started taking classes and dove in.

Ann: Scott and I complement each other well. I am the details partner in our venture. I crunch the numbers, and with my expertise in marketing and graphic design, I handle the branding. We are constantly bouncing ideas off each other. There are some areas where our strengths and talents overlap, and we navigate well together.

Deciding on a business name was actually pretty challenging. We tossed around a lot of ideas. It's hard to think of something that hasn't already been trademarked. Scott has an obsession with old-school magic, and I love turn-of-the-century vaudeville and burlesque. We started thinking about things related to these interests and the time period. There was such a circus culture then. We just started writing down names of things that were associated with that, and we came up with High Wire. The name had a fun connotation, good graphic potential, and we could get a trademark for it.

Distilling as a craft

Scott: When I was making pies, my philosophy was to use the best and freshest products, and that was what made them stand out from the rest. In starting this distillery business, I was consumed with questions and doubts about what I could do that would set High Wire Distilling Co. apart from what the guys in Kentucky and Tennessee were doing. We started thinking about using local ingredients for distilling. I didn't want local to just be a gimmick. Our product

Our mission is to provide convenient sales opportunities to food producers and to give household consumers convenient access to local food.

towns. My firm designs a variety of ways to incorporate agriculture into an urban core with rooftop gardens, community gardens, and a town square with a garden plot. As the town expands out from the core, we create spaces for small hobby farms, and then larger and larger agricultural plots.

The most difficult part of my transition from North Carolina to South Carolina was the lack of a local food system. When I arrived, local food was not abundant or easily accessible, so I planted my own garden and helped start a farmers market, which I managed for four years.

Within the next few years, more farmers markets started up in the area. This was actually detrimental to the farmers. Fearing they would lose their market share, farmers felt obliged to attend all of the markets. Manning a booth nearly every day of the week prevented them from spending time on their farms, and the competitive and oversaturated markets encouraged a few of the farmers to source produce from non-local farms and mix it with their own. With reselling and poor transparency, the market culture became tense. Fortunately my farmers market was small, and I had good relationships with all of our venders, but I was aware of the farmers' stress. I wondered how farmers could reach a larger audience without needing to sit at a farmers market booth each and every day.

I reached out to Garrett Budds with the Beaufort Open Land Trust. Garrett was successfully working on farmland conservation efforts, and we began developing ideas for a tool that could bring farmers and consumers together in an online platform. Garrett, his wife Katie, my wife Lauren, and I became partners.

We researched and contacted people around the country who were running online farmers markets. I asked individual farmers strategic planning questions about products, quantities, getting the product availability right, storing, refrigeration, and delivery. We found that the drawback of the online model is that it eliminates customer and farmer face-to-face interactions. We tried to remedy that by also having a storefront for shopping, meet-your-farmer

events, and classes in cheese making, bee-keeping, and more.

In 2011, we launched Sea Islands Local Outlet (SILO), an online direct-to-consumer local food company. Our mission is to provide convenient sales opportunities to food producers and to give household consumers convenient access to local food. Our website provides an accessible marketplace for locally sourced produce, meats, seafood, dairy, breads, baked goods, and more.

Farmers—our first priority

Local food can be a huge economic engine for a community because the farmers, distributors, and consumers all benefit as money is exchanged and remains within the community.

Part of the inspiration for starting SILO was a book called *The Town that Food Saved*, about the citizens in a small Vermont town who worked together to create a robust local food culture, and thereby provided a profitable economy for the entire community. At SILO, the farmers are central; we want them to be sustainable. We strategize with them about which products are in demand, and how to specialize and grow incrementally so they can meet that demand. Because we know the weekly demand through online orders, the farmers only harvest what we have pre-sold.

Everything purchased from SILO is local and naturally grown, meaning free from pesticides, synthetic chemicals, hormones, and antibiotics. We don't require organic certification, unless the farmer is marketing their product as organic.

How it works

Our online farmers market is a combination farmers market, food co-op, and Community Supported Agriculture (CSA). Our members pay an annual fee of $50, which helps pay some of our expenses. Unlike a CSA, our customers only order items they choose and are not required to order each week.

By Saturday evening of each week, SILO partners

post the amount of each item they have available for delivery on Thursday of the following week. Household customers place their online orders between Sunday morning and Wednesday at noon. The producers package and deliver the ordered items to us on Wednesday afternoon or Thursday morning.

From Wednesday afternoon until Thursday evening our schedule is very busy—it is complete chaos for about twenty-four hours. After the producers deliver their products, we sort for each order and pack each customer's bag for Beaufort and Charleston deliveries. The orders are kept in the cooler overnight. Thursday morning more goods are added to the orders, and any frozen items are put in a cooler. By 10:30 a.m. Thursday, we head to Charleston—about a ninety-minute drive—for our delivery locations there. When we arrive in Charleston, more order items are added to the orders from GrowFood Carolina, the Charleston Cheesehouse, EVO Bakery, and others.

SILO's role is to provide consumers a venue for purchasing everything local, and farmers a place to sell their products. It is very encouraging to see farmers expanding the amount of land they have under cultivation, and to see a new crop of farmers emerging on the scene. We are working hard to make buying local sustainable for the whole community. ❧

Glenn Roberts
Carolina Gold Rice Foundation and Anson Mills

Dr. Brian Ward
Sustainable and Organic Research Scientist

Dr. Merle Shepard
Emeritus Professor of Entomology

Glenn Roberts *is unquestionably a renaissance man with an insatiable curiosity. He has been a musician with the San Diego Symphony, a chef, a restaurateur, an Air Force pilot, a world sailor, a dressage rider, a truck driver, a restorer of historical buildings, and he laughingly refers to himself as a science groupie. Today, he is an agricultural visionary with a keen focus on the terroir and culture of regional heirloom grains.*

His farm and mill, Anson Mills, grows and sells certified organic farros, including the rare

▲ Above photo: Glenn Roberts.

Farro Piccolo. Other products include Sea Island Red Flint Grits, Stone Ground White Grits, Sea Island Red Peas, Carolina Gold Rice, and Charleston Gold Rice. Glenn was one of the founders, and is now president and CEO of the Carolina Gold Rice Foundation. Traveling around the country and world, Glenn fulfills the foundation's mission of preserving and restoring Carolina Gold rice and other heirloom grains, along with promoting research and educational activities on heirloom grain culture and heritage. Like his drive for learning, he has boundless energy for this noble cause.

I called Glenn with the intention of meeting in Columbia, South Carolina, to learn about Anson Mills. Instead, he suggested we meet a little south of Charleston at the combined facility of the United States Department of Agriculture's (USDA) Agricultural Research Vegetable Laboratory and Clemson University's Coastal Research and Education Center. The facility was opened in 2003 by an act of Congress, thanks to South Carolina's influential former senator Fritz Hollings. It is one of the most advanced agricultural research facilities, and as part of the USDA, all the work is in the public domain.

Glenn introduced me to world-renowned scientists, Dr. Brian Ward and Dr. Merle Shepard, who shared their behind-the-scenes research on soil, seeds, weeds, diseases, and pests, as well as their work to promote sustainable food production.

***Dr. Brian Ward** is a research scientist with Clemson University's Coastal Research and Education Center. Dr. Ward specializes in increasing historically significant, very rare seed for biosecurity, and he also conducts organic research in legume, grain, and vegetable rotations. His mission is to research cultural practices in agriculture that growers can adopt in order to dramatically increase sustainable and organic production across South Carolina.*

***Dr. Merle Shepard** is emeritus professor of entomology with Clemson University. He served for eight years as head of the Entomology Department of the International Rice Research Institute in the Philippines and as team leader for a project on integrated pest management in Indonesia. Dr. Shepard's research interests are centered on the biological control of insects, integrated pest management (IPM), and pollinating insects.*

Resurrecting Carolina Gold rice

Glenn: My introduction to rice production, not rice farming, but actual production, was right here. The Clemson University Organic Research Farm is where I saw my first real and healthy rice field. The Carolina Gold Rice Foundation works with Dr. Ward and Dr. Shepard at this facility, where research is being conducted on organic Carolina Gold rice production, historical rice field recovery, and the restoration of other heirloom grains and agricultural practices.

The history of Carolina Gold rice is long, rich, and colorful. This varietal of rice was introduced to Charlestowne around 1685. The legend of its origin

▲ Brian Ward.

in South Carolina is that the seed grain was a gift from a foreign ship's captain to a Charlestowne physician who cured the ailing crew of sailors. During the antebellum years, Carolina Gold rice was a thriving commodity on the coasts of North Carolina, South Carolina, and Georgia. In short order, it became a culinary delight and was exported in massive volumes worldwide, bringing enormous wealth to those coastal communities. After the Civil War, the rice industry and culture were nearly destroyed. But what really ended rice production was the two consecutive catastrophic hurricanes in 1910 and 1911. With the first hurricane, the crop seed was lost, and with the second one, the seed reserves were lost.

In 1988, Dr. Shepard came to this facility from the International Rice Research Institute. At that time, we were searching for the Carolina Gold rice seed. Dr. Shepard called a friend and research leader with Agricultural Research Services (ARS) in Aberdeen, South Dakota. As the principal research agency for the USDA, he thought they might have the seed. Fortunately, Dr. Shepard was right, and his friend sent some seeds to the lab here in Charleston.

Creating Charleston Gold

Merle: While meeting with the world-renowned agronomist, geneticist, and rice breeder, Dr. Gurdev Khush, I extolled the virtues of Carolina Gold but discussed two problems—it lodges, or lays down, in heavy wind or rain, and its yields are weak. Dr. Khush asked about the positive qualities of the rice, whether I liked the color, and if I wanted it to have a more aromatic taste. Answering affirmatively to his inquiries, he replied, "Maybe we can do something about that." He, along with Dr. Anna McClung, the top geneticist for rice production in the United States, worked together to improve Carolina Gold rice. Using Carolina Gold as one parent, they crossed and back-crossed it with high-yielding Green Revolution rice parents. After twenty-five successions of cross-breeding and back-crossings, by 2005, the selection was narrowed down to its progeny, which we named Charleston Gold.

After creating Charleston Gold rice, we started propagating the seed with the intention of making seeds available to farmers and keeping the seed in the public domain. However, a food company got their hands on Charleston Gold with the intent of claiming it as their intellectual property and privatizing it. We spent years and significant resources hiring lawyers to fight that company and keep the seed public. We eventually recovered the rice and its Charleston Gold name.

Glenn: Dr. Shepard's involvement enabled the return of Carolina Gold rice and the creation of Charleston Gold rice. In 2005, I contracted with the Texas Rice Improvement Association to produce the Charleston Gold seed. The first commercial seed was available two years later. Since then, I have been giving the seed to rice farmers like Jimmy Hagood, Campbell Coxe, and many others for their first crops. Once they are successfully growing it, they begin to purchase the seed. I still give seed to new rice growers, like Lucie Kulze and organic farmers in the Upstate. I want this seed to be used for the greater good, and it is the Carolina Gold Rice Foundation's goal to keep it in the public domain and make it abundantly available and accessible.

Conserving and securing ancient grains

The seed room at this facility holds a treasure of ancient and heirloom seeds. A few of the many grains here are Abruzzi rye and emmer and einkorn wheat.

Emmer, which means mother in Hebrew, is the second-oldest grain on earth. Einkorn, also known as farro, is the oldest grain. New carbon dating analysis estimates it at 20,000 years old. It was introduced into America by Italian growers and is now grown here in South Carolina, as well as in Texas, Virginia, New England, and Canada.

Abruzzi rye is probably the most widely planted ancient grain in the world. It is allelopathic, meaning it produces a biochemical to prevent other plants from competing with it. It is persistent and can tolerate temperatures to just above freezing. It takes its name from the town of Abruzzi, Italy, where the Jesuits, after leaving Rome in the eleventh century, hid in caves to escape persecution. The only grain they could grow there was rye.

The quality of the seed stock, especially for these ancient grains, is due to the scientists here at the lab and research center. Dr. Ward makes sure the seeds stay healthy and are conserved. There is a set of preventive measures designed to reduce the risk of the loss of seed stock, and he is the biosecurity point for these seeds. There are six biosecurity points in North America, two of which are in Canada.

At Anson Mills, we work closely with the research center and Dr. Ward. Once Dr. Ward is satisfied with the research, development, and achievement of desired seed characteristics, we roll it up into

▲ Brian Ward, Merle Shepard, and Glenn Roberts.

seed production and distribution. In addition to collaborating with Anson Mills for the last three years, Dr. Ward has also been producing seed himself and donating it to deserving farmers through Clemson and the USDA. The Carolina Gold Rice Foundation and Anson Mills donated more than 160 tons of rare landrace seed in 2015 and will donate more than 200 tons worldwide in 2016.

Over the next two decades, the scientists here will primarily be focused on food bio-density—small, fast-growing crops, high in nutrition, that react vigorously in sustainable systems. One of the most bio-dense nutritional foods on the planet is rice. Black rice, for example, was such a valuable grain that for hundreds of years it was the currency used to pay taxes to the emperors of China. Black rice matures quickly, has a very high anthocyanin content, and like other red, purple, and blue vegetables, fruits, and grains, it is very high in antioxidants. Today, black rice could have high potential for third world production and nutrition. Sadly, the Brazilian geneticist conducting all the research on black rice died. The technicians at his seed company sold the remaining core seed stock, and his research has disappeared.

Black rice likely grows in some rural areas of South America. If the seed could be found and developed for production, that heirloom grain would be a boon for world nutrition.

Research and science improving agriculture

Brian: The Coastal Research and Education Center is comprised of scientists from the USDA and Clemson University who work in our research laboratories, greenhouses, and test plots. The primary goal for the research center is to grow more nutritional and healthier plants per acre, while reducing petrochemical input from fertilizer and pesticides. We have four departments—Agronomy, Pathology, Entomology, and Horticulture. Agronomists are scientists who work with soils. Pathologists work with fungi, bacteria, viruses, and nematodes. Our entomologists work with insects, focusing on Integrated Pest Management (IPM) systems that use bio-controls rather than pesticides. The horticulture department, using classical breeding techniques, is working to improve crop resistance to diseases, fungi, and pests, while also improving nutritional value and yield. My work incorporates the research of each of these fields to take old and new plants and improve their resistance, quality, yields, and nutritional value.

I am also Clemson's chief southern-region researcher for a new system of growing rice, called the System of Rice Intensification (SRI). It is a method of growing rice similar to growing vegetables, where rice is grown in a raised bed in moist ground under plastic or natural mulch with drip tape irrigation near the plants' roots. It uses the least amount of seed and water, and the yields are very good. It may be the rice growing system of the future.

One of my colleagues, Dr. Richard Hassell, PhD, professor of Horticulture, is currently grafting watermelons. We solely employ classical breeding, taking the pollen from one plant and crossing it with the flower of another. With the watermelons, we are grafting one vigorous plant with another that has rootstock resistant to soil-borne diseases. Prior to these types of advancements, highly toxic methyl bromide was used to sterilize diseases in the soil. Methyl bromide not only destroys disease, it destroys the health of the soil. It also destroys the ozone layer that protects the earth. This graft will eliminate the need to apply petrochemicals to the soil to grow these watermelons.

Our work is for conventional research purposes, and all of it is designed for sustainability. Most growers are conventional growers and use petrochemicals. The work we do focuses on reducing the use of chemicals and increasing sustainability in farming. A significant component of this work is to educate growers on new practices and more sustainable alternatives.

The magic of polycropping

Brian: In 2015, I was conducting the first formal polyculture research in the nation, here in the Clemson University field plots. Traditionally, farmers in the Western world plant and harvest items separately and in sequence. Here, we are experimenting with polycropping and have planted twelve key plant species together. Each complements the others, both in a foliar terrestrial sense, aboveground, and belowground in the rhizosphere. The rhizosphere is the layer of soil directly influenced by the roots and surrounding microorganisms. In our polycropping studies, we observe above and below the surface.

▼ Polycropping.

The ways plants complement each other is like magic, and it also affects flavor and nutrition. The research center recently acquired a quarter-million-dollar piece of equipment, an HPLC (high-performance liquid chromatography) that allows me to conduct aromatic studies and prove, on a peer review basis, the impact of polycropping's relationships on flavor and nutrition. HPLC analyzes what's going on under the soil, so I can identify and better understand the interactions of plant hormones and enzymes. HPLC also allows me to observe and better understand soil bacteria and how it communicates with microbes and plants. This communication is called quorum sensing. Interrelationships that occur in polycropped soil are very different from what occurs in the soil of a monoculture field.

Systemic Acquired Resistance (SAR) is an example of quorum sensing. SAR is a whole-plant resistance response. If a caterpillar with a certain protein in its saliva bites a leaf, the plant's cells have receptors that sense that the protein is harmful. As a result, the plant begins to produce secondary metabolites through glandular oil cells in its leaves to repel the caterpillar. The metabolites rupture and expel a gas, which stimulates the rest of the plants in the field to produce the same repellant, preventing the caterpillar from feeding on the entire field. This is the kind of magic that occurs, and HPLC will allow us to better understand it.

Conventional versus sustainable

Our mission is to promote the sustainable production of grains, vegetables, and row crops. Although I give lots of talks to farmers about the benefits of growing organically, it is more important to grow sustainably. We want growers to sustain their operations by having healthy soils and being good stewards of the land. Sixty percent of the growers in South Carolina are sixty years of age or older. Most of them shun organic, even though all farming was organic pre-1950. I'm trying to help them understand that, in addition to environmental sustainability, the profit margin for growing organically is thirty percent greater than growing conventionally. So it is also more financially sustainable. The dollar is always the bottom line.

Organic certification takes three years. But for a field to be optimally healthy after non-organic practices have damaged the soil's microorganisms, it truly takes up to ten years, and that is with heavy cover cropping. The organic certification process is undeniably onerous, but the long-term, sustained rewards are seen in the land, in the environment, and in farm revenue.

For comparison, we have conventional plots and polycropped plots. The fields with not a weed in sight are the conventional plots; they have used chemicals. Almost all agriculture is done like this.

My polycropping field is a stark contrast. After harvesting Jimmy red corn, we planted crimson and white clover, French black oats, French rye, Nora wheat, emmer, peas, and camelina. In three weeks, you won't be able to see the soil. When the crimson clover sets seed and senesces, or dies back, the nitrogen in the nodules of the root system is released. This happens at the same time the Nora wheat is maturing, so the wheat benefits from the added nitrogen. Furthermore, this polycropping also provides habitat and a food source for beneficial insects and pollinators. Planting sequential pollinator crops will exponentially increase and help recover the wild bee and other necessary populations.

We are working with farmers to promote organic and sustainable methods of enriching their farmland. Converting a conventional chemical field into a field with living organisms in the soil takes years, but a small investment in cover cropping will reap rewards. Along with polycropping, the rotation of legumes with grains and vegetable crops will significantly improve the soil.

Glenn: You probably know about farming the "three sisters"—growing corn, beans, and squash together. Aboveground, the corn provides the trellis for the beans, and the squash leaves shade out the weeds. The three are complementary below the surface as well. The "three sisters" technique is polycropping, but there aren't just three sisters, there are hundreds of sisters. The complementary combinations are endless.

A grower's soil is like an artist's blank canvas, with many possibilities and beautiful results. I'm often asked by people that I meet how they can get more involved with the food system, and my answer is to go plant something. Try growing tomatoes in a container on your back porch. Plant a small herb garden, or wildflowers in your backyard to attract butterflies and bees. Just plant something, fill the canvas, and enjoy. ❧

Teresa and Rustin Gooden
Bulls Bay Saltworks

For millennia, salt was valued for trade and currency. "Not worth his salt" referred to the trade of salt for slaves in ancient Greece, and in religious practices, "salt of the earth" referred to one's purity. For Rustin and Teresa, who live a simple, self-sufficient life—growing vegetables, raising livestock, and keeping honey bees—sea salt has become a thriving business. Upon harvesting seawater from the pristine waters of Bulls Bay, Rustin manages the salt making process, while Teresa handles the business administration, packaging, and deliveries with the help of their two employees.

Salt of the Earth

Rustin: Teresa and I have been a team since we met in our mid-twenties. We were seasonal tour guides, guiding river rafting trips in Alaska during the summer and canoeing, kayaking, and hiking trips in the Florida Everglades the rest of the year.

We settled for a while in Portland, Oregon, where I was finishing a degree in biology, and Teresa was participating in a beginning farmer apprentice program.

Teresa and I pride ourselves on our self-sufficient and thrifty lifestyle. We try to live sustainably and organically. We grow, make, and build whatever we can. Our plan was to create a garden, raise livestock, and live a totally self-sustaining life in Oregon. But in 2011, I was offered a job as a park ranger on the

are magnesium sulfate and magnesium chloride—nigari. Nigari is the substance used to make tofu from soy. It is basically Epson salt, and while great to soak your feet in, it is too concentrated and bitter to eat. I drain the nigari off and only harvest the sodium chloride. I clean the unwanted crystals off the salt in a concentrated brine without the use of chemicals. After it is clean and dry, I separate it into flakes and crystals, and move the salt into the drying room.

From there, some flakes and crystals go into the smoke shack. To create our Bourbon Barrel Smoked Flake, I use aged bourbon barrels to create the smoke. Today I'm smoking fifty pounds of salt crystals in these barrels, which will take up to thirty hours. Our Bourbon Barrel Smoked Flake is our best seller. It adds a simple, subtle smoky flavor.

I didn't have a playbook for how to make salt. I mostly figured it out along the way, and my background in science and chemistry became very relevant. We tried and failed, tried and failed, tried and got something right. There have been many learning opportunities. Mistakes have led to more efficient salt making techniques, some of which are proprietary. And then there are the little things. After we lost a couple hundred gallons of water due to a hole in one of our liners, we learned to use smaller tubs. That mistake had positive results, because water heats up and evaporates faster in the smaller tubs. Gravel floors aid in drainage, but also increase evaporation. We also learned that the greenhouse has too much humidity to dry salt, so we developed a proprietary drying method that is efficient, and leaves a consistent moisture content all the way through the salt.

Serendipity led to success

Teresa: Right now, in our packaging area, we have about 400 pounds of different types of salt, which we harvested before leaving last week for a food festival in Baltimore. We need to get it packaged before tomorrow, when Rustin leaves for a two-day festival south of here, and I attend a shrimp festival nearby.

After the salt is completely dry and some of it is smoked, we move it to a commercially inspected facility where we weigh, package, label, and store it. Our Charleston Sea Salt, Bourbon Barrel Smoked Flake, and Red Mash Sea Salt (with a spicy kick to it) are sold as flakes or crystals in jars, grinders, or sampler packets. Our salt grinders are refillable. We also have a Carolina Margarita Salt. Everything we do is done by hand.

As a food producer, we are monitored by the USDA and must comply with the registration, verification, and certification regulations. We hired an inspector to help us design a facility to meet the compliance restrictions. In keeping with USDA regulations, we have five sinks—one for utility, one designated for wash, one for rinse, one for sanitation, and one for hand washing. One-tenth of this room consists of sinks! All the surfaces—floors, walls, and ceilings—have to be sealed and washable, and every light fixture has to be enclosed.

Currently we distribute through the local food hub, GrowFood Carolina, and through a regional distributor. We have a growing number of accounts across twenty-six states and have quickly expanded from local customers to restaurants and specialty stores coast-to-coast.

Although Rustin and I fell into the salt making business with a serendipitous smoked salt discovery at our pig roast five years ago, we had always wanted to start a small business. We are working hard and always improving. We realize people make a choice to support Bulls Bay Saltworks. We are so appreciative of our many customers and our community for being so supportive. Hopefully by example, we will inspire others to try something new, to start a small local business, and to follow their dreams. ❧

Walter Earley
Hickory Bluff Berry Farm

There are people we meet in life that seem to bubble with joy. It shows in their eyes and all over their faces. Walter and Cathy Earley are that kind of people. They showed me around Hickory Bluff Berry Farm, which grows far more than their well-known strawberries. They also took me into their beautiful home, which the two of them built by hand—starting with the basics, cutting down trees to clear the land. Walter and Cathy are can-do people, and when farming—more specifically the weather—tries to trip them up, they get up, dust off, and persevere with that joyful, can-do attitude.

The "Earley" years

After World War II, my dad worked in the oil fields of Oklahoma before returning to this area, where my grandfather was a mule trader and farmer. I was four years old. We lived in the old farmhouse on this property, which was built in the late 1800s.

There was no indoor plumbing, no central heat, and, of course, no air conditioning. We were poor and had little extras, but it didn't seem to matter, because everyone else we knew was poor, too. We had a wood-burning stove for heat and an outdoor hand pump for water. We lived off the land and grew commodity crops—cotton and tobacco. When I wasn't in school, I helped on the farm. I fed the animals, hauled firewood, and worked in the fields. And whenever I could get away with it, I would sneak off to go fishing or hunting.

When I was ten years old, I sold boiled peanuts and shined shoes. At fourteen, I worked at a gas station and later in a grocery store until I graduated from high school. My mom passed away when I was sixteen, so life was hard for a good while until I met my wife-to-be, Cathy. She and her family brought me through some very difficult times, for which I am forever grateful.

I'll never forget my high school science teacher, Mrs. Julia Cross, and her husband, Russell, the superintendent of schools. Recognizing my love of the outdoors and farming, they helped connect me to a $300 grant to send me to horticulture school in Charleston after graduation. Cathy and I got married, and after a year in horticulture school, I enlisted in the Navy. I was sent to Morocco and served as an assistant fire chief.

After the Navy, we returned to the farm, which I inherited from my dad. I took a job with the USDA Soil Conservation Service in 1974, and farmed part-time—growing corn, soybeans, and wheat on about a hundred acres. I spent the next three decades with the Conservation Service. The first twelve years, I worked with farmers on land issues like drainage, erosion, wildlife management, and conservation measures, while continuing to serve in the Navy Reserves one weekend a month. I was later transferred to another county, a couple hours away from the farm, and came home on weekends. Farming from that distance became too much, so I put the farm in maintenance mode by planting the open fields in loblolly pines, a commercially important tree for timber.

Upon retirement in 2005, Cathy and I returned to my childhood home to start Hickory Bluff Berry Farm. That first year, we built our home. We hired someone to pour the foundation, a local contractor framed it, Cathy's brother did the electrical, and we

▼ Checking for blemishes.

We frost protect with overhead irrigation. Once the water coats the flowers, they can't get any colder than the freezing point of 32°F, even if the air temperature dips below 20°F.

hired out the plumbing. Otherwise, we built it ourselves. We cut down ninety trees from our farm and brought in a portable sawmill for the job.

Building a strawberry farm

With our home built, it was time to begin our retirement with a little farming. We intended to start a landscaping nursery, but the economy and housing market fell apart in 2008, so we tried our hand at strawberries, a specialty crop harvested in April and May. We contacted Clemson Cooperative Extension Service for technical assistance, and our area extension agent came to assess how serious we were about farming. He told us exactly how to grow strawberries, where to purchase the rootstock, how and when to plant, and how to fertilize, irrigate, and use plastic mulch. We had a great first crop of strawberries until the rains came at harvest time and ruined them all. We could do nothing but throw thirty-gallon barrels full of strawberries in our woods and prepare for the next season. That was the disappointing start to Hickory Bluff Berry Farm. But we persisted! And we have been strawberry farming for almost ten years.

We plant in October. Strawberries can be planted as plugs, as whole plants, or as rootstock—a little mass of roots with no leaves. We prefer rootstock. We planted by hand for years, but a couple years ago, we bought a mechanical planter, which punches holes in the plastic mulch at the right distance and depth. That has allowed us to increase our strawberry production by another full acre. We are now planting 43,000 strawberry plants on three acres.

Depending on how warm the winter is—and some of our winters have been very warm—the strawberry blossoms appear in February and March. Once they start blooming, we need pollinators. We have five honey bee colonies on the farm to provide that critically important service. Once the berries start blooming, we must become especially vigilant and protect against freezing weather. If the temperature drops below 32°F, the flowers will freeze and ruin that crop of strawberries. More flowers will bloom,

but then we would be weeks behind the early market, and we strive for those early market margins when strawberry supply is low and demand is high.

Our vigilance with the temperature starts in the field with a thermometer probe in a strawberry flower. An alarm wakes me when the temperature drops to just above freezing. Then I head to the field to monitor the temperature. We frost protect with overhead irrigation. Once the water coats the flowers, they can't get any colder than the freezing point of 32°F, even if the air temperature dips below 20°F. It's important to keep the overhead irrigation running until the temperature gets above freezing the next day. There are some years when I have to frost protect four or five times a season, and others when I never need it.

Rain won't damage the strawberries until the fruit is ripe, and no rain in April and May is ideal for strawberries. Once ripe, strawberries are negatively affected by rain and humidity. In that case we must spray a fungicide weekly to prevent the fruit from mold and rot. We skip spraying if they don't need it, because we prefer to minimize our usage of chemicals. Furthermore, the spray is expensive. If we must spray, we only spray on Saturdays after the U-Pick has closed, since we are not open on Sundays.

Beyond berries

Hickory Bluff is known primarily as a berry farm; we harvest blueberries and blackberries, too. But Hickory Bluff is more than just berries, and we have a wide range of diversification in our crops. We plant, grow, harvest, and sell twenty acres of other specialty crops—broccoli, cabbage, kale, collards, squash, beans, cucumbers, okra, heirloom tomatoes, melons, and other items. As far as deciding what to grow each year, we meet with GrowFood Carolina, the local food hub, for crop production planning, and we also meet with our other customers to determine their needs. Our biggest obstacle is labor, but we have been fortunate to find dependable labor when we need it.

We sell our produce in a variety of ways. Our daughter, Karen, does our marketing through social media. She and our son, Chris, sell at farmers markets and help with our thriving U-Pick and farm stand, both open daily except Sundays. We have a farm-to-school program with the Berkeley County Schools, and we deliver to GrowFood Carolina twice a week. Working with GrowFood has allowed us to triple our production in five years from a few acres to fifteen acres. GrowFood has also simplified our lives. In addition to helping with crop planning, they do all the marketing, sales, and distribution to restaurants and retailers on our behalf. That allows us to focus on farming.

Hard work, great rewards

A typical day for Cathy and me is long, long, long. Today, for example, I started at six o'clock in the morning. We have an order going out to the Berkeley County Schools, which we packed in the cooler last night. At seven o'clock, I loaded a truck with broccoli, cabbage, and strawberries for GrowFood. We have five workers picking in the fields today. By nine o'clock each morning except Sundays, customers start arriving at our farm stand and U-Pick. I depart for the GrowFood warehouse around noon, which is an hour away. We also have three or four workers

handpicking through all the fruit to check for blemishes and packaging them according to their destination. Open pulp containers are used for restaurants and farmers markets, and clamshell containers with our label are used for retailers. All of this is done with care and according to food safety procedures and regulations. Fridays and Saturdays are farmers markets, which require packing, loading, setting up at the market, and then unloading when we return home in the late afternoon. Our days are long, but very satisfying.

This year we started hosting school field trips in an attempt to help the next generation learn the importance of farmers and how their food is grown. This has become one of the more enjoyable and rewarding parts of what we do.

Cathy and I are in our sixties now, and the demand for our fruits and vegetables continues to expand. Hickory Bluff Berry Farm has become a family business lately since our kids have both become very engaged with the farm's operations. Cathy and I will continue farming until we can't do it anymore, because we love it. Now that the kids are involved, it is even more fulfilling. We've built a family farm, and it is gratifying to know it will carry on for another generation. 🌿

Bill Livingston and Jeff Massey
Livingston's Bulls Bay Seafood

Livingston's Bulls Bay Seafood is located on Jeremy Creek in the historic town of McClellanville, South Carolina. The seas were too rough for a venture on the boat during my first visit, so Bill Livingston and his son-in-law, Jeff Massey, gave me an extensive tour of their company docks. With calmer weather the following week, I returned to head out with the clamming crew. We departed Jeremy Creek and traveled nine miles through Clubhouse Creek, Oyster Bay, and Cowpens Creek to the state-permitted clam lease on the backside of one of the barrier islands, adjacent to the pristine waters of Cape Romain National Wildlife Refuge.

I experienced the whole process from planting seed clams to harvesting mature clams. Once back at the dock, there was culling, grading, bagging, and tagging for sale. Fortunately, both visits were during soft shell crab season, so I slipped down the road to TW Graham's, the small local seafood restaurant for out-of-this-world delicious delicacies—can't get any fresher.

Outstanding Resource Water, outstanding seafood

Bill: My family has always been in the seafood business. Starting at the age of fourteen, I have been a crabber, oysterman, shrimper, an eel and catfisherman,

▲ Above photo: Jeff and Bill.

and a seafood dealer. Clamming is the last addition to my repertoire. I bought this commercial dock and opened Livingston's Bulls Bay Seafood in 1995. I sell soft shell crabs, shrimp, oysters, and clams directly to the public, restaurants, and retailers.

Livingston's Bulls Bay Seafood provides seafood according to the season. Clams are year-round. Soft shell crabs and oysters are harvested in the spring. Summer is shrimping season. Oysters and shrimp are harvested in the fall, and oysters during the winter.

We have state leases that permit us to grow clams and oysters in Bulls Bay and Cape Romain, both designated with the highest water quality classifications available—Class One Wilderness Area and Outstanding Resource Water. There is no better seafood than what we grow right here in these pristine waters.

Challenges from land and sea

Mother Nature throws a generous amount of problems at us, from hurricanes and nor'easters to predation. When Hurricane Sandy hit, it created a new inlet with the shifting sand smothering our clams. Then a couple of nor'easters hit, and again, our leases were slammed. Clams are food for stingrays, red drum, black drum, conchs, and a ray called the "clam crusher." We try to protect them from predators by growing them in mesh bags.

Another challenge we face is development. Coastal property is extremely valuable. When real estate booms, waterfront properties become highly sought after—commercial docks shut down and condos go up. It is hard to blame people who choose to sell their docks and coastal properties for a significant sum after working tirelessly as fishermen or clammers their entire lives.

But I think our biggest potential threat today is offshore drilling. No matter what anyone says, if they drill for oil here, it will cause problems for us and anyone else whose livelihoods depend on the coastal waters. We are extremely concerned.

Peelers and busters

Soft shell crab season only occurs for a short period during the spring, which allows the species to continue breeding throughout the summer. On a spring moon tide when the water temperature rises above 70°F, the crabs will breed. Crabbers bait crab pots with a male crab, and the females, searching for a "date to the prom," come in hordes. There may be as

Some regulations are important, but if regulators say NO to raw seafood products, then who are the real losers? And who will be the winners—producers in Japan and China! Supporting local needs to happen by purchasing local and also by advocating for local. Our livelihoods depend on it.

many as twenty-five females to one pot. If there is a red line, called the bloodline, down her rearmost leg, then crabbers know she is going to shed (peel) within the next couple of weeks. At that point, I buy the peelers.

I keep the peelers in saltwater tanks kept at creek temperatures. Peelers become busters when their shells are beginning to bust open for the molt. We constantly check each tank for the vulnerable busters, because if we don't move them to another tank, other crabs will kill them. When the busters start their molt by backing out of their shells, we put them into what we call super buster tanks. At this point they are most fragile, so it is important to keep them isolated with crabs in exactly the same stage. By law we are required to record every crab for food safety reasons and have both a shedding permit and a wholesale dealers license.

We also buy shrimp from shrimp boats that tie up at our dock. However, we are a sulfite-free dock and won't allow any shrimpers to use our dock if they use chemicals. Sodium bisulphate is a chemical preservative that many shrimpers put on their shrimp to keep them healthy looking. Many people are allergic to it. We use Everfresh, a citric acid, instead of a chemical preservative.

Fostering a healthy ecosystem

Jeff: Livingston's Bulls Bay Seafood started farming clams in 1999, a year after I joined the business. When we got our first clam lease, it was a giant mudflat. Cultivating clams and oysters dramatically improves the water quality, because clams, oysters, and other bivalves are filter feeders. They consume suspended particles in the water column and contribute to water clarity. With clearer water, sunlight penetrates the water column and an entire biological community flourishes—phytoplankton and zooplankton, the microscopic foundation of the aquatic food web, thrive and attract a host of fish,

shrimp, stingrays, and birds. Planting clams on our lease restored and continues to foster the ecosystem's health.

Initially we had our own hatchery, raising clams from spawn. The average clam releases a million eggs each time it spawns, but spawning is way too time consuming, so now we buy seed clams from a hatchery. The first time Bill bought seed, he paid $1,500 for 50,000 clams. They were microscopic and were contained in just one folded washcloth. Bill opened the washcloth in one of the tanks to release the seed clams, and we couldn't see a thing. Everyone looked at him like he was nuts. Two years later we were successfully harvesting clams. The survival rate of a clam in the wild is one percent of one percent of one percent—basically one in a million. But by cultivating them in protective bags, we beat those odds by a long shot.

We place 10,000 seed clams in each "nursery" bag, made from a woven polyester mesh with four-millimeter holes and plant, or attach, them to a specific spot on the lease. Depending on the growing season and time of year, it will take three to six months before we bring the nursery bag in from the lease and transfer the clams into ten- to twelve-millimeter "grow-out" bags, and replant them back on the lease. They will remain there for about two years. We have nursery and grow-out bags in all stages of development, and we plant the bags chronologically in a grid, keeping meticulous computerized records of precise locations and dates. The giant mudflat has certainly been transformed.

Harvesting and marketing clams

The high tides here are six to eight feet, so we schedule our year-round planting and harvesting around low tides. Harvested clams are washed on the boat to remove sand and silt. Back at the dock, we rewash them in a tumbler using fresh water, which makes the clams close tightly. The tumbler cools the clams and removes unwanted debris and shells. We work under a sunscreen tarp, which keeps the birds away and provides some shade.

Next, the clams go into the grader where they are counted, separated into four grade sizes, and dropped into bags at the mouth of the grader. The bags float in a tub of water so the clams won't break as they drop in. Once tagged, they are sold in 200-count bags that are color-coded based on the clams' size. Off to market they go with individual barcodes on each tag, letting the consumer know the date, time, location, and person who harvested them. Fortunately, there is a lot of mechanization for these processes.

Bill: We also grow and sell cluster oysters on state-permitted leases. South Carolina oysters grow in clusters; single oysters come from Louisiana. We are required by South Carolina Department of Natural Resources to replant the shells, because if you look closely, you will see that new oyster seeds are already growing on these shells. We cull in place, which means rather than throwing the entire oyster cluster in the basket, the crew takes the time to knock the dead shell off and throw it back in the water. This keeps more shell in and around the oyster reefs, which promotes new growth. We've been doing this for a while, but this practice became law this year.

Oysters have always been easy to sell, but when we started clamming, we had lots of competition from other clammers in Charleston, so we found better year-round markets in towns to the north of us. We also sell our clams to Whole Foods for their distribution center in Roswell, Georgia. They order and pick up clams twice a week.

Support and advocacy

Jeff: I wish consumers cared more about where and how their seafood is produced. It is important to buy from local fishermen and farmers, and also to encourage state agencies to support the local farmers and fishermen. We need more common sense when it comes to regulations. Some regulations are important, but many of them are based on assuming the worst-case scenario from a food provider. If regulators say NO to raw seafood products, then who are the real losers? We, the local fishermen are, as are you, the consumer. And who will be the winners—producers in Japan and China! Supporting local needs to happen by purchasing local and also by advocating for local. Our livelihoods depend on it. ❧

▼ Planting clams.

Lucie Kulze
Origin Farm

Lucie is an enthusiastic, energetic, and cheerful young farmer. Since childhood she has had a strong urge to be a farmer and maintain the integrity of her family's historical planta-tion. Through a variety of different agricultural apprenticeships and her own test acreage, she is exploring, developing, and creating her future farming plans. She is concerned about land access for new farmers, hopes to connect farmers with landowners, and, as a way of giving back, she wants to eventually provide apprenticeship opportunities to other new farmers.

Cultivating a lifelong love

I was born with a natural affinity for plants. I re-member being fascinated by my very first plant, a jade, in preschool. In seventh grade, my mom planted an herb garden, which I soon expanded with lettuce, collards, and broccoli. By high school, I was hooked on vegetable gardening. I spent week-ends at our family property, Plum Hill Plantation, working in the garden and walking in the woods.

Eat Dirt! was my high school senior thesis, born from my passion for nature and growing food. I started a school garden and grew lettuce, carrots, radishes, dill, cilantro, collards, kale, sugar peas, and cucumbers. I exceeded my goal of connecting people to nature through growing food. The garden also created community by bringing people together that otherwise would have not bonded—the lunch ladies, janitorial staff, freshman, and upperclassmen. It became my sanctuary, and it made my junior and senior years much more tolerable.

My first mentor, Elizabeth Beak, is a consultant on food-based urban projects. One of her projects was the Medical University of South Carolina (MUSC) Urban Farm. She guided me through *Eat Dirt!* and connected me to my first high school summer job at Rebellion Farm. During that apprenticeship, an eye-opening "ah-ha" moment struck me when I realized that everything about farming—sowing, potting, applying drip tape, placing tomato cages, washing, harvesting, helping with deliveries, all of it—made me feel happy, fulfilled, and connected to the land. I had a true passion for farming. It wasn't just a hobby; I knew my direction in life.

Alternative education

Rather than attend college, I've been exploring different agricultural experiences by apprenticing with innovative farmers across the Southeast. My apprenticeships have introduced me to all forms of farming and agricultural practices—conventional, organic, biodynamic, permaculture, polyculture, and animal husbandry. I've met so many wonderful farmer-mentors.

I took a permaculture course and learned to design agricultural spaces from an innovative perspective. Through careful observation of the geography of the land, I learned how to integrate the inherent features that exist in a specific space into a better and more natural way for growing. Mimicking nature's

Many people have the desire to farm, but don't have the financial means to buy or lease land. . . . landowners may be willing to lease some of their unused and farmable land to the next generation of farmers.

patterns is a fundamental component of permaculture. Rather than planting against nature, if farmers observe the space—soil type, drainage, orientation of the sun, moisture, and wind—before planting, then they can accentuate the ecology of that specific environment, developing agriculture that is low input and less energy intensive. This is the foundation through which I will develop my future farm someday.

I spent my first three apprenticeships with farmers who were predominantly growing vegetables. My final apprenticeship, during the winter of 2016, was at Full Circle Farm in northern Florida where I tried my hand at animal husbandry. They produce nutrient-dense, grass-fed dairy products from Devon-Jersey crosses, forest-raised pork, pasture-raised eggs, meat chickens, lambs, and goat milk. My experience there forever changed my plans for my farming career. I learned that, if managed properly, livestock recondition the health and productivity of the land and the surrounding ecology. Cultivating a diversity of plant and animal species—polyculture—rotational grazing, soil re-mineralization, and other techniques are restorative. Soil is rebuilt rapidly by returning carbon and encouraging a phenomenal habitat in which soil microbes thrive. I fell in love with the dairy cow-grass symbiosis. It's a mutually beneficial relationship, and in fostering this, we can restore and manage land while also producing milk and meat—only from grass!

Farming modeled after nature

Another vitally important part of my farming education comes from Masanobu Fukuoka's *One Straw Revolution*. Fukuoka had a no-till rice and barley dry cropping system. In the winter, he grew clover and barley. The clover provided nutrients for the barley; the barley provided food and biomass to mulch the rice. He sowed the rice into the standing barley and after harvesting, left the barley straw on the field. This system maintained and increased soil fertility year after year.

Fukuoka never added external fertilizers and never had pest issues or weeds—all because he had healthy soil. It was healthy because he mimicked natural systems. He returned all the plant material (except for the grain) to the field, and he never tilled the soil. Tilling oxidizes the soil, causing aerobic bacteria to eat the organic matter, and eventually the soil will collapse. Tillage also promotes weed germination. Conventional fertilizers and all the "cides" (insecticides, pesticides, etc.) create hard soil, because they kill the microbes in the soil that keep it aerated. It is no longer soft and fluffy like a no-till mulch system, a forest floor, or a healthy pasture. Because Fukuoka modeled his system after nature, his book has had a powerful and influential impact on me, and I believe it could change the perspective of many farmers.

Rehabilitating antebellum rice fields

My first commercial crop was rice, because of the historical, ecological and cultural benefits of producing it. My inspiration arose from what I learned from Fukuoka and *One Straw Revolution*. But rice farming became a real possibility for me when I met Dr. Brian Ward at Clemson University's Coastal Research and Education Center and Glenn Roberts, founder of the Carolina Gold Rice Foundation.

We still have antebellum rice fields at Plum Hill Plantation, but some of the impoundments are too old to effectively flood the fields for rice. The dikes eroded, and much of the fields reverted to perennial marsh grasses. My family received a grant from the North American Wetlands Conservation Act to help renovate the dikes, canals, and trunks, which will allow us to flood the fields for rice production and for the benefit of wildlife.

I decided to start rice production with a five-acre field. Since the field had reverted to perennial marsh grasses, I disked and rototilled it, then drilled in the seed. This introduced oxygen to the soil, and unwanted sesbania, a flowering plant in the pea family, germinated along with the rice. Although sesbania is a nitrogen fixer and produces a lot of biomass, its huge stalks inhibit our ability to use a small combine. Normally flooding kills sesbania, but we were a few days late getting water on the rice, and the sesbania grew above the water line along with the rice. We were able to get rid of the sesbania by mowing the fields in late summer. Rice, being a grass, grew back, but the sesbania died, especially after another flooding. This added a lot of extra work to my first attempt at rice production.

Just when our rice was ready to be harvested, the unprecedented October 2015 rains let loose on the Lowcountry, and we were inundated with twenty-three inches. We were only able to salvage about a half acre of rice, which we harvested by hand in waist-deep water. Dr. Ward, friends, and family came to help harvest. We waded into the water with sickles to cut the rice and stacked it in floating totes. After a day and half of hand harvesting, we took our rice to Anson Mills. There it was dried, threshed, cleaned, sifted, hulled, and some of it was polished. We ended up with white and brown rice and middlins. Middlins are the rice grains that crack during the milling process and are delicious when cooked as rice grits. The season would not have been a success without the generous help of Glenn Roberts at Anson Mills, Dr. Ward, and my family and friends.

Restorative farming

In addition to rice, I am focusing on how to develop the rest of my farm using the lessons gleaned from my farm apprenticeships and Masanobu Fukuoka. Plum Hill Plantation has a pasture that I would like to farm, but it is exposed to the sun, wind, and elements. The sun will scorch the vegetables, and the winds will desiccate the greens.

First, I'll have to create shade and windbreaks. I plan to set up a perennial-annual polyculture, because growing annual food alone is not resilient or regenerative. I will build swales along the land's contour to catch rainwater and prevent erosion, and on the downside of the swale, I will plant fruit and nut trees. The perennial trees and bushes—persimmons, pears, blackberries, muscadine grapes, pecans, chestnuts, blueberries, and figs—will do well in this region and will provide shade and a windbreak for the annuals. I will also have livestock to restore the health and productivity of the land.

Permaculture design may take more work up front, but in the long run, it creates a farm that requires less external input and is more resilient, economical, and regenerative. The land gets better year after year, which is the exact opposite of today's agriculture systems.

Creating opportunity

One of the biggest obstacles to new farmers is land access. Many people have the desire to farm, but don't have the financial means to buy or lease land. And many farmers only need one to two acres. This dearth of accessibility to land is a concern of mine; not everyone is as fortunate as I am to have access to family land. I want to help connect farmers with landowners. Most landowners don't know about this dilemma, and if they did, they may be willing to lease some of their unused and farmable land to the next generation of farmers.

My mission is to eventually have a diverse working farm that heals the land, produces nutrient-dense foods, and coexists with native ecology. I also want it to be a place of learning for other aspiring farmers. Since I have had the opportunity to attend workshops and programs around the country and intern with farmers, I would like to give back and provide similar experiences for other prospective farmers.

I named my farm Origin Farm because it was conceived through my process of understanding myself. My chosen profession of farming emerged from a deep place within me. It is my desire to take care of this family land, Plum Hill Plantation, that I love and for which I have such a deep connection. Farming is not my job; it is my way of life! ❧

Mike Lata
FIG (Food Is Good) and The Ordinary, Chef

Including Mike in this book was a great last-minute decision. Not including him would have been a great oversight. For the past three years, as I was collecting these stories, my instinct had been telling me to include him, but I was afraid of being too heavily weighted with legendary all-star chefs—a unique problem to have! Fortunately, other interviewees encouraged the decision and helped set up the interview. Mike's four-year-old son, Henry, accompanied him to the interview, and was a perfect delight. I didn't have a chance to get a shot of Mike at either of his wildly popular restaurants, FIG (Food Is Good) or The Ordinary, but this late spring afternoon shot in street clothes will certainly suffice.

Mike was awarded the James Beard Foundation's Best Chef: Southeast in 2009, FIG restaurant has consistently been voted as Best Restaurant by local Charlestonians, and his seafood hall and oyster bar, The Ordinary, is anything but ordinary. It has already won local and national praise, and was nominated for the James Beard Best New Restaurant in 2013. Mike's commitment to the support of local fishermen, oystermen, clammers, crabbers, shrimpers, farmers, and foragers is extraordinary.

A pivotal moment

I didn't go to culinary school, and I have no classical training. But the makeup for a chef must be hidden somewhere in my DNA.

As a kid growing up outside Springfield, Massachusetts, I spent a lot of time with my grandmothers. My maternal grandmother was French, and she fancied herself a cook, but it was from my paternal Polish grandparents that I acquired the experiences that most informed my culinary future.

My Lata grandmother could make five meals out of one chicken, and her garden was bigger than her house. With these grandparents, I learned to pick beans, hoe potatoes, and pickle vegetables. We often made meals based on our Polish heritage, and I would help hand-roll noodles and stuff cabbages. Our meals were garden fresh, simply prepared, and delicious—the kind of food you never forget. Food was the center of the family.

When I was fourteen, I worked at a drive-up hamburger stand, packing orders and serving ice cream. I soon realized that the kitchen culture was what I wanted to be part of, and I asked the owner if I could become a short order cook. I immediately liked the kitchen—the teamwork, the sense of urgency, and the fast pace.

Through high school and into college, I continued to work in restaurant kitchens. I wasn't focused on any certain style of restaurant or cooking; my focus was on supporting myself. I was studying broadcast journalism in Boston and doing well, but I was worried about all the educational debt I was accumulating, especially since I wasn't really sure what I wanted to do. So I transferred to University of Massachusetts at Amherst (UMass) to save on tuition.

A very pivotal day was the day I skipped class to watch Julia Child speak at UMass. To a standing room only audience, she talked about where food has taken her and how she experiences life through the lens of food—leading her to travel, learning about new cultures, developing personal knowledge, and fueling her passion. I felt she was speaking directly to me. I quit school with the intention to become a chef. I started doing seasonal work in both Martha's Vineyard and New Orleans, where I met a girl, and eventually I followed her to Atlanta.

Creating a signature niche

I was twenty-one when I landed in Atlanta and started

working as a line cook at a reputable restaurant. Within a year, the chef-owner made me chef de cuisine. As chef de cuisine, I was responsible for everything in the kitchen—ordering the food, creating the menus, and managing the kitchen staff. I felt the owner had prematurely given me too much responsibility, but he was absent, and the restaurant was in my hands.

Without the benefit of a culinary school education or an apprenticeship under a culinary mentor, I didn't have the prior opportunities to create a unique style, a depth of resume, or a repertoire of signature dishes. I had a blank canvas, and it was up to me to figure out how to make a go of this promotion while also making the customers'

experience unique and unforgettable. I recalled my experiences with my Polish grandmother—harvesting fresh food and cooking simple meals. I knew one thing for sure—super fresh food tastes super good. My instincts directed me to fashion my own niche. I decided to be a curator of the highest quality local ingredients and to make simple, yet elegant dishes. This would be my signature.

Now my task was finding the freshest, most nutritious, and highest quality food sources. Fortunately, I stumbled on the Georgia Organic Growers' Association, which consisted of about thirty local farmers. Every Sunday, the farmers would fax their available produce to a central person, who would fax the farmers' list to chefs. The changing availability of those weekly items—ten pounds of purple Cherokee tomatoes, forty ears of white corn, a bushel of okra, and many pounds of blueberries—became the brush strokes for my blank canvas.

At the weekly farmers market, I started developing relationships with the farmers and visiting them on their farms. Occasionally I would do chef demonstrations at the market using their produce. The farmers became my friends, and in the process, I created a style of cooking that focused on their harvests.

One of my new farmers market friends—I visited her goat farm often—happened to be the food editor for the *Atlanta Journal Constitution*. Her pages started telling the story of a young chef in town

The most meaningful thing for me as a chef is the relationships I have developed with an entire family of local farmers and fishermen.

who was using fresh local vegetables. One night I was featuring a "Soir des Legumes" dinner, when out of the blue CNN showed up and filmed me during meal prep. In short order, I was on the map.

Milling corn in the kitchen

Meanwhile, the director of operations for the Anson-Garibaldi Group, Glenn Roberts, was searching for a chef for Anson Restaurant in Charleston. He was interested in starting a local food program in Charleston and contacted the woman in charge of our Atlanta cooperative, who recommended me. Glenn and Anson courted me for about six months, but I really was not interested in leaving Atlanta. I was ready to decline the offer when, on my last visit in December of 1997, Glenn took me to Celeste Albers' farm. She was eager to farm for restaurants in a way that complemented what I wanted to do with farmers. Celeste was the deciding factor, and in early 1998, I moved to Charleston to be the chef at Anson.

Over the next couple of years, Glenn and I did a lot of good work together, establishing Anson as a great restaurant with me as its chef. We focused on locally and seasonally driven menus. We were able to source local seafood, meats, eggs, and produce, but we lacked local corn and rice. Glenn started driving around, scouring the South for heirloom grains. Once, having found an heirloom corn in Tennessee, he came through the back door of Anson's kitchen with the bag of corn and a handheld table gristmill. "Let's make grits," he said. I reminded him that we served grits to about 400 customers per night, and we needed four gallons of it. But that night, through his persistence, we figured out how to create one dish using his freshly ground corn. Recognizing the need for a gristmill, Glenn Roberts' renowned Anson Mills was born.

A moving target with untold variables

With the kind of volume we had at Anson, and by committing to a seasonal menu, I honed my skills

around preparing meals "a la minute"—with total spontaneity. There are so many variables in that process. Imagine you are having a big dinner party, and at noon you are waiting for your local farmer to arrive. You have no idea how much of each vegetable he will have, or if his tractor ran out of gas during harvesting, and you will get nothing. This is very nerve-racking.

Once the food comes in the back door, there are restaurant protocols about receiving, prepping, and properly handling it all the way to the meal. After seeing, feeling, and often tasting the products, I determine the entire menu, right then and there. The menu goes to print, I educate the cooks on how to prepare the meal, and then educate the servers. Then we hope that we have enough product to get us through the entire night's service. Every night becomes an intense experience, because every single part of the process is a moving target with untold variables.

I realize that when a farmer brings in their produce, they are bringing in the pride of their hard work, and I am very respectful of that. And yet, it isn't as simple as knowing that a farmer is delivering ten pounds of beans. I need to know how long the beans have been growing, and if they are from the same bean plants he picked last week. If they are the same, then they are going to be too mature and won't work for the dish I was thinking about creating. I'll still buy the beans, because I'm committed to supporting the farmer and keeping the menu local, but because the texture and taste will be different, I'll need to adjust what I was thinking about and create an appropriate dish for that texture and taste.

Some chefs may tell farmers that they can't use their harvest because the carrots are too crooked or the arugula is too hot. I will use whatever the farmer brings me, and I will figure out what to do with it. Maybe I'll make a pesto or soup from that arugula. However, when there's an opportunity for improvement, we must have a dialogue to inform each other of our needs to create a better product. There must be a clear understanding of the quality produce, meats, and fish that I am looking for. It matters to me as a chef what time of day the lettuce gets picked, and how quickly the field heat is removed. What makes sense in the field does not always produce the best results in the kitchen. I work with my farmers and fishermen to help them understand and achieve the best quality product that I need.

We—the chefs and farmers—each want the other to do well. Mark Marhefka, of Abundant Seafood, and I worked a long time together to set and meet each other's expectations. You would think a grouper is a grouper, but it is not. If a fish is bruised or its flesh is not firm, then I cannot use it as a fillet, but I can use it in a stew. How a fish is handled after it comes out of the water makes all the difference. Mark has developed a superior technique for handling and storing fish, and the quality of his fish is unrivaled.

Part chef, part entrepreneur, full-time farmer advocate

At Anson, I was working eighteen hours a day, getting lots of press, and breathing life into the restaurant. But I was ready to become more than a chef; I wanted to become a partner. Proposing that we reclaim Southern cuisine in Charleston, I drew up a business plan that would take Anson to the next level. At that time, no one was cooking solely regional cuisine, so I proposed that we would be the ones to do it at Anson. We'd make the best shrimp and grits, crab cakes, or pimento cheese—with such integrity that we would change the dining experience. But the owners of Anson just couldn't get their heads around how to make this transition.

It was time for me to move forward and pursue this dream of creating a restaurant inspired by and reflecting the seasons, the farmers' fields, the fishermen's catch, and the region's culinary heritage. Anson's assistant manager, Adam Nemirow, totally understood my vision and became my partner. It took us over a year to find and secure investors and the right location, but in April of 2003, Adam and I opened FIG (Food Is Good) in downtown Charleston.

From the moment our doors opened, FIG's mission has been to provide our guests with an unforgettable experience. We achieve that by having a dedicated, knowledgeable, and caring staff; we source seasonal ingredients from local farmers and fishermen; and we serve honest, straightforward food that celebrates the Lowcountry's culinary traditions. This simple philosophy and approach has led to FIG's great success over the years.

Although fear of failure has always been a recurring challenge for me, FIG's sustained success encouraged Adam and me to open another restaurant a decade later. So in 2012, we launched The Ordinary. One part chef and one part opportunist, I recognized there was a massive gap in the market for a fancy seafood restaurant and oyster bar—a restaurant very different from the style of seafood that is offered at tourist venues. We decided to create a great seafood restaurant celebrating local purveyors of the sea—fishermen, crabbers, clammers, shrimpers, oystermen. The taste of raw oysters depends on the salinity of the ocean, which varies significantly down the East Coast. At The Ordinary we provide our guests with authentic experiences to taste the merroir—the taste of the local waters—of oysters and other seafood. Five years after opening our doors at The Ordinary, our fancy seafood hall and oyster bar is thriving, as are the local clammers, oystermen, crabbers, shrimpers, and fishermen whom we source from and to whom we are dedicated.

The most meaningful thing for me as a chef is the relationships I have developed with an entire family of local farmers and fishermen—Mark Marhefka, Celeste Albers, and many others. I feel lucky to have cultivated this kind of connection and high level of trust with our vendors. It is also rewarding to feel like I have had an influence on their product, to help them make it better before it gets to my restaurants and to their other consumers. FIG and The Ordinary's successes can be attributed to the purveyors, the guests, and the team cooking and serving the food. Together, we have raised standards and quality for an unforgettable experience.

So much of who I am as a chef started with my grandmother—harvesting from her garden and cooking straightforward, seasonal, fresh food with simplicity and integrity. I don't know how to do anything else. If you gave me asparagus in December that had been grown in Nicaragua and asked me to make a meal, I wouldn't have a clue what to do with it. ❧

Patrick Myers, Kent Whetsell, and Josh Brooks
Landsdowne Dairy and Lowcountry Creamery

I met Patrick, Kent, and Josh in their creamery production kitchen, a refurbished restaurant next to a gas station off an interstate highway. The three business partners
meet every Saturday to make their Lowcountry Creamery products. After observing their
yogurt production, we piled into Patrick's truck and drove a couple miles to Landsdowne Dairy,
where we wandered through a pasture of happy Jersey cows and toured the milking barn.
I returned a second time and met with Kent to learn more about the cows and milk production.

Reviving the family dairy

Patrick: Landsdowne Dairy was my family's working farm for four generations, until my dad shut it
down in 2004 due to the milk industry's negative
profit margins. Around that time, there were more
than 130 dairies in South Carolina. Now, a decade
later, there are only about 60.

▲ Above: Josh, Kent, and Patrick.

Most of the milk consumed in South Carolina is
imported. Large out-of-state dairies, due to their economies of scale, have lower labor costs and lower input costs of land and feed, allowing them to produce
more milk for less. Therefore, it is cheaper for dairy
plants in South Carolina to import milk from across
the country rather than pay local farmers to produce
it. This outside pressure has caused many dairies to go
under, and sadly the milk that South Carolinians are
consuming is coming from farther and farther away.

Large out-of-state dairies, due to their economies of scale, have lower labor costs and lower input costs of land and feed. Therefore, it is cheaper for dairy plants in South Carolina to import milk from across the country rather than pay local farmers to produce it.

Despite these odds, my friend Kent and I both grew up and worked in the dairy industry, with exposure to lots of different aspects of it. Kent, a graduate of Clemson University with a degree in animal science, is a fourth-generation farmer. He worked on dairy farms for fifteen years and was a parlor manager at Clemson University's dairy. I have a master's degree from Clemson in animal physiology with an emphasis on ruminant nutrition. I work for a feed company as a dairy nutritionist and work directly with dairy farmers on their ration formulation. Kent and I started thinking about creating a business together.

Fortunately, my dad didn't sell our farm, and the bones and infrastructure of the recently closed dairy were still sound. Thanks to my family, we moved forward with our business plan pretty quickly.

In 2010, Kent and I formed a partnership and leased Landsdowne Dairy from my family. We purchased dairy cows and reawakened the dairy operations. Learning from my dad's experience, we knew we needed to wean our dairy away from total dependence on contract sales. But first, we had to get the dairy up and running.

Happy and healthy cows

Kent: Landsdowne Dairy has 220 Jersey cows, and we are currently milking 180. Jersey's milk is very high quality, because it has more fat and protein than other dairy breeds. We maintain consistent milk production by staggering breeding throughout the year, and have fifteen to twenty cows calving each month.

After the calves nurse to receive their mother's colostrum, they are weaned and are bottle-fed with lightly pasteurized milk twice a day. Each mother cow produces about six gallons of milk per day, which is about five times more milk than her calf can consume.

We milk our cows at 5:00 a.m. and 5:00 p.m. Our equipment enables us to milk ten cows at a time, and the milking itself only takes five minutes per cow, but the entire process—preparing, milking, and cleaning up—takes four to five hours each morning and evening.

When the cows enter the milking parlor, we clean their udders and manually attach the vacuum-operated machines, which produce a pulsating action on the cows' teats. The milk is transported through tubes into a big receiver jar, then pumped through a filter and into a 2,000-gallon tank, where it is kept between 38°F and 42°F.

In addition to feeding our cows a high-quality feed, we rotate them between our forty acres of pasture, where they spend four to five hours every day, year-round. We also have a free-stall barn in which the cows roam freely, eat, drink, socialize, rest, and sleep in open stalls. All of these factors contribute to happy, healthy cows and the sweetness of their milk.

From price takers to price makers

Patrick: To sell milk commercially, dairy farmers are at the mercy of the wild fluctuations of the market. Milk is traded on the Chicago Board of Trade, and the price is determined by multiple factors that impact our current economy—from China's powerfully fluctuating purchases to the Russian embargo on the European Union (EU). When Russia, the largest importer of milk from EU dairies, placed a food embargo on the EU, all the milk destined for Russia had to find new markets, which caused supplies to rise and prices to plummet, not only affecting EU dairies, but the rest of the world.

While Landsdowne Dairy is as local as it gets, global factors impact the price we get paid for our milk. We have a contract with a milk co-op. Every other day, a big tanker picks up around 16,000 pounds of raw milk from us and takes it to a plant where it is commingled with milk from other dairies to be pasteurized, homogenized, and sold. This gives us some assurance for steady income, but we want to find a balance between contracting out our milk and creating some of our own products to sell on a local market.

Right now we are price takers, but our goal is to become price makers. We seek to create some independence through our creamery products and sustain the dairy's future by not being totally dependent on the global market. We don't want to grow Landsdowne into a huge commercial dairy, we want to build value into our milk products.

Value-added products

In 2012, we hired a consultant and conducted a feasibility study to determine if there was a market for us to create an artisan creamery. There was, and to start on a small scale, all we needed was a Department of Health and Environmental Control (DHEC)–permitted commercial kitchen. So we bought and repurposed this vacant restaurant. In 2014, with a third partner, Josh, who is a banker and self-declared foodie, we created a new partnership

and established Lowcountry Creamery. By 2015, we were selling yogurt.

Greek yogurt is popular, so we started there. Technically, Greek yogurt is a probiotic cheese. Using small-scale forty-five gallon batches of raw milk, we lightly pasteurize it by slowly bringing the temperature to 147°F for thirty-two minutes. This light pasteurization preserves the flavor and essential enzymes. To this we add a culture, incubate it, strain out the whey, and package it. We are constantly experimenting, learning, and improving. Each time we make yogurt it is a little different, which contributes to its artisan quality.

When we started making yogurt, the creamery business was only using half a percent of our milk production. A year later Lowcountry Creamery has built a brand, expanded our range of products to include full-fat yogurt, non-fat yogurt, crème fraîche, whole milk, chocolate milk, and buttermilk. Now, we are using five percent of our milk production.

All of our products containing fat are non-homogenized. Here's a little-known fact—our bodies absorb more fat from homogenized milk products than from non-homogenized milk products. Homogenization breaks the fat down into smaller globules so it will become suspended in the milk. Our bodies absorb more of the fat due to the polarity of the fat globules, which now attract proteins. Because our bodies want to absorb the protein, they absorb the fat too. Not so with non-homogenized milk products. Therefore, drinking our non-homogenized 4.8–5.2% milk, your body will likely absorb just a quarter of the fat, whereas drinking homogenized 2% milk, your body will absorb about ninety percent of the fat. And there's no doubt about it, milk products with fat are a lot tastier than non-fat products.

Rewarded by local communities' support

Producing great quality milk and making value-added products is one thing, but it's to no avail without having a way to market and distribute them. Fortunately, there is a local food marketing and distribution hub, GrowFood Carolina, which sells our products to chefs, restaurants, and retailers. The more they sell, the more our creamery grows, which allows us to use higher and higher percentages of our milk production. In turn, we become less dependent on prices set by the Chicago Board of Trade. We become price makers.

The trending of our creamery business in two short years—up and to the right—is a dream realized. After my family's dairy was closed for six years, it is rewarding to have it up and operating again. Our products are high quality, nutritious, and delicious. Our cows are happy and healthy. The work is labor intensive, but rewarding. And we are proud that the local community is appreciating and purchasing our products. Like our creamery business, we hope the buy local trend—up and to the right—continues! 🐄

Marc Filion
Keegan-Filion Farm

Well known in the Lowcountry, Keegan-Filion Farm is a family farm that raises pastured, hormone-free, steroid-free, antibiotic-free chickens and turkeys, as well as
heritage Tamworth hogs and grass-fed beef in humane, sustainable, and environmentally safe
ways. As I spent time with Marc on his farm and with his animals, I got an up-close understanding of the true costs of food production—the time, resources, and care required to raise
poultry and livestock in such a responsible way. Marc and Annie are dedicated to humanely
and sustainably producing our food. In turn, we as consumers need to make it sustainable for
them to do so!

From idealistic to realistic

My grandfather was a chicken farmer in Rhode
Island, and I always wanted to farm. When Annie

▲ Above photo: Marc and Annie.

and I got married, we had an idealistic view of farming. In 1986, we tried our hand at raising hogs, but
we hung up that venture after about five years.
We were selling to Smithfield through their buying station, and when farmers sell through a buying
station, they must take the price that is offered that

day, even if it is below the cost of production. The market for hogs had collapsed, and we were losing money on every hog we sold. We decided the best thing to do was shut down, because there were no direct sale market opportunities at that time.

We began farming again in 2004. We work just as hard, and probably harder now, but we diversified our production and decided that we would be in control of setting the prices for our animals. Today, we sell our eggs, broiler chickens, turkeys, hogs, and cattle via direct marketing channels only.

Nurturing livestock with quality care

Annie and I work hard and take great pride in the way we nurture our animals with the best food, fresh water, clean and spacious living spaces, and pasturage.

We have fifteen head of cattle—Black Angus, Charolais, and Black Baldies, which are a cross between an Angus and Hereford. We get six- to eight-month-old steers, and a neighboring farmer raises them for us. They graze on grass for the next twenty to twenty-four months before we take them to the processor. I sell thirty-five head of cattle a year.

We keep about thirty heritage Tamworth sows. They are a breed from 1800s Europe, known for their great marbling and delicious bacon and pork chops. The hogs are pretty easy. I only need to spend about twenty minutes a day feeding them in the morning and evening, but I do always keep my eyes on them. One of our sows is three weeks away from farrowing. Average gestation is 114 days—three months, three weeks, and three days. When she gets closer, we will move her to the farrowing house, give her a bath to disinfect her, and watch her closely. I bred her with our two-year-old Tamworth boar, but I'm getting rid of him because he is too aggressive. Unfortunately, we can't sell him for meat because boar testosterone produces a foul-tasting meat. Sows, females that have had piglets, can be used for sausage. Young six- to eight-month-old gilts (females) and barrows (castrated males) are used for other pork cuts.

More than eighteen acres are dedicated to raise hogs, but we limit their pasture area to ensure we always have fresh ground. Every couple of months, we rotate them onto new acres that have been planted with nutritious cowpeas, wheat, oats, rye, collards, and turnips. The hogs have a house with a misting system to keep them comfortable and cool.

We raise both layers and broiler chickens. Our laying hens, Production Reds and Highland Browns, come from Amish farms in Pennsylvania and Ohio. Gathering, washing, and crating eggs is very labor intensive, and takes up to three hours per day.

Our broiler chickens are a cross between a Cornish breed and a Plymouth Rock to give us a Cornish Rock Cross. I have a standing order of 325 chicks per week. When a chick hatches, it has enough nutrients to last 72-98 hours. The chicks are delivered through the postal system when they are two to three days old. The post office calls me at 5:00 a.m., and I go get them immediately. When the chicks first arrive, the most important thing is to hydrate them. I give them electrolytes and vitamins the first day, which helps build a strong immune system, and probiotics for four weeks to put healthy bacteria in their gut.

All of our baby chicks are raised in a housing unit called a brooder. It has five levels, each with fifty chicks. Each level has two sets of lights, for illumination and for heat when necessary. We keep the temperature at 95°F for the new chicks and drop it about a degree per day for five days. We continue to drop the temperature five degrees a week for the four weeks they are in the brooder. At three weeks, we start conditioning them to go outside.

We monitor our chicks closely and keep detailed logs on everything in the brooder house, because when you don't use antibiotics, there is no room for error. The chicks graduate into the pasture at four weeks; however, weather is the limiting factor for everything we do. If the ground is wet, we'll hold them in the brood house a couple extra days.

Once they are on pasture, our chickens are able to scratch, peck the grass, and roam freely inside "chicken tractors." The chicken tractors are pens on skids that we move to fresh grass each day. Chicken tractors protect the birds from possums, coons, foxes, hawks, coyotes, and worst of all, domestic dogs. During hot weather, we put a shade cloth over the chicken tractor and a soaker hose in it to keep the birds cool. In the winter, we put a tarp over it to protect them from the wind, and if it is really cold, we'll put propane tanks in the chicken tractors to provide more heat. Because they move each day, the chickens are naturally fertilizing the grass, which we will cut as hay for the cattle. We send them to market after eight weeks, which is about three weeks longer than meat birds raised in an industrial chicken house. This is because we don't give them antibiotics or other growth-promoting feed additives.

Since we don't use antibiotics in any of our livestock's feed, it takes us sixty percent more time and resources to raise each animal before sending it to be processed. Time, labor, and food are money.

We also receive 125 turkey poults per month from a hatchery in Pennsylvania, and the process is much the same as for the chicks.

We raised 350 turkeys for Thanksgiving last year and another 750 for ground turkey and turkey sausages. Turkeys sold for Thanksgiving are between fourteen and eighteen weeks old. We let the birds raised for ground turkey and sausage grow another six weeks until they weigh around fifty pounds.

Each week I get half of a tractor-trailer of chicken feed—fourteen or fifteen tons—delivered to the farm. I would need 400 acres to grow this amount of food myself. Our chickens eat corn, soybean meal, vitamins, and minerals. We don't add any animal proteins—bonemeal or blood meal. And although Annie and I vehemently protested genetically engineered foods from the moment they first appeared in 1993, our feed is unfortunately genetically

modified. Soybeans are ninety-eight percent GMO, and corn is ninety-three percent GMO. I recently found and tried a non-GMO corn and soybean feed, but it was so expensive that we were unable to remain competitive in the restaurant market. Chefs couldn't pay the extra price. We lost money for several months and had to go back to GMO feed.

Additionally, our birds are not organic because, like non-GMO feed, organic chicken feed is very expensive. Our prices would have to be way over market. Furthermore, there isn't an organically certified processing plant in South Carolina, and one processing plant can't process both organic and non-organic meat because of cross-contamination. Our processor, Williamsburg Packing in Kingstree, is certified humane, which is very important to us.

Keegan-Filion Farm doesn't use any antibiotics, steroids, or hormones. Actually, steroids and hormones are illegal in chicken, pork, and turkey, so when you see these three meats advertised as steroid and hormone free, it is just a marketing ploy. And although the use of antibiotics in feed is legal and causes the animals to develop faster, we do not use them. If we were to give our hogs antibiotics, they would grow more quickly and be ready for processing in about five and a half months. That is sixty percent less time than it takes us to raise them without antibiotics. While this would benefit us economically, we are opposed to using antibiotics for raising animals.

One of the reasons Annie and I started raising chickens and livestock without antibiotics, steroids, and hormones in 2004 was because some of our friends' daughters experienced the early onset of female reproductive functions around the age of nine. Doctors are seeing this more frequently, as early as age seven in some girls. When the pituitary gland produces hormones at such an unnaturally early age, it seems logical to draw this corollary deduction—if what we consume has been fed antibiotics to encourage quick development, then might this produce the same results in humans?

A day in the life

Every morning we are in the brood house taking care of our chicks and turkey poults by 6:30 a.m. After breakfast, the pig nursery gets hosed clean, and we feed, water, and check on the hogs and cattle. Every four hours, we re-check and water the chicks. The chicken tractors get moved, and the garden and store are tended. In the evening, the feedings happen all over again. And, if it is really cold, I check on the chicks throughout the night.

On Tuesdays, we load the trailer with chickens ready for processing, and the following morning at 5:00 a.m., I leave for Williamsburg Packing—100 miles away. After unloading the chickens, I drive back to the farm to load the hogs and run them to the same processing plant. Every Wednesday, I travel 400 miles and spend eight hours in the truck, in addition to loading and unloading the animals. I also stop along the route to meet a farmer from the Happy Cow Creamery. We distribute their milk, butter, and cheese to our farmers market customers.

Six months ago, our son Jesse started farming with us full-time. He does a lot of our building and maintenance projects, makes sales calls to chefs, and delivers to the Charleston and Columbia restaurants. On Mondays, he and I take the refrigerated truck back to the processing plant to pick up the packaged meats from the week before. We sort and organize our chicken and pork packages for the restaurants, farmers markets, and our store. We get back to the farm around 5:30 p.m., unload items for the store, load nineteen cases of eggs, and get ready for Tuesday morning's Charleston, Summerville, West Ashley, Mount Pleasant, and James Island deliveries.

On Fridays, we pack for two Saturday farmers markets. On Saturday, Annie leaves for the Summerville market at 6:00 a.m. I get to the brooder room at 5:00 a.m., and leave for the Port Royal farmers market around 6:45 a.m.

Along with Jesse, we have two full-time employees. They help with all the chores on the farm and man our farm store, which is open Monday and Friday from 1:00 to 6:00 p.m.

A little chicken history

Pre-World War II, people didn't eat chicken the way we do today. Chickens were kept primarily for eggs. The birds were scrappy, mostly foraging on yard insects and kitchen waste. They fared poorly in the winters due to the lack of sunlight and vitamin D, had a high mortality rate, and were not meaty. During World War II, the military was sending beef and pork to the troops, but the troops and the American public were in need of more food and protein. To reduce the pressure on food supplies, President Roosevelt appealed to the citizenry to create Victory Gardens and raise chickens for meat, because they grow to an edible size in a short amount of time. At that time, the Department of Agriculture started sending day-old chicks to poultry raisers through the U.S. Post Office, which is still the method of chick delivery today.

Are family farms sustainable?

Up until two years ago, I was a regional manager for a large company, traveling a lot and living in motels. I gave up the salaried job so Annie and I could farm together. Somehow Annie was doing all of this herself—feeding, moving livestock, picking up from the processing plant, making deliveries, calling on chefs, and going to farmers markets. I don't know how she did it, but I'm grateful that we are enjoying farming together now, and I am really happy that Jesse decided to join us.

With the increased help around the farm, Annie can handle the books, communicate with the chefs, answer email, and manage the daily activities on the farm and our meat share program. Annie and I have not had a day off in two and a half years, but we

▼ Poults inside a turkey tractor.

are getting close to having the luxury of being able to take a little break.

Last year we raised 15,000 broilers, 1,200 turkeys, 400 hogs, 35 steers, and collected probably more than 100,000 eggs from our laying flock. When Annie and I first started farming again, our sales were ninety-six percent to restaurants and four percent to individuals and families. Today, our sales are basically split down the middle to both restaurants and families. We certainly like this trend, because selling a clean product to people who care about their health is key to our farm's mission. Overall, our farm has continued to grow and has finally reached a level that allows us to sleep at night knowing we can sustain a living.

Annie and I both spent lengthy careers in the corporate sector. Annie was in manufacturing and distribution. I was in upper-level management of a $40 million corporation and in charge of a $12 million division. We are convinced that our business experience has allowed us to be as successful as we are. We are constantly looking at ways to improve our operation, manage our cash flow, and set long-range goals to ensure our continued success. Knowing how to farm is obviously key. Knowing how to handle the financial and business part of the farm is just as important—especially because the nutrition and care we provide our livestock is expensive and time consuming. Since we take significant extra effort and don't use antibiotics in any of our livestock's feed, it takes us sixty percent more time and resources to raise each animal before sending it to be processed. Time, labor, and food are money. We do our best to keep our prices as low as possible, because we want everyone to be able to afford healthy, humanely raised food.

The true costs of raising livestock must be considered in the pricing. We pay $1.10 for a chick, $3.80 to process it (kill and pluck), another $1.50 to have it cut up into legs and breasts, and $0.25 per vacuum-sealed bag. That is almost $7.00 per bird, and that doesn't include feed, labor, or transport costs. We raised 15,000 birds last year. Selling chicken for $3.95 per pound, we only gross $1.50 per bird, not including any labor costs. A local farmer can't compete with agribusiness giants like Tyson, Pilgrim's Pride, or Perdue that sell their birds for $1.95 to $2.25 per pound. Local farmers, too, must make a profit to stay in business.

Sadly, most consumers don't understand the externalities, the hidden costs of raising an animal with the high degree of quality and care that we provide. We've had people stop by our store and walk away because they were unwilling to pay $3.95 for a dozen eggs! For farms like ours to survive, we must have broad and consistent community support. Consumers must look beyond the dollar cost of food and seek to understand the TRUE cost of their food. Cheap food is cheap for a reason.

Many people tout the value of local food with words of support, but don't put their money where their mouth is. Knowing and trusting your farmer, understanding how livestock are raised, and consistently purchasing our products will enable local farmers to remain in business. Annie and I love farming, but it has to be a sustainable livelihood. The community must be dedicated to buying locally; it's the only way local farming can be sustainable.

Cash flow is an issue for farmers, because farm loans are due in one year. Oftentimes, it seems like all the year's income goes into financing the farm's growth, then paying the loan, and not into the farmer's pockets. It can seem impossible to get ahead. That is why many farmers today must maintain another job in addition to farming.

Are we sustainable? We dreamed about having this farm; we have a lot invested in the land and our animals. We are proud of what we do here at Keegan-Filion Farm. We raise and sell healthy and delicious food. But the bottom line is this—we too have a bottom line. ❧

Campbell Coxe
Carolina Plantation Rice

*C*ampbell was milling Jimmy Hagood's Lavington Plantation rice the day I visited. Campbell and a handful of others are growing rice from seeds that were originally provided by the Carolina Gold Rice Foundation (CGRF). The CGRF produces and provides pure true type starter seed free of charge to qualified Southern growers when they begin farming Carolina Gold and/or Charleston Gold rice.

From cotton to Carolina Gold

I'm a seventh-generation farmer and have been farming Plumfield Plantation on the Great Pee Dee River for more than three decades. I grew thousands of acres of cotton, but several years ago the cotton market became more unpredictable and less cost effective. I looked for a new crop that I could take straight to the consumer without being a victim of the commodity markets' wild, uncontrollable fluctuations.

My cousin grows rice in Arkansas, and after many duck hunting trips there, I became inspired to mimic his method of rice production—pumping water from a nearby river into a flat field. Although rice had never been grown on my inland farm—hours from the tidal waters of South Carolina's coast—I am next to the Great Pee Dee River, which comes up every year and deposits a huge amount of alluvium. Like the Nile, the Great Pee Dee gives us rich, deep topsoil that just happens to be perfect for growing rice.

I started planting Della, a long-grain aromatic

Even though the work is hard and farming doesn't generate a huge financial gain, I'm proud to be bringing back an heirloom crop, and I'm proud of the quality of the products that I am providing the consumer.

rice, in 1996. I began with ten acres, then twenty, and every year since I've been increasing the acreage. Plumfield Plantation has about 250 acres in rice production now.

Rice grew well on Plumfield, but the closest rice mill was 870 miles west of here, in Arkansas. While inconvenient and inefficient, I sent my rice to be milled there for five years, until diesel fuel soared to four dollars per gallon. I quickly realized that I would be out of business unless I built my own mill. So I built a mill in 2001. Not long afterward, through the generosity of the Carolina Gold Rice Foundation's seed sharing, I planted my first crop of heritage Carolina Gold rice.

The story of Carolina Gold

Carolina Gold rice is a biblical grain, or a landrace grain, which means it grew indigenously and has never been messed with and never hybridized. It is a native grass, and Carolina Gold rice brought massive wealth to Charleston beginning in the late 1600s. Coastal South Carolina was the largest producer of rice in colonial America for more than a century. In the 1700s, ninety-eight percent of South Carolina's rice was being shipped around the world. However, Carolina Gold rice and the rice industry completely disappeared after the Civil War due to the demise of slave labor, the lack of financial capital, and two major back-to-back hurricanes, which destroyed the crop and depleted the seed stock.

In 1988, after a comprehensive search, the original Carolina Gold rice seed was found at the principal research agency for the USDA in Aberdeen, South Dakota. Somehow, and fortunately, seed had been buried in a USDA seed bank vault to prevent its extinction.

Carolina Gold rice has some major production deficits. It is not disease resistant, it has a low yield, and it lodges, meaning the rice falls over with wind or rain. Lodging prevents a combine from getting under it and properly harvesting the top heads of grain.

Over the period of a decade, research scientists Dr. Merle Shepard, Dr. Anna McClung, and Dr. Gurdev Khush experimented and created an improved version of Carolina Gold rice. It was bred with a highly aromatic Indian basmati rice, creating a new rice, Charleston Gold, in 2008. It has a shorter stalk that does not lodge as easily, it produces a higher yield of rice, and it has broad-spectrum disease resistance. Plumfield Plantation has been growing it successfully ever since.

Carolina Gold and Charleston Gold rice seeds are both certified non-GMO (genetically modified organisms) and are registered and certified by the Texas Rice Improvement Association. I make sure to keep enough reserve seed in the event of a tragedy, which was fortunate because during Hurricane Katrina, our seed source in Beaumont, Texas, lost their stock of reserve seeds. There are vaults around the world that harbor seeds for just such a crisis, although it takes years to recover the volume of production.

From the field to the mill

We plant our rice on dry fields in early May. As the rice matures, we add water to the field, called stretch water, which inhibits weeds. When the rice is about six to eight inches tall, we add more water. The water kills the weeds, but not the rice, because rice is a semi-aquatic grass. Rice wants its head out of the water, but when preyed upon by armyworms and stinkbugs, we can flood the fields, submerge the rice for a couple of days without harming it, and kill the pests. The water also stabilizes the temperature, keeping the head of the rice at a constant 78-80°F. Stable temperature is a positive factor for pollination, because rice won't pollinate above 100°F.

We harvest the rice in the fall. Birds, in particular the bobolink—its species name is *oryzivorus* (from the Latin *oryza*, "rice," and *vorare*, "to devour")—will take it all if we don't get it harvested in time. October is supposed to be the driest month in South Carolina, but we had more than forty inches of rain this past

October, with twenty-five inches falling within a three-day period. I lost about half of my rice production due to the floods.

At harvest time, we test for moisture. If the rice is harvested too soon, there will be too much moisture in the grain, and it will ferment. Batches of paddy rice usually have a moisture content of around eighteen percent. We put the grain into silos that have perforated floors with air blowing through them to get the moisture level down to eleven percent before milling it.

Milling begins after harvest, and we mill daily until January or February. The rice is conveyed by an auger from the grain silo into my 1961 truck, which drives about a hundred yards and unloads into the mill. The rice is put into the seed cleaner, which removes all the debris—leaves, sticks, stones, insects—anything other than rice. Then it moves into the husker, which has two rubber wheels running at different speeds. The rice moves between them, and the friction removes the husks. The husker replaces the mortar and pestle of long ago. At this point, it is brown rice.

From the husker, the rice is conveyed through a machine with a porcelain disk that spins and uses pressure to polish the grains. Polishing removes the bran, converting the brown rice into white rice. The bran is shot from the polisher into large bags for by-product uses. The white rice then proceeds through a grader, which removes broken kernels. Lastly, because we don't bleach any of our rice, we run the rice through the polisher again.

Ten thousand pounds of pre-milled rice only yields 6,000 pounds of milled rice. The other 4,000 pounds are byproducts—bran and broken kernels. These byproducts are valuable, and we sell them for a profit, rather than waste them. The bran is very high in protein and fiber and is sold for animal feed. We sell the broken rice kernels as "middlins," locally known as rice grits (normal grits are made from corn), or we make rice flour (a gluten-free product).

The rice is stored in a cooler in 2,000-pound bag totes. It's packaged as orders come in. Carolina Plantation Rice is Green-E Certified, meaning that everything we use for packaging has been recycled. Our packaging is hand-sewn using 100 percent American cotton. As a local producer, I feel that it is important for our operation to use only local packaging, too. Furthermore, the energy we use to produce our products is from a local and renewable energy source—EPA-endorsed landfill methane gas.

The history of white rice

The only difference between brown rice and white rice is the milling process. Brown rice requires less milling. After the husk is removed, the rice is cloaked in the bran, which has a brownish color and contains all the fiber, vitamins, and nutrients. Centuries ago, when barrels of rice were shipped around the world, brown rice would spoil because it maintains its natural oils and will go rancid without refrigeration. Removing the bran left a white rice, which could be stored long-term and shipped worldwide. This process for removing the bran made the rice very valuable, and consequently, polished white rice was considered to be the rice of the wealthy.

The business of rice

I have five employees, and each wears at least four different hats. All of my employees are locals, and I want to make sure they have year-round employment. In the winter, when we aren't busy with rice production and milling, I run a commercial hunting operation. Some of the employees become guides, and the others cook meals for the hunters and maintain the grounds, facilities, and equipment. One needs to be creative to keep a place like this going and keep everyone employed.

Cutting out the middleman seems like a good idea, but there's a lot more to the process than meets the eye. I am responsible for everything—from the field to the customer's shopping cart. The rice needs to be stored and dried in the silos, milled, stored again in refrigeration, packaged, marketed, sold, and shipped.

Our first marketing hurdle was to convince customers to switch from buying cheap rice with a long shelf life to a gourmet heirloom rice that requires refrigeration. Fortunately, chefs mostly drove that promotional and educational campaign, showcasing Carolina Gold's rich heritage. Ten years later, when Charleston Gold rice was introduced, people simply weren't ready to recognize another new rice product. Personally, I don't think Carolina Gold is as tasty as Charleston Gold, but I grow it because people ask for it. And although the price is the same, Carolina Gold's yield is half. So this is a marketing hurdle I continue to work on to overcome.

The Internet has brought the world to my swamp, allowing me to distribute my products anywhere in the world. I don't need a brick and mortar store to be able to compete with gourmet shops like Dean & Deluca in Soho, New York.

In addition to website sales, Carolina Plantation Rice sells our Carolina Gold, Charleston Gold, Charleston Brown Rice, middlins, rice bran, white cornmeal, yellow cornmeal, fish fry mix, rice flour, stone-ground white grits, and dried iron clay cowpeas to GrowFood Carolina, the local food hub. GrowFood markets, sells, and delivers to local chefs and the larger grocery store chains. We also wholesale directly to retail stores and gift shops; Carolina Plantation Rice products make great souvenirs!

Regulation overkill

The most concerning things about the entire rice growing process, and farming in general, are the regulations. The state and federal governments are starting to regulate us to death. The South Carolina Department of Health and Environmental Control (DHEC) wants to know the source of every drop of water I use in my fields. I installed GPS monitors on my intake pumps, and each one is permitted by DHEC. Fortunately, we have been here for generations, so Plumfield Plantation has been grandfathered a certain amount of water. The amount of water used by farms like mine is a drop in the bucket in comparison to corporate agribusiness and the manufacturing industry's total water consumption. The paper mill three miles upstream is using hundreds of times more water than I use, and they are releasing gray water back into the system. I have no gray water, but I am under the same regulations, or more, than they are.

No one is lobbying on my behalf. I have no advocates in the state capital or Washington, D.C. Industry and corporate agribusiness are the big consumers of water, not my rice plantation. Small farmers need a level playing field. We don't want to be regulated out of business. Who would consumers buy their rice from then—large industrial-sized farms in Arkansas, Louisiana, Texas, China, or India? It is important that consumers know this and purchase from their local farmers.

What I love most about my job is that I am on my farm all the time. I work, hunt, fish, and thoroughly enjoy my life. Even though the work is hard and farming doesn't generate a huge financial gain, I'm proud to be bringing back an heirloom crop, and I'm proud of the quality of the products that I am providing the consumer. When I was growing cotton, no one told me how much they liked my cotton. But growing heirloom rice, people make a point to tell me how much they enjoy it. It makes me feel so good to produce quality products that people love! 🍃

Josh Johnson
Old Tyme Bean Company

Experiencing the whirlwind of Josh's day with him made me realize again how generous the people featured in this book are with their time. After meeting his wife, Amanda, sons Corbin and Henry, and his father-in-law, Bates, I climbed in Josh's truck to see acres and acres of peanuts, cotton, corn, and butter beans; equipment sheds with a variety of planters, sprayers, and combines, and more sheds with processing equipment to separate, clean, and package various crops for sale. What became very clear to me was that I was spending time with not only a farmer, but a talented mechanic and a motivated entrepreneur. Josh's wonderful sense of humor, down-home expressions, and easy manner were a delight. And the butter beans I ate from the pod in the field were outrageously delicious.

A passion for farming

I grew up on a small tobacco farm near Myrtle Beach. My daddy says, "Farming is a disease of the mind and soul," so I guess I'm genetically predis-

posed to the farming disease. I attended Clemson University, joined Alpha Gamma Rho (a national agricultural fraternity), and graduated with a degree in Agricultural Economics in 2004.

My degree consisted of traditional economics

We had to abandon another ten acres with low production. . . . The economic return must cover the cost to harvest.

classes followed by a specialization in agricultural production, where I learned everything from hogs to corn to cotton. I learned about the Chicago Board of Trade, puts and calls, and how to manage a farm. Although I had been farming with my daddy for years, this degree better prepared me for the business side of farming. I am always thinking about the economics of each acre I grow. Farming is my passion, but it is also my business.

After meeting Amanda, I left my family's tobacco farm and started farming with her father, Bates Houck. Houck Farms was originally a cotton farm, and the farmhouse was a stagecoach stop between Charleston and Columbia. Our children are the fifth generation on this farm. I hope they will want to become farmers too, but I don't want farming to prevent them from being actively involved in sports programs and extra-curricular activities. I was sorry to miss those pursuits in my own childhood.

Amanda's grandfather, S. H. Houck, was a dairy farmer, and Bates bought his dairy business in 1980. In 1988, Bates participated in the federal government's billion-dollar buyout to reduce surplus milk. One of the requirements of the buyout was to remain out of milk production for five years. So Bates moved solely to row cropping—growing corn, peanuts, and cotton.

When green is gold

This year, to our repertoire of crops, Bates and I are adding fifty acres of butter beans—also known as green baby lima beans. We have 700 acres in cotton, 400 acres in corn, and more than 800 acres in peanuts. From the end of April through the beginning of June, all we do is plant. We start with peanuts and move into cotton. We run two or three planting tractors from 8:00 a.m. until 7:00 p.m. for about twenty to thirty days, depending on the weather. With all the work involved for each of these commodity crops—from planting to cultivation to harvest—there simply isn't time to market a specialty crop like butter beans. Had the local food hub, GrowFood Carolina, not been interested in selling my butter beans for me, I wouldn't be growing them.

Butter beans hold a special place in my heart.

My Grandma Mary is a big part of the reason I'm in the butter bean business. When gardening season came around, she would buy a little sack of butter beans and say, "Honey, we will need something to eat this winter, so we're gonna plant us some butter beans." She would chop out a divot in the dirt with her hoe, and I would put beans in each hole, give a gentle push for good seed-to-soil contact, and then loosely cover them up. When they grew a couple inches, we would plant another row, continuing to stagger four or five plantings like that. And then when winter came, she would cook the butter beans—that I helped grow.

Beyond these tender memories with my grandma are the economics of butter beans. Butter beans are gold. Demand for them exceeds their supply, because they are very susceptible to weather and difficult to grow. If they were easy to grow, then the supply-demand dynamic would be different. I want to grow something that everyone wants, but a crop in which other farmers are not willing to invest—equipment, labor, time, and patience.

Butter beans are self-pollinating. They have what is called a perfect flower with both male and female parts. Although bees are not mandatory for their pollination, they do stimulate the plants to produce more flowers. We go through great pains to avoid spraying anything that will hurt our beneficial insects.

Butter beans do not love extremely hot daytime temperatures, and the blossoms won't tolerate night-time temperatures above 75°F. If the temperature only drops to 85°F at night, that perfect flower will abort, resulting in a beautiful bush with no beans.

The flowers are indeterminate, meaning they never terminate, or stop making flowers and beans until something causes the demise of the plant. Therefore timing for the best harvest requires some experienced guesswork. When we harvest, about three percent of the beans have dried up, and the rest are still green and premature. We strive to time the harvest to maximize our yield. The difference between harvesting this morning and tomorrow afternoon can make all the difference between a mediocre harvest and a great harvest.

Another reason most farmers don't want to grow

butter beans is they need to be hand cultivated due to a weed that grows with them that resembles a legume. Because the weed's flower turns into something that looks like a pea, the mechanical harvester picks it like it is a pea and the mechanical sheller will shell it like a pea. I would end up with that rogue seed mixed in with my butter beans. Therefore the time-consuming and labor-intensive work of hand weeding is required.

A toss of the dice

Growing butter beans is a big gamble. We plant fifty acres in six different plantings, and we bet that at least one of the plantings will yield well. In the past year, we unfortunately abandoned one five-acre planting due to an onslaught of deer. The deer ate about fifteen percent of the butter beans, and while it doesn't seem like a lot, harvesting the remaining eighty-five percent would not have been cost effective. We applied for and received an out-of-season game permit from the warden in order to protect future crops from deer. We also had to abandon another ten acres with low production, because there weren't enough butter beans to make it worth picking. The economic return must cover the cost to harvest. As discouraging as abandonment of a field is, the upside potential is great. We've had some fields that yielded 100 bushels per acre and sold for $30 per bushel; $3,000 per acre is a darn good return.

A farmer must figure out not only how to farm

and how to sell, but how to maintain the equipment. Whenever Bates and I find a spare minute, we work on our equipment. The old adage, "necessity is the mother of invention," is certainly true when it comes to farm equipment, which is a substantial capital investment. When I go into a John Deere store and see a new piece of equipment selling for $300,000, I have no choice but to come home and figure out a way to keep my current equipment going. We recycle parts from old equipment and reconfigure according to our needs. We also purchase equipment from other farmers who have gone out of business. I recently repurposed an old trailer; I insulated it and hooked it up to an air conditioning unit to create a refrigerated storage and delivery vehicle for my butter beans. I keep it at 45°F. When it is time to deliver our butter beans to GrowFood Carolina, I unplug it and take it for the hour drive to Charleston.

We were able to modify our harvester and sheller to suit our needs, too. The harvester is designed to pick any bush that is knee-high or lower. It will harvest peas, butter beans, and string beans. It is indiscriminate as it rakes everything off each bush—leaves, vine, and bean pods. A fan sucks the light debris away and deposits it back on the field. From the field, the butter beans go into a sheller, which rotates, shakes, and drops individual butter beans onto a conveyor belt. They are hand-sorted, bagged, and weighed. Butter beans have a shelf life of a week, but GrowFood sends them to a processor for blanching, and then freezes them to sell throughout the year. This is great for me, because by extending sales, I am able to get paid year-round.

I am trying to make a good living, leave the land in better shape than when we inherited it, and give my children a nice springboard into the next generation of farming. And I hope to do a good job. Growing and selling butter beans combines my passion for farming, my memories of Grandma Mary, and my understanding and implementation of effective business practices. It also allows me to enjoy many meals with Grandma Mary's favorite butter bean recipe. It's not a family secret. She would fry bacon, add butter beans, and stir them in the bacon grease. Then she added water and salt and boiled for twenty minutes. I love to share this recipe with others. It turns out so good, it ensures continued demand for my butter beans! ❧

Father Stan and Brother John
Mepkin Abbey Mushrooms

*D*riving onto the grounds of Mepkin Abbey, a Trappist monastery, I could feel a calmness sweep over me. The driveway is a beautiful allée of live oak trees leading into a property beautifully landscaped with native plants, and on this early spring day, a profusion of azalea blossoms. I met with Father Stan, the abbot, and Brother John, the cellarer—business manager. Brother John oversees all things temporal (secular) at the monastery—the grounds, the retreat house, and the abbey's mushroom business.

Sitting on a bluff overlooking the Cooper River, a thirty-five-mile meander north of Charleston, this property was given to the Catholic Church in 1949 by Henry and Clare Boothe Luce, who had used it as a hunting preserve. Clare Boothe Luce engaged the renowned landscape architect Loutrell Briggs to create the beautiful and contemplative gardens where the family is buried. To maintain the property and keep it open to the public, the monks generate income from a variety of sources. In addition to the timber leases established by the Luces,

▲ Above photo: Father Stan.

the mushroom production, columbarium, retreat center, and gift shop are important income sources for sustaining Mepkin Abbey.

From the rule of St. Benedict, Trappist monks welcome guests as they would welcome Christ. Therefore, after walking the grounds with Father Stan and visiting the mushroom houses with Brother John, I was invited to noon prayer followed by lunch in the guest refectory. At Mepkin, the monks balance the cloistered and contemplative life with frequent visitors.

Monks and mushrooms

Brother John: Trappists, by tradition, are involved with agriculture. In years past at Mepkin Abbey, we've had Jersey milk cows, Angus beef cattle, and a chicken operation. Since 2008, we've been growing oyster mushrooms. At that time, we were the only farmers in South Carolina growing oyster mushrooms.

Oyster mushrooms are very labor intensive, because they are so sensitive to airborne contaminants and pollen, and they can become damaged easily.

We combat this with an intensive filtration system, changing the filters in each mushroom house at least four times each day.

In 2014, we added shitake mushrooms to our production. Shitakes are sturdier, have a longer shelf life, and are not as sensitive as oysters when being handled. Each variety of mushroom requires special temperatures, lighting, air movement, and moisture. Fortunately, we have the help of a local farmer, Jimmy Livingston. As our mushroom manager, he's able to oversee the complex operations.

▼ Brother John with shitake mushrooms.

Farming is an integral part of our monastic life. Working with the land inspires each of us. It provides a balance of mind, body, and spirit, which is central to the grounding nature of prayer.

To grow oyster mushrooms, we purchase manufactured spawn (spores) and mix the spawn with wheat straw, cottonseed hulls, and some secret supplements. (Of course, some of the procedures for growing our mushrooms are proprietary.) This mix is stuffed into black plastic bags with holes, and small mushrooms start emerging in two weeks. They fruit for about ten days, go into hibernation, and then fruit again. After the second fruiting, the spent mix goes into our compost.

In the wild, shitake mushrooms grow on logs, but we purchase synthetic logs containing spores from a source in Pennsylvania. We soak the logs in water for two hours, and then the mushrooms fruit for seven days. We give them three days of rest, re-soak them, and they re-fruit again for another seven days. We soak them one last time, and get a third fruiting. The first fruiting is always the most productive. Because mushrooms are age-sensitive and each new stage requires a different environment, they must be transferred into another room for each successive fruiting.

Mold is our biggest problem, because airborne mold competes with mushrooms' mold. To prevent airborne mold, our heavily insulated Quonset huts—semicircular corrugated metal buildings—are hard cell insulated, which is non-permeable, and the temperature is kept at 62°F. Mushrooms need ninety percent humidity to grow, but conventional air conditioning pulls the humidity out of the air. Therefore we have devised a special, and proprietary, way of keeping our buildings cool without removing the humidity.

Each week we sell about 700 pounds of oyster mushrooms and 700 pounds of shitake mushrooms. Considering how little an individual mushroom weighs, that adds up to a lot of mushrooms! Mepkin Abbey sells to local grocery store chains, but the bulk of our mushrooms are sold to Limehouse Produce, a local distributor that sells them to local restaurants. We also sell dried mushrooms at our gift shop with directions for rehydrating.

The Trappist tradition

Father Stan: Brother John and I have both been at Mepkin for nearly six decades—since we were seventeen years old. There are sixteen monks in the community, and we usually host about a dozen guests.

We were prayerful about choosing this mushroom farming endeavor. We researched thirty-nine different options and arrived at mushroom cultivation because it provides necessary income and fulfills other important fundamentals of our Trappist tradition.

It is important for Trappists monks to play a valuable role in our outside community, and one of the ways Mepkin Abbey does so is by providing healthy food. As dietary fiber, both oyster and shitake mushrooms provide great health benefits; they are high in vitamins, minerals, and proteins, and oyster mushrooms might provide cholesterol lowering molecules.

Additionally, by growing mushrooms, we are engaged in full life-cycle reutilization. We take what is considered agricultural waste—wheat straw and cottonseed hulls—for use as our growing medium. When the mushrooms finish fruiting, everything, except the black plastic bags used for the oyster cultivation, goes into the compost pile. The compost then nourishes our vegetable garden that feeds us. We find this full-cycle reutilization inspiring.

Our monastic life, modeled on the life of St. Benedict in 640 AD, has three pillars—prayer, reading, and community life. We are not hermits or armchair scholars. Farming is an integral part of our monastic life. Manual labor is important, because the human spirit needs this physical dimension that creates energy, nourishes health, and inspires contemplation. Working with the land inspires each of us. It provides a balance of mind, body, and spirit, which is central to the grounding nature of prayer. However, we feel strongly that getting our hands in the dirt and connecting with nature must be both productive and beneficial to our life at Mepkin Abbey as well as the greater community. Our mushroom farm fits beautifully with the goals of our Trappist tradition. ✿

Jimmy and Johnna Livingston
Wabi Sabi Farm

Jimmy and Jo, owners of Wabi Sabi strawberry and vegetable farm, were the first farmers I visited after starting this book project. It was a perfect beginning. I knew that if others were going to be as open, friendly, and fun, I may never be able to stop meeting and interviewing farmers. With the enormous amount of work they each had that first day I visited—planting, pruning, harvesting, washing, packing, and getting products off to market—I was touched that they so generously made time for me and invited me back again. On my second visit, I walked alongside Jo as she worked nonstop on the very long squash rows. Afterward we went to the washtubs where the red and white onions, harvested earlier in the day, were being washed by Jo's mom and some other employees. Jo helped pack the onions so Jimmy could deliver them to GrowFood Carolina later that morning for distribution to local chefs.

From sickness to health

Jimmy: We started Wabi Sabi Farm in June 2011. For seventeen years prior to that, we had a successful screen print business. Prolonged exposure to chemical solvents made me very ill. My last year in the print business, I ended up in the doctor's office or hospital forty times. I finally realized that it was time

142

It is disheartening when a customer comments, "It's not worth that price. I can find it cheaper elsewhere."... Local farmers are not getting rich. To be viable as farmers, we must sell for enough to cover the costs of growing, harvesting, and getting it to market. Farmers, too, must be able to make ends meet and make a decent living.

to listen to my body and adopt a lifestyle that would restore my health. It was time to return to our roots.

Jo and I both grew up very close to where we are today. Jo was raised on a commercial tobacco farm, and I was raised on the Cooper River. When I was young, my family sold catfish, but it became near impossible to sustain a livelihood on freshwater fishing, so they migrated a little east to the sea and are now in the commercial fishing business—selling clams, oysters, soft shell crabs, and shrimp.

Jo and I looked for a good community and a healthy lifestyle in which to raise our kids. We gravitated to the fresh air of the country, where we could take root and try our hand at farming specialty crops—vegetables. Fortunately, ten years prior to leaving the screen print business, we invested in these twenty acres, which was part of a 110-year-old farm. We let the land lie fallow to recover from the previous farmer, who had grown a monoculture crop of corn, had bleached the soil with liquid nitrogen, and exposed the bare topsoil to harsh winds and weather. The land also was riddled with an invasive nut sedge, which can only be controlled by hogs or major chemicals. We chose to use hogs.

Upon purchasing the land, we planted cover crops—cowpeas and naked oats. Naked oats have a long root system that breaks up the hardpan—the hardened, impervious layer of dirt and clay—and successive plants will trace the oats' root path. We worked in stages, one section at a time, growing cover crops and turning them back into the soil to reconstitute the fields.

We raised the soil's pH by adding lime, one bag at a time. There were no lime providers nearby, and we were too far for anyone to deliver less than twenty tons of lime. We didn't have a big truck, so Jo and I made lots of little trips and hand-poured lime, bag by bag. Ten years after purchasing the land, we had grown healthy soil. Now we could start growing vegetables.

We needed a farm name to register with the state. We read an article in *Mother Earth News* about Wabi Sabi, a Japanese philosophy that life and beauty are imperfect and transient, and that it is best to embrace those imperfections and make the best of them. That spoke to us, so we adopted the name, Wabi Sabi Farm.

Careful cultivation

Jo: I enjoy just about everything about farming—planting, weeding, harvesting, and experimenting with new vegetable crops. But then there is okra. Okra is like fiberglass; it's covered with tiny spines that will irritate your skin. To harvest okra, I must outfit myself in heavy clothes, long sleeves, high boots, and gloves, which in 100°F summer heat is pretty intolerable. Beans give me a headache too. I love to eat beans, but picking them is torture for me. We aren't growing okra or beans anymore!

Squash are so tender that I wear gloves when I'm harvesting them. If my fingernails were to slightly nick them they would develop a brown blemish in a couple of days. Blemished produce is rejected by most consumers, so we harvest with care. As I pick, I cull. Any squash that is imperfect, didn't pollinate properly, or looks unhealthy gets tossed between the rows. They will be raked up and fed to the pigs later today.

Maintaining clean plants is one way we avoid disease. We also space mildew-prone plants, like squash, farther apart, which allows the breeze to flow through and cuts down on the chances of disease.

We use plastic mulch on many of our beds. Mulch is a euphemism that farmers use for the black plastic stretched tightly over fruit and vegetable beds. Plastic mulch in combination with drip irrigation has many advantages—it warms the soil allowing for earlier planting, reduces weeds, retains moisture, and keeps the soil from splashing on the plants during a rain. Preventing the soil from getting on the plant leaves is one way to reduce the possibility of soil-borne diseases. For our tomato plants, we use a shiny chrome mulch, which reflects the sunlight to the undersides of the tomato leaves and prevents damage from harmful thrips and moths. Thrips are tiny sucking insects that hide under the leaves and spread viruses. The reflection from the chrome effectively deters these pests, so we don't have to use chemical pesticides.

People often ask if we are certified organic. What I wish they would ask is: Did we put any chemicals on this plant? The answer most likely is, no, we have not. Jimmy and I take all precautions to prevent problems so we won't need to use chemicals. We work hard to have healthy soil, maintain clean plants, provide good airflow, rotate our crops, use companion plantings, and suppress pests by using Integrated Pest Management (IPM), which encourages beneficial insects. After all, the reason we sold our screen print shop was to escape chemicals. Nevertheless, we have chosen to forego organic certification because it is a burdensome task and time-consuming process.

I also wish consumers would be knowledgeable or ask about the seasonality of crops sold at the farmers markets. Not all vendors are selling seasonal and local produce; some have purchased produce elsewhere and are reselling it as if it had been harvested from their farm. Educated consumers help our business, because they know that what we are selling is in season and was just harvested from our farm. They also understand that farm products that are freshly harvested are more nutritious than those that have been transported from far away.

A diverse customers base

Jimmy: Early this morning while it was still cool, I came through our rows of squash and harvested squash blossoms for the local food hub GrowFood Carolina. These ephemeral blossoms are coveted by Charleston's chefs, and we get a great price for them. Yesterday I delivered forty flats of strawberries to GrowFood, and later this morning, I will deliver ten fifteen-pound boxes of red and white onions, broccoli, and squash to GrowFood.

In addition to distributing our bounty through GrowFood, we also utilize other sales channels. By marketing directly to the public through our farm stand, U-Pick, our website, Facebook, and various

nearby farmers markets, we create a diversity of revenue streams. And to supplement our income further, I manage Mepkin Abbey's mushroom production.

Wabi Sabi has many loyal and interested consumers who come to our farm and to our farmers markets. Jo and I are passionate about farming and get great satisfaction from providing customers with the best quality and most delicious fresh produce. It is disheartening when a customer looks at one of our products, like a head of broccoli, that we are beaming with pride about, and comments, "It's not worth that price. I can find it cheaper elsewhere." This happened again recently, and the person tried to bargain me down in price.

Yes, she can find cheaper broccoli in most grocery stores—grown on an industrial-sized farm and shipped from 1,500 miles away. Because of the economies of scale, that broccoli will sell for less than what the farmer in her neighborhood can grow it for. But she will not know the farmer who raised the imported broccoli, nor will she know whether the broccoli was grown in healthy soil microorganisms or with chemicals, nor will her dollars support her local economy, nor will she have the nutritional benefits of eating truly fresh produce. She will have just used her dollars to support a farm 1,500 miles away rather than the farmer next door.

Local farmers are not getting rich. To be viable as farmers, we must sell that head of broccoli for enough to cover the costs of growing, harvesting, and getting it to market—the seeds, the tractor, the fuel . . . not to mention our labor. Farmers, too, must be able to make ends meet and make a decent living. We want customers who are as dedicated to us as we are to them.

Agritourism has recently become one of our best revenue sources. Wabi Sabi's annual Strawberry Jam, which will occur this Saturday, is a fun-filled day of appreciation for our customers. We expect 500 people this weekend. They come to pick strawberries and experience the farm, our cows, chickens, and pigs. We bring in a local band, cook hotdogs, and have a sunflower maze for the kids to run through. The day provides a fun and down-to-earth understanding of where food comes from, along with community camaraderie.

Embracing the imperfections

Jo: We are passionate about nurturing the land, having our hands in the dirt, and harvesting fresh and nutritious produce for our family and community. We believe that this is how we are meant to live. The fresh air and exercise contribute to our physical and emotional health, and we enjoy farming as a family.

In the evening after a wonderful day of productivity, when the kids are doing their homework or playing around the house, I love wandering out into the serenity of the fields with my basket to gather the fruits of our labors for our dinner—beautiful purple eggplants, squash, onions, and big red tomatoes. We are so humbled and grateful to be working this productive ground. Life is full of imperfections, but we have found the perfect life for us. ❧

was really going on. Many kids were going to the corner store for their dinner. Here, on this side of downtown, the nearest grocery store is more than a mile away, which classifies this area as an urban food desert. It was a powerful realization.

I wondered how we at Taco Boy, which was the first of the three restaurants I opened in this neighborhood, could do something to promote access to fresh, local food. It would be a way to give back to the community. I wanted to provide something positive and healthy that would bring everyone together. My first thought was a community garden in the neighborhood.

My mentor, restaurateur and philanthropist Jerry Scheer, encouraged me to talk to the principal at Mitchell Elementary School, a Title I school that is

down the street from my house. Title I is a federal grant program that supports elementary and secondary school students living in areas of high poverty. I didn't really have a clear picture of where the conversation was going to go, but I wanted the kids to have access to fresh produce. Principal Dirk Bedford was very open-minded and interested in alternative methods for inspiring kids to learn and to eat healthy. He heard me out, and suggested that we establish a school garden program with the third graders.

My first adventure in the classroom to introduce the program was a real eye-opener. I excitedly announced, "We are going to create a garden and grow produce." Their teacher, Ms. Black, interrupted and asked, "Who knows what produce is?" There was no response, so I jumped in with a hint, "You know,

▼ Mitchell Elementary students and Green Heart buddies.

it's in the grocery store in the produce section." Ms. Black rocked me with her next question, "Have any of you ever been to a grocery store?" In a full classroom of eight- and nine-year-olds, there were only four children who had been to a grocery store in their lives!

Giving back to the community

In 2009, we started The Green Heart Project. On Thursday mornings, six members of the Taco Boy management team, some College of Charleston student volunteers, and I would meet with the third grade classes and their teachers. Working with the students, teachers, college volunteers, and the local community, we realized that this project was not only about fresh, healthy food, it was about community.

I watched the kids' personal transformation as they took ownership in their garden. So many benefits came out of building a garden together. They learned to work as a team, that hard work—like growing and harvesting food—is rewarding, and that classroom lessons could be incorporated outdoors. They met new members in their community, including college students. They also gained the new experience of eating fresh vegetables, which they shared with their families.

The Green Heart Project has grown and evolved in a manner we never envisioned. It was such an immediate success that it expanded to include all the grades at Mitchell Elementary, and we created three additional programs—class time in the garden, an after-school program, and a summer program.

The Green Heart Project is not in the school's budget. Our restaurant, Taco Boy, has been in a private partnership with Mitchell Elementary and is the primary financial underwriter of the program, in combination with the schools' parents.

Six years after initiating our first program at Mitchell Elementary, The Green Heart Project has launched four more garden programs in local elementary schools around Charleston. Each Green Heart Garden has a local business sponsor that funds that garden for the school year. We started with my restaurants sponsoring three schools to make sure the model would work, which allowed us to iron out the kinks. The Green Heart Project received its 501(c)(3) status, established a board, and now has four full-time employees. Within the next couple years, we envision making this model available so any school, anywhere county-wide can replicate it.

The Green Heart Project has been transformative for the kids, their teachers, the schools, those of us who have volunteered in the program, and the greater community. For all of us involved, growing food at local schools has nurtured our hearts, our bodies, and souls. 🍃

Drew Harrison
The Green Heart Project, Director

The Green Heart Project is a small nonprofit that creates school farms to connect kids with fresh, locally grown produce. It serves as a vehicle to teach students lessons about hard work, respect, and success—all while creatively reinforcing their classroom curriculum. Their first project began in 2009 at Mitchell Elementary School, a Title I school in Charleston, South Carolina. Sponsored by local restaurants, businesses, and individuals, The Green Heart Project is a model for growing food, minds, and community. I had the opportunity to join Drew and the students at Mitchell Elementary on three different occasions as they were planting, weeding, and harvesting from their urban school's farm.

Growing food, growing minds

I was one of The Green Heart Project's first volunteers six years ago. On my first day, a truck dumped a load of donated soil on the street in front of Mitchell Elementary. Using cinder blocks to form beds and transporting countless wheelbarrows full of dirt, the third graders, other volunteers, and I built the garden from the ground up. After volunteering for a year, I became the project's first employee. In 2014, we received our 501(c)(3) nonprofit status, and I became the executive director. Partnering with the

Planting and cultivating a seed, watching it grow into a living plant, and eating it as nutritious food is a new experience for these kids, and it fills them with pride.

Westside Neighborhood Association and the City of Charleston, the garden has expanded to a plot of land across the street.

The Green Heart Project conducts hour-long classes for each grade throughout the school year. Each session begins the same way. We circle up, talk about the rules of respect, give buddy introductions, and split into small gardening groups. Our mantra is RESPECT, a focus of every session: respect yourself, respect your Green Heart buddies (be that a person, a bird, or an ant), respect the garden, and respect the bigger garden of the earth. Sharing and eating healthy vegetables cultivated from the garden is one way of respecting yourself and others. Another way is through our Green Heart greeting—giving an earnest handshake, making eye contact, and using a proud voice of introduction.

Breaking into small groups with Green Heart buddies, the activities range from garden maintenance to harvesting. A program manager works with the teachers ahead of time to incorporate their curriculum into the garden's living laboratory. Typically, garden work is coordinated with math and science classes, but lessons are also tied to other disciplines like creative writing. Oftentimes lessons occur spontaneously, like when the third graders were studying food webs, and there was an infestation of aphids in the garden. The aphids were eating the collard greens, and the ladybugs were eating the aphids. Learning is much more powerful and information is easier to retain when it happens through real-life experiences.

Although the farm is an educational tool, it is primarily about growing and eating healthy foods. The fourth grade classes harvested seventeen pounds of freckled romaine and some butter crunch lettuce today, and because the farm is GAP (Good Agricultural Practices) certified, the lettuce will be served in the cafeteria tomorrow.

Expanding opportunities

Since the garden is most prolific during the summer, we offer ten to fifteen of our most engaged students the opportunity to become ambassadors of the garden and participate in our summer program. Their counselors are paid interns from the College of Charleston, who have to fundraise for their own salary. Along with garden maintenance and harvest, weekly field trips allow the students to experience farm-focused businesses, attend farmers markets, and eagerly spread the word about The Green Heart Project.

One day our campers harvested heirloom tomatoes, sweet basil, carrots, and bell peppers and took them to Monza, a local pizza place, to sell the bounty. The chef paid for the produce and then invited us in for a delicious pizza lunch using our garden ingredients. What an eye-opener it is for students to realize that the garden's delicious fresh food is also valued monetarily.

The Green Heart Project also provides a Healthy Hearts Culinary and Nutrition program at Mitchell Elementary. We select eight to ten students for a six-week course; they are required to bring a parent or guardian to every class. The goal is to teach the basics of nutrition and how to prepare a meal from scratch. A specialist from Whole Foods Market conducts the cooking and nutrition class. Whole Foods sponsors the class and provides the majority of the ingredients necessary to prepare the dishes using some of our garden produce. The class demonstrates that eating a healthy, nutrient-dense diet is both delicious and possible on any budget. Additionally, we work on skills such as safe food handling and prep, knife skills, bulk cooking, and more. It is a fun and highly effective class for both students and adults, and it creates positive changes.

I remember one of our early participants in the Healthy Hearts Culinary and Nutrition classes who was initially timid about tasting any of the fresh vegetables from the garden. By the end of the six-week session, he was so inspired by his newly learned culinary skills that he started cooking for his family. Now he is in the local high school's Culinary Arts Program, and he recently helped cater our Healthy Heart Harvest Dinner.

Green Heart's "Friend-Raiser Fund-Raiser" Healthy Heart Harvest Dinner is our annual end-of-the-year event celebrating the hard work and dedication that our students, volunteers, and partners have put into making our program successful. It connects our community with our youth through food. We collaborate with Chef Ira Hill's Burke High School Culinary Arts Program. Chef Hill has integrated the catering of events into his curriculum, and his students prepare the Harvest Dinner meal. Last year, we had more than 850 attendees from the community, the schools, the neighborhood association, and our restaurant sponsors—all partners in making The Green Heart Project a success!

More than a garden

In addition to the many visible benefits of this program, it is important to recognize that there are a number of intangible benefits, too. The kids, many from low-income homes, are spending time with volunteer mentors from the College of Charleston and developing relationships with college students. These relationships make college seem attainable, when it might not otherwise have been on their minds. The summer program's introduction of kids to farmers, businesses, and chefs opens doors to new worlds and opportunities. Already some of our first students are working at restaurants that supported our program.

Our program at Mitchell Elementary has been so successful that we have replicated it in four additional schools throughout Charleston, and plan on replicating it throughout the state. Planting and cultivating a seed, watching it grow into a living plant, and eating it as nutritious food is a new experience for these kids, and it fills them with pride. It has changed their perspective on what food is, where it comes from, and the value of healthy eating.

Observing the transformation of our students each year is priceless. When they enter the program they are so disconnected from food that when a volunteer plucks a leaf from a plant and eats it, there are groans of disgust. Something coming from the ground is seen as dirty. By the end of the year, they are eating freshly pulled carrots, grit and all.

Over the years, we have built gardens and grown food, and in the process we have grown a movement. Neighborhood and college student volunteers, along with financial sponsors from restaurants, businesses, banks, and food distributors, have joined together in the support of growing food, growing minds, and growing a healthy and vibrant community—The Green Heart Project. ❧

Kevin Shaw
Georgia Olive Farms

The "buy local" philosophy can vary from person to person, but I think of it as concentric circles rippling outward. I ventured to southern Georgia—the longest trip of any taken for this book—to visit Georgia Olive Farms.

In the late 1700s, Thomas Jefferson sent olive tree varietals to South Carolina, but the climate was too cold, and they didn't survive. Yet there are similarities in the climates of the Mediterranean olive-producing countries and South Carolina's neighbor, Georgia. Today, ninety-nine percent of America's olive oil is imported from Greece, Italy, or Spain, with the remaining one percent coming from California. So Kevin's olive oil—grown, harvested, and milled only four hours from Charleston—certainly qualifies as local olive oil!

I spent half a day with Kevin and his family learning about their farm. I came away with gifts of grits and olive oil, and three small olive tree saplings, which with a little nurturing are still thriving.

Continuing a family legacy

I grew up on our family farm in Lakeland, Georgia. My granddad introduced my cousins and me to all things agriculture, including livestock, which we butchered and packaged ourselves. My dad sold insurance, but he farmed on the side with his brother. I thought I would go to medical school, but after a summer internship at Emory University, I knew I wouldn't be able to tolerate working indoors, and I needed to get back to the farm.

For years, Shaw Farms has been growing cotton, peanuts, and corn. In the late 1990s, my wife, Gayla, and I started growing twenty acres of an heirloom variety of white corn called Trucker's Favorite for grits and cornmeal. It is non-GMO and the same variety my granddad grew years ago.

Gayla and I initially gifted grits to our friends, a hobby that we eventually grew into a business—Gayla's Grits. We've significantly increased production, and now they are distributed both wholesale and retail around Georgia. Our primary selling points are that we grow and mill our own corn (most millers purchase their corn from other farms), and Gayla's Grits are gluten free. Corn is gluten free, but if it is milled using the same stones as wheat, the stones can't be sanitized to prevent gluten cross-contamination. By growing and milling our corn here, we can ensure the quality of our product and provide chefs with the exact coarseness of grind they request.

Starting a new legacy

Around the same time Gayla's Grits was starting, my cousins Jason and Sam and I, along with our friend Berrien Sutton, formed a farm partnership. We wanted to diversify beyond cotton, peanuts, and

We wanted to diversify beyond cotton, peanuts, and corn into a product that would free us from volatile contract markets and give us additional cash flow.

corn into a product that would free us from volatile contract markets and give us additional cash flow. We considered blueberries, but our area already had many acres of blueberries. Meanwhile a local farming friend, realizing there was an overlap in some of his equipment for juicing blueberries and milling olive oil, successfully planted olive trees and milled the oil. We decided to take a calculated risk and try our hand at olives, too.

We started Georgia Olive Farms in 2008 with eighteen acres, and in the past few years, we have expanded to 100 acres. We hope to eventually plant another 1,000 acres, but we want to do this in stages as we learn more about growing olives.

We each contribute different talents to this new business venture. Jason is in the insurance business, and he is a state representative. He handles all the marketing and media. Sam is a banker, and he handles the finances. Berrien, an attorney, handles the legal work, and I am the farmer. At harvest, we all pitch in to ensure the successful production of quality Georgia Extra Virgin Olive Oil.

A European olive in the American south

Olive farming requires large capital investments. We plant and maintain 600 trees per acre, which initially cost $5,000 per acre. We drove our first harvest to Texas for milling, and two years later, we were milling with our own equipment from Florence, Italy. The new equipment was very expensive, but fortunately we received a grant to help pay for a portion of it.

Georgia Olive Farms buys thousands of cuttings from California each year. We keep them in our greenhouse until we are sure we won't have any more cold weather. Ninety percent of the olive trees in our orchard are Arbequina, which originated in Spain. The other two varietals are Arbosana, which also has its origins in Spain, and Koroneiki of Greek origins. Koroneiki is supposed to be the hardest to grow, but is the varietal that is performing the best here in Georgia.

We use a system started in Barcelona about twenty-five years ago of super high-density planting and mechanical harvesting. This system eliminates hand harvesting and pushes the trees to maturity faster. The trees produce fruit in three rather than seven years.

White flowers appear during the first part of April, and the fruit is set by the end of May. They are wind pollinated and don't require bees, although pollinators help facilitate pollen movement, especially in times of low winds. We mechanically harvest the olives in mid-September by driving the harvester over the top of the olive rows. On average, we harvest three tons of fruit to the acre, which will yield about ninety gallons of oil. We continue to learn more each year, and hopefully we can increase our yields to that of California, which reaches nearly 300 gallons per acre.

Olives must be milled within twenty-four hours of harvest to limit oxidation. Harvested olives are dumped into a hopper where a number of separating and cleaning processes begin. The de-leafer removes most debris, and a plume of water further separates and cleans the olives. After cleaning, the olives are dropped into the hammer-mill, which grinds the olives, including their flesh and pits, into a paste.

The thick paste is slowly conveyed into a machine called a malaxer, where paddles slowly massage the paste, releasing the oil. From the malaxer, the paste is pumped into a horizontal centrifuge, called a decanter, which separates the oil and water from the pulp. From there it goes into a vertical centrifuge for further separation. Then we rack the oil in large cone-bottomed stainless steel tanks. Racking allows the remaining water and sediment to fall to the bottom of the tank where it can be drained from the oil. This process clarifies the oil and lengthens its shelf life. Finally, the oil is bottled, packaged, and distributed.

The next oil barons

Our first harvest was done by hand. We sent some of our olive oil to chefs in Charleston and Savannah.

Sean Brock at Charleston's Husk Restaurant was the first chef to call us. He said, "I have a proposition for you. I'm speaking at the Southern Foodways Alliance in Oxford, Mississippi, and I would like to showcase your olive oil." A farmer can't get much more of a boost than an endorsement like that from a James Beard Award winning chef in front of the audience of that esteemed group. His support also led to a story in a 2012 issue of the magazine *Garden and Gun* titled "In Georgia: The Next Oil Barons—Georgia farmers produce the South's newest cash crop." Between Sean Brock and *Garden and Gun*, Georgia Olive Farms was on the map!

We sell two olive oils: our Georgia Arbequina Extra Virgin Olive Oil and our Chef's Blend Extra Virgin Olive Oil. The blend ratio varies every year, consisting mostly of Georgia Arbequina, with smaller percentages of Arbosana and Koroneiki. Until our production reaches higher yields, we will need to supplement our Arbosana and Koroneiki with oil from California. By expanding our acreage each year, eventually we will meet the demand.

Georgia Olive Farms Extra Virgin Olive Oil is available at numerous boutique markets on the East Coast and large retailers like Whole Foods, Kroger's, Harvey's Supermarkets, and Target. The most convenient method of purchasing it is online.

Most people have no idea what goes into producing quality food, nor are they aware of a farmer's enormous capital investments. I hope our story sheds some light on the value of family farms. Artisan foods require extra effort and a higher cost of production. Family farms like ours have the ability to be innovative. For example—we were only farming commodity crops for decades, but then we added specialty corn for grits and cornmeal, and now olives for delicious olive oil. Massive farms don't do that. But if massive corporate farms swallow up diverse family farms like ours, then we lose that innovation potential and opportunity for production diversity. And when that happens, we all lose. 🐚

Casey Price
Jeremiah Farm

In order to see the entire morning routine, I arrived at Casey's micro-dairy and educational farm a little before the goats' breakfast. After most of her chores, Casey enthusiastically and patiently taught me to milk Skyler with a squeeze, press, and release rhythm. Then I watched her as she finished the milking, and filtered, bottled, and chilled the goats' milk.

Casey offered me a taste. I'm allergic to the protein casein present in all animals' milk and have never liked the taste of milk, yogurt, or cheese, but I wanted to try a sip of raw goat milk. It was out of this world—deliciously sweet!

Casey is a natural teacher and happily leads visitors on educational tours of the gardens and livestock operation. She teaches people how to make their own cheese, kombucha, kefir, and yogurt, as well as other farmstead life skills. As I was leaving, a young couple arrived to purchase some goats.

Our journey into goats

My husband, Tim, and I have lived at Jeremiah Farm on Johns Island for almost fifteen years now. When we first arrived, we didn't have a name picked out for the place. Tim was reading the book of Jeremiah and in Chapter 29: 4-7 it said, "Build houses and settle down; plant gardens and eat what they produce"… so we became Jeremiah Farm.

We live a sustainably minded life and grow most of our own food. We have a robust vegetable garden and raise chickens. It was Tim's idea to get a dairy goat to provide us with a gallon of milk a day— enough for our family of four.

I figured that goats are more manageable than cows, much smaller and easier to keep, but still, I wasn't sure I was up for the extra work of keeping a goat. The next day, my Bible reading from Proverbs said, "And the goats will provide the price of the field and milk for your household and all of your maidservants." I was open to accept this sign and decided to pursue the idea.

That was when I started seeing "goat milk for sale" signs posted around the island. I wrote the phone number down and called Mr. Davis, a farmer in his eighties. I'll never forget that January day in 2002. Our children were three and five years, and Mr. Davis's goat Jan stepped off his front porch, walked up to our car, and promptly knocked our son, Branch, on his bottom. Fortunately, Branch just laughed, so everyone else did too. The rest of the visit, Jan adoringly trotted at the children's side.

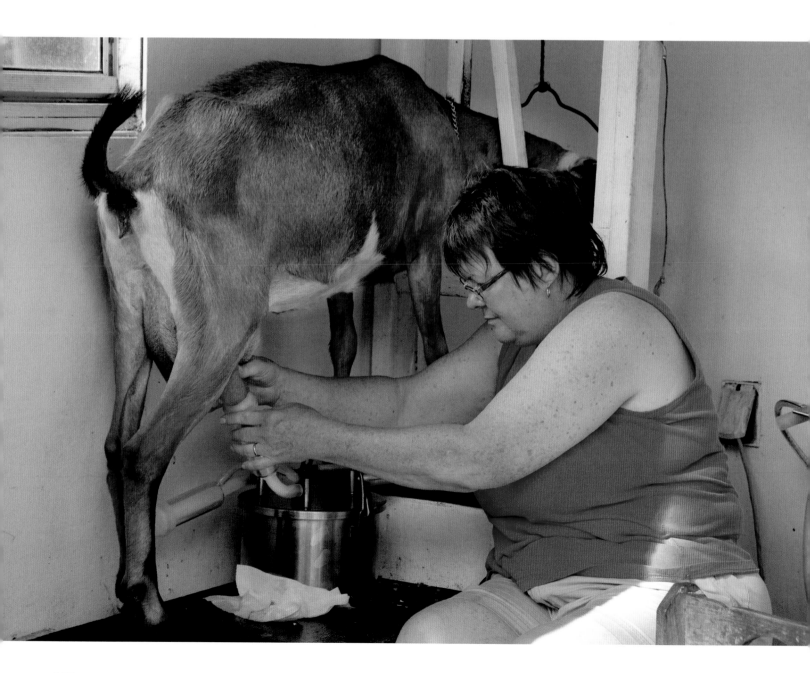

Without a doubt, there will be those days when it is raining, your boots are being sucked off by the mud, you have a sick goat, you have no customers, and there are ten gallons of milk in the refrigerator.

Mr. Davis shared his knowledge of goats with us. He showed us his freezer full of frozen milk and explained that his goat was currently "dry," so last fall he froze milk to get through the winter. He "dries a goat off" in the fall after she becomes pregnant to allow her to restore her body before kidding again in early spring. Once she kids, the milking commences.

He offered us a taste of raw goat milk. Our children each downed three glasses, exclaiming that they loved it. Tim loved it, and I figured I better have a taste, too. I love milk, but had never had goat's milk before, and my expectations were not high. I took a sip and said, "Wow, this tastes like milk, but sweeter!" Now every week I hear that same refrain from my farm's visitors.

A crash course

After our visit to Mr. Davis's farm, Tim and I decided to get a doe and buck. The doe would produce a perfect amount of milk for our family. Since I knew next to nothing about raising goats, I headed to the library. I hadn't even finished the book, when I saw an ad for dairy goats in the *Market Bulletin*, the South Carolina Department of Agriculture's bimonthly sales bulletin. The next day, I picked up our doe and buck in my mini-van. The woman told me the doe was pregnant and should give birth in about a month. I surmised that would give me time to finish the library book and figure out what I was doing. What a rookie I was!

Two days later, I came down to feed the goats and found that Rosey had given birth. I immediately called Mr. Davis, my goat mentor, asking him what to do. He asked if the baby was nursing. I said yes, and he said, "Okay, I'll be over in a couple of days." A couple of days!

Sure enough, two days later, Mr. Davis arrived with his milk stand, his bucket, and his supply kit. He cleaned Rosey's udders, gave her some penicillin (because that is what the old-timers did back then), showed me how to milk her, and said he wouldn't leave until I had finished. I was a nervous wreck, but I was able to get the hang of it fairly quickly. He told me that the kid would only need about a quart of milk a day, and a doe could give up to a gallon each day. We decided to milk Rosey and bottle-feed baby Ruby. That way we would know Ruby was getting what she needed, and we would have what was left over.

The next year, we bred Rosey and Ruby. What started with one doe rapidly increased to two milkers, then five, then nine. Today we have twenty goats, Nubians and Alpines. Because each of our goats has a distinct personality, we name all of them. The two breeds are easy to tell apart, because the Nubians have long floppy ears and Roman noses, and the Alpines' ears are upright with both sexes having a goatee. Nubians are known for their sweet nature and sweet milk, while Alpines are a bit more standoffish, but give a higher volume of milk.

Breeding, milking, and meticulous care

We breed our goats in August, after the does are eight months old and at least eighty pounds. Kids will be born within five days before or after the 150-day gestation period. I rarely need to assist a goat with birthing, but I remain close by just in case.

I start milking after the kids have nursed for forty-eight hours and received the colostrum. Milking increases a doe's production and relieves her udder pressure. I only milk once a day for the first eight weeks, then wean the kids, and start milking twice a day. Each milker will lactate for seven to ten months. After they have been bred again, I'll dry them off so they will have three months of rest before another milking season starts.

Without any encouragement, each of our does climbs up on the milking stand. We invested in a milking machine when I began milking five goats twice daily. The machine mimics hand milking by pulsing and squeezing. While one is being milked, I prepare the next goat on the other milking stand and continue going back and forth with goats on the two-stand system until all are milked. The process takes about six minutes per goat.

I use two five-quart milk pails. As soon as one

is full, I take it into the bottling room and start filtering and bottling milk. My first bottles are in the chiller within twenty minutes of milking. The chiller is a converted freezer that holds water at 33°F. Iced water is the fastest and most economical way to chill milk on a small-scale farm. The milk drops to 40°F in less than an hour. After milking, all the equipment is cleaned and sanitized.

There are a number of factors that contribute to our sweet milk. Nubians and Alpines naturally have especially delicious milk. We chill our milk quickly and keep it refrigerated at 35°F. This will maintain maximum freshness for ten to fourteen days. We take great care of our goats. We make sure they get good food to maintain their health, wellness, and milk production. We treat our goats gently and keep meticulous health charts for their vaccinations and worming.

A very important part of caring for our goats goes to our two Great Pyrenees, Hannah and Ben, who guard our livestock. Goats and chickens are prey animals, and our biggest predators are feral dogs, bobcats, and raccoons. Our Great Pyrenees are bred to instinctively protect our goats, and they have certainly earned their keep.

Hard times happen

When we started goat farming, our vision was simple; we wanted to provide milk for our family. Over time, our goals changed. Initially, we didn't see ourselves providing a service to the community, but within a couple of years, folks suffering from various ills, who can benefit from raw goat milk, began to contact us, and we got our permits to sell so we could meet their needs.

Farming and running a dairy is very hard work, so it is important to know why you are doing it and who you are doing it for. Without a doubt, there will be those days when it is raining, your boots are being sucked off by the mud, you have a sick goat, you have no customers, and there are ten gallons of milk in the refrigerator. At those times, it is really helpful to remember why you are farming. Hard times happen, and when they do, you've got to focus on your vision.

Just one sip

People are hesitant to try raw goat's milk because it is outside their normal experience. I love changing their minds, as it only takes one sip to get the delicious flavor. More people around the world drink goat's milk than cow's milk. However, if you see goat's milk at a grocery store, beware. It most likely has been pasteurized and simply will not taste the same, nor have the same health benefits.

Pasteurization became common in the 1920s, and unfortunately many people believe that milk—cow or goat—is unsafe if it has not been pasteurized. During the Industrial Revolution era, as the urban population began to encroach on rural pasturelands, farmers started supplementing their feed with waste grains from distilleries. Cows are not designed to eat grain unless the grain is growing on the grasses they are eating. A diet of grain changed the pH in their rumen and suppressed their immune system. This unnatural diet caused the cows to get sick, and people got sick from drinking their milk. To kill the bad bacteria, milk was brought to a high heat—pasteurization. The problem is that pasteurization also kills the good bacteria along with vitamins and the enzyme lactase, required for properly digesting the milk.

Consumers have been led to believe that to be safe, milk must be pasteurized. However, raw milk is easier to digest because the enzymes and good bacteria have not been destroyed in the pasteurization process. When purchasing raw milk, it is important to know your farmer and know that they have been certified to sell raw milk. Jeremiah Farm has passed the strictest of safety standards licensing us to sell raw, non-pasteurized milk.

We have a range of customers who visit our dairy farm—those who love raw goat's milk and want to support local food, and others who want to connect with the farm experience, understand where their food comes from, and know their farmer. We also have customers who want to restore their health, parents with infants and special needs children, and people with allergies, Crohns disease, ulcers, and other digestive problems. Some come to learn how they can live more sustainably. We welcome them all, and love sharing our experience and our delicious goat milk.

Urbie West
Rest Park Farm

W ith nearly fifty acres under production, Rest Park Farm is one of the largest specialty crop farms that I visited. It's beautiful and historical with a rustic old barn at the property entrance, as well as the 1872 phosphate mine shed, which was moved to the farm in 1893. Adjacent to the shed is the rail spur from which the farm shipped its produce. Now abandoned, the rail spur will soon be converted to a Rails-to-Trails corridor connecting bikers and hikers from the coastal town of Beaufort to the farm, opening the door for agritourism.

Urbie explained the burdens that the FDA's 2011 Food Safety Modernization Act's (FSMA's) requirements can place on a small family farm. National food safety protocols are important, but much of the regulations and programs that fall under the act, like the Good Agricultural Practices (GAP) certification system, were created to address food safety on industrial-scale farms.

▲ Above photo: Ashby and Urbie.

Rest Park Farm would still be able to sell through our CSA, farmers markets, and roadside stands without GAP certification.

GAP is a food safety certification that audits for possible sources of contamination to food—in the field, in the packing facility, and during storage or transportation. Primary to GAP certification is traceability. It is incumbent on me as the farmer to come up with a system so each box of produce can be traced to a specific field on a specific day. It requires logs for everything—cleaning equipment, service records for the cooler's compressors, protocols, standard operating procedures, and more.

I've been resisting GAP certification for two primary reasons—time and money. We already keep reams of logs—documenting field rotations, spray charts, cooler temperatures, the amount of sanitizer in the field wash, and the time it takes to get from the field to cooler. I work sixteen-hour days that start at 4:00 a.m. I don't know where I'm going to get the time to add extra monitoring and documentation each day.

Second, our packing shed, like many in the South,

is open on all sides. However, ours dates back to 1893. We love our historical shed. But, to receive GAP certification, it will be more economical to build a new packing shed than to up-fit this one. I'm frightened about what that will cost us. Initially I thought it would be around $70,000; however, our new Clemson extension agent gave us a set of plans to build a mobile satellite shed. It would enable us to meet GAP requirements for specific crops and could be built for around $7,000—considerably less than up-fitting the old shed. I have been dragging my feet, but I know I need to bite the bullet.

Ashby is slowly convincing me that we must become GAP certified if we want to farm into the future.

Floods, heat, and hurricanes

In addition to his business sense, Ashby is a hard-working partner with solid convictions. He had to talk some sense into me last fall, when I was ready to quit farming altogether. We had three back-to-back seasons that no business model in the world could have planned for. In the fall of 2015, we had twenty-four inches of rain, which flooded our crops. In early June of 2016, the temperature reached 110°F and burned up everything in our fields. That fall, we were hit with Hurricane Matthew. Our crops were decimated. I can't tell you how many tears I shed in that field.

Rest Park Farm was unable to deliver CSA boxes to our 600 members for five of the twelve weeks in our CSA season. Even more disheartening than the three successive seasons of weather-related crop failures and the struggle to fulfill CSA memberships were the irate and spiteful emails we got from some of our members. One would think that the type of person who would sign up for a CSA would be more in touch with the vicissitudes of weather and its impact on local farmers. I was amazed, and really saddened, by the total lack of understanding.

Farming is a passion for Ashby and me. We love planting, harvesting, and knowing that people are eating the fresh and nutritious vegetables that we worked hard to grow. We are conventional farmers with a conscience.

We want consumers to learn to eat local, seasonal foods. It is ultimately up to the consumer to decide if they want local agriculture and if so, to understand the harsh reality of all that is required for a small specialty crop farmer to create superior food—the costs of seeds, equipment, and labor; compliance with food safety regulations; sixteen-hour days; and surviving the impacts of extreme weather. Small and mid-sized farms are not the recipients of the $25 billion in farm subsidies from the federal government. Our income is solely dependent upon consumers' choices, and we hope everyone will choose local. ❧

Before going to print, Urbie called, and with great sadness he told me that the farm's expenses were outweighing its revenues; he and Ashby were closing shop.

Frasier Block
Johns Island Farmers Market

I love going to the Johns Island Farmers Market. Nestled under the trees at the forest's edge on Charleston Collegiate School's campus, it has such a down-to-earth feel and a strong sense of community. Manager Frasier Block's enthusiasm makes everyone feel welcome as she sets the stage introducing household consumers and chefs to local producers of produce, eggs, meat, milk, pasta, cheeses, and bread. In addition to starting and operating the Johns Island Farmers Market, she works on projects for the nonprofit Johns Island Conservancy—seeking to preserve the rural character of the Sea Islands—and she and her partner, Blue Laughters, care for the garden at the Children's Museum of the Lowcountry. She also manages to find time to be a ballroom dancing instructor. Frasier touches her community with her smile and boundless energy.

Finding my passion

After graduating from the College of Charleston with a corporate communications degree, I worked in

▲ Above: Blue Laughters and Frasier Block

the private sector, but found my heart wasn't in it. I needed to find, listen to, and follow my passion. I spent a couple of years working on different farms in the area through the nonprofit Lowcountry Local First. In the process, my admiration for farmers grew, but I realized I would rather support and promote

Vegetables can lose fifteen percent to fifty-five percent of their nutrients within a week. So by time food has shipped over a thousand miles, has been on grocery store shelves, and then in the household refrigerator, its nutritional value and quality has depleted.

them than be one. Meanwhile I was hearing consumers talk about their desire to buy food locally, and I wondered how I could use my communications education and agricultural experience to become a liaison between farmers and consumers. My affinity for the land, farmers, and local foods pointed me in the direction of starting a farmers market, and my passions blossomed.

Having worked on local farms and manned farmers market booths, I had developed relationships with farmers, vendors, small businesses, and entrepreneurs who I knew would be interested in the Johns Island Farmers Market. I had the network, but no idea how to start and manage a farmers market. I studied how other farmers markets worked and what didn't work, compiled feedback from their customers, and just figured it out. I obtained help with legalities and safety issues from an event company that I had worked with previously. Blue and I spent four months pulling it all together and launched the Johns Island Farmers Market in January 2014.

Johns Island was the perfect spot for a farmers market. It is a rural island consisting of quality farmland, and it's one of the few places in the Charleston area that not only didn't have its own farmers market, it didn't have a central gathering place for the community. A weekly farmers market with community activities would provide a way to pull the community together.

Because there are dozens of farmers markets around Charleston, we needed to create a niche of our own—something that would set us apart from all the others. The Johns Island Farmers Market is the only market in the area that operates year-round. It makes plenty of sense, because in our climate, the ground never freezes and something is always growing. In the winter, we have cabbages, kales, collards, and root veggies along with year-round local eggs, grass-fed organic meats, raw milk, nuts, artisan breads, pastas, and cheeses, butters, jams, jellies, honey, and more. We also have innovative farmers growing food year-round using hydroponic and aquaponic agriculture.

Connect, learn, interact, enjoy

Johns Island is the fourth-largest island on the East Coast. There is immense pressure to develop this beautiful rural island, which would irrevocably alter the land's use away from farming. As the availability of developable land around Charleston decreases and the price of land escalates, Johns Island's rural future is in great jeopardy. All the more reason to bring people together, make strong community bonds, and introduce consumers to their local farmers and artisans! Supporting the livelihood of our farmers, building awareness, and putting our dollars back into this farming community may help hold development pressures at bay, while also providing consumers with the freshest and most nourishing food.

We want vendors to be dedicated to this market, and we want it be their storefront so they don't have to invest in brick and mortar. Even if they only have a small backyard farm, we encourage and support local growers who want sell their products here. We are always open to accepting new vendors. Recently a farmer stopped by with a trailer full of watermelons—the tastiest I have ever had—and of course we wanted him to be a part of our farmers market. This is precisely how we support local people and the local economy.

The Johns Island Farmers Market has recently been chosen as one of two markets in South Carolina to receive a grant from South Carolina Eat Smart Move More Coalition. This two-year grant will allow our farmers market to be SNAP eligible. SNAP is the Supplemental Nutrition Assistance Program, formerly the Food Stamp Program, that provides food purchasing assistance to low-income individuals and families. We feel this grant will expand our reach and enable us to be more inclusive to the whole community. Everyone can benefit from fresh, local, sustainably grown foods.

We strive to make the Johns Island Farmers Market more than just a place of transactions, but a place where people can connect and learn from each other. Interactive events change each week and include chess games, pony rides, and fitness programs. We offer classes, demos, and activities, which provide a personalized way to introduce healthy cooking, sustainable education, and community-building experiences.

Clemson Extension Master Gardeners are present each week with information on sustainable gardening practices. Patrons can bring soil samples from their home gardens to be tested for a soil assessment. A local beekeeper sells honey weekly and occasionally sets up an observation beehive to demonstrate the importance of bees and pollination. Our local garden club holds their biannual plant sale here. The Haut Gap Middle School brought their school orchestra and played one Saturday and returned another week with their steel drum band. The Antique Tractor Society has tractor shows and demonstrations twice a year. Along with farm and local artisan products, we have food trucks, live local musicians, a bounce house, plenty of seating, and free parking. Hanging out, having fun, and most importantly, getting to know one another as a community is happening weekly at our farmers market—it's so fulfilling to see!

Growing Connections

Blue and I are the only full-time market employees. We have created, organized, and managed this farmers market for the past three years. We frequently visit our farmers on their land, pull and taste their carrots, see their chickens roaming safely protected in a lush field and observe and learn about their sustainable growing practices.

According to University of California studies, vegetables can lose fifteen percent to fifty-five percent of their nutrients within a week. So by the time food has shipped over a thousand miles, has been on grocery store shelves and then in the household refrigerator, its nutritional value and quality has depleted. This is another reason to buy freshly harvested foods from local farmers. One of our main challenges is showing people that almost everything on their shopping list can be sourced locally and sustainably, provided they are willing to eat seasonally. It's also important to keep our flow of dollars local, which boosts the local economy and supports all our friends and partners in our community.

Now in our fourth year, my passion to connect our hard-working local farmers with educated local consumers continues to be a success for all parties. Relationships continue to develop. The Johns Island Farmers Market allows people to make choices that support their health, support local farmers and artisans, support local farmland, and invest in our community. For that, we are delighted! ❧

Tami Enright
The Bee Cause

I simply cannot write a book about the ingredients of a robust food system without expounding the vital role of honey bees. Our food supply world-wide depends on the transfer of pollen from a plant's male reproductive parts to a plant's female reproductive parts. Fertilization of agricultural crops sometimes occurs by wind dispersal, but the most reliable way nature cross-pollinates from one plant species to another plant of the same species is through pollinators—honey bees, bumble bees, butterflies, hummingbirds, bats, and others. And honey bees provide us with the extra gift of honey!

I met Tami, executive director of *The Bee Cause* at the observation hive in the resource room at Charleston Collegiate School on Johns Island. After visiting with Tami and the Head of School, Hacker Burr, a group of third graders joined us. Together we observed the queen, foragers, nurses, and a variety of hive activities.

Sadly, after two successful years with a very healthy hive, Charleston Collegiate School lost their entire colony to a countywide aerial spray of a lethal, non-species-specific insecticide in an attempt to curb the mosquito that carries the Zika virus. Had beekeepers across the *county known, they could have protected their bees by preventing them from foraging for a specific time. The school is waiting to receive a new hive in the spring.*

Life-changing introductions

"No, no, no!" I said to my friend who wanted me to attend an Introduction to Beekeeping workshop. "I barely do gardens, and I don't do bugs!" "But," my friend replied, "your garden is struggling because you don't have any pollinators, and the pollinators are struggling, too." I reluctantly attended the weekend course with her. Three days later, I enthusiastically ordered two beehives. Fortunately, my husband and our kids, aged four, five, six, and seven, were pretty excited, too.

I joined the local Bee Association Club—there's one in every town—and ordered beekeeping suits for my kids. A couple months later, a screened shoe-box of 5,000 honey bees and one queen showed up on my doorstep. My new hobby soon turned into teaching beekeeping at a nearby school and managing beehives for some farms. My kids started teaching their friends, and we learned to make lip balm from the wax.

When the Savannah Bee Company opened a retail store in downtown Charleston, a friend of mine, who grew up with the owner, Ted Dennard, asked me to come along to the grand opening. I thought I would impress him when I told him that all four of my kids had bee suits and were involved with our bees. He enthusiastically told me that he had four kids, and they were beekeepers, too. Initially our conversation revolved around our kids and their interests in bees, but soon it evolved into wondering how to connect more kids to bees and beekeeping. A couple weeks later, we met to expand upon that conversation.

Ted, I learned, was introduced to beekeeping when he was twelve. He kept bees during high school and college, and he taught beekeeping to village farmers in the Peace Corps. Ted is committed to educating children and adults about the vital role honey bees play. He hired me to partner with him to start a nonprofit, which we aptly named, The Bee Cause. Leveraging Savannah Bee Company's back office for legal, insurance, and marketing support, I developed

▼ Jay, Luke, Ellis, Alistair, and Tami.

Thanks to The Bee Cause, kids understand that much of the food on our plates is due to the pollinating activities of these important insects.

a business plan and applied for The Bee Cause to become a 501(c)(3) tax-exempt entity.

Growing hives and growing minds

With the mission of educating kids about honey bees and their valuable role in our world, we installed our first pilot observation hive in a local elementary school in October of 2012. By watching the colony's activities through glass without disturbing the bees, the students and adults learn about bee activities. With the curriculum we provide, they begin to understand how important bees are to the food on our plates. And they begin to think more carefully about how we interact with nature in our own backyards. They become more connected to nature and, therefore, become good stewards.

Since that first pilot, the program has taken on a life of its own. We installed six pilot programs in both Charleston and Savannah public schools. As The Bee Cause grew, other school districts felt more comfortable joining. After four years, we have almost 200 schools in the program nationwide.

When a school asks to partner with us, the first step is to visit the school and verify that they have an accepting environment, a willing administration, and truly want to participate in the program. Someone at the school needs to be super-passionate, and we want to know the school will be dedicated to caring for the hive and utilizing it. If the school is a good fit, we find an ideal location for the hive and provide our Bee Wise Educational Materials and Resource Guides. This curriculum provides teachers with learning opportunities in math, science, writing, reading, and research—all related to bees and beekeeping. The school also partners with the local bee association to work with a bee mentor who will be a hands-on resource, visit every two weeks, and gather honey.

Most folks don't think that bees and kids go together. There are different species of bees, and generally honey bees have a gentle disposition. It is surprisingly easy to get kids interested in honey bees, and it's rewarding to introduce them to something they can find fulfilling, productive, and fun. Today, with the fear around kids' allergies, from peanuts to gluten to bees, introducing our program can be tricky. We provide very comprehensive safety manuals and training courses on how to manage and take care of the bees.

Schools receive their observation hive free of charge. About a quarter of the schools agree to sell honey as a fundraiser to pay for the installation of an observation hive in another school of their choice. This *Pay it Forward* initiative supports the The Bee Cause's mission to install honey bee observation hives in 1,000 schools. The Savannah Bee Company donates the honey; the school sells the honey for $15 per jar, with $10 for *Pay it Forward*, and $5 to help pay for the upkeep of their own hive.

From a school's perspective

Hacker Burr: The Bee Cause fits well with Charleston Collegiate School's project-based, hands-on experiential learning approach and with our outdoor program. We recognized right away that a hive would reinforce our foundation in science and nature and complement our small on-campus farm. There were no obstacles to the program—it didn't change our insurance, and it came as a *Pay it Forward* gift from a local coffee distributor.

Our observation hive is providing us endless learning opportunities. One of the four pillars of Charleston Collegiate School is financial literacy and entrepreneurship. Additionally, we seek to incorporate community service into our learning activities. The beehive provides a forum for us to engage our students in both.

For three days during carpool drop-off and pick-up times, our third graders raised $1,400 selling honey. The students handled it all. They crunched numbers, made change, tracked inventory, and sourced more product. They learned how to make a sale—looking the customer in the eyes, shaking hands, and thanking them for their purchase. Through our honey sales, we were able to *Pay it Forward* and provide a hive to another school on Johns Island.

We like pushing our students out of their comfort zones to facilitate learning. The observation hive allows us to talk about fearing things we don't comprehend; it promotes curiosity and encourages understanding to overcome fear.

The program has been such a success that a local beekeeper is now keeping six outdoor colonies here, and we recently applied for a grant to get beekeeper suits for our students.

A window into the world of a honey bee

Tami: Bees are programmed to gather both pollen (their source of protein) and nectar (a carbohydrate). Pollen is stored for the off-season, and nectar is used to make honey. The bees collect the pollen in their pollen baskets—a flattened area fringed with hairs on the bee's hind leg, used for carrying pollen. When they return to the hive, they transfer the pollen to another bee that packs the pollen into cells in the hive for storage as a future food source. Bees suck nectar from flowers and store it in their honey sacs (a second stomach) until they return to the hive and release it to be made into honey. In the process of gathering both pollen and nectar, the bees pollinate the plants.

Lots of hobby and commercial beekeepers use chemicals in their hives to treat for pests and other predators. Mites are usually the biggest problem in a traditional beehive, but because we can see into our hives, we can treat pests before they become a big problem.

Beetles also will get into the hives, but the bees can defend themselves. They will herd and confine the beetles and then push them through thin screens at the bottom of the hive. We are adding slide-out beetle traps to hives this spring, which can be pulled out and cleaned.

Looking into our hive, we can see a couple of the forager bees doing a waggle dance to communicate where they have found pollen. The dance is like a map to show the other bees where the food can be found. All the bees in the colony watch the foragers do their waggle dances, and determine which dance is strongest. And that is where they will go to forage.

It is easy to find the queen because I have put a red dot on her for identification. Her abdomen is much larger and longer than the others. She goes from cell to cell laying approximately 2,000 eggs each day. She must lay so many eggs to grow the hive, because worker bees only live about six weeks. Each egg is the size of a comma and will hatch into a larva in three days. Nurse bees clean the cells and feed the larvae pollen and honey. After six days, a little brown cap will form over the top of each cell, and the larvae will pupate. Two weeks later, the cap cracks open, and a worker bee emerges. When a worker bee hatches, the first thing she does is clean the cell so it will immediately be ready for the queen to lay more eggs. She is born with that innate behavior.

Reasons to bee hopeful

Tami: Honey bee populations started to significantly decline around the late 1990s. A mix of factors contributes to their decreasing numbers—a chemically driven agricultural system, transporting bees around the country to pollinate different agricultural crops, parasites, and climate change. The honey bee is a small part of a much larger ecosystem, and the entire system is being set off balance by these challenges. Fortunately, the international community is working toward promoting biodiversity and sustainable agricultural practices, and tracking the effects of pesticides. It will only be through continued research, education, and awareness that we will be able to improve honey bee habitats, and in turn, our own food system. Of course, introducing children to the value of honey bees is a big step in the right direction.

I love being in front of the observation hive with a group of students. It brings me such joy to watch their excitement and hear how proud they are to recognize and understand different bee activities—nursing, waggle dancing, and the queen laying. It also fills me with hope for the future of these and other struggling pollinators. Thanks to The Bee Cause, when these kids are outdoors and see bees foraging, they will have a totally different reaction and an appreciation. Rather than being fearful, they are curious, respectful, and caring. They have become more connected to nature and have become wonderful ambassadors for the plight of pollinators. Now they understand that much of the food on our plates is due to the pollinating activities of these important insects.

I started out with one beehive seeking to pollinate my own garden, and now, with The Bee Cause, I am dedicated to replicating school beehives 1,000 times, and hopefully more! 🐝

Jim Rathbun
Brickyard Point Farms

Lady's Island, a barrier island off Beaufort, South Carolina, is a hidden agricultural jewel. In April, I met Jim along with his trusty companion, Kona, a very friendly pitbull, who reluctantly gave me enough room to join Jim in the golf cart for a tour around Brickyard Point Farms. I saw acres of pecan trees, learned about cultivating, harvesting, and shelling pecans, and was the fortunate recipient of delicious, freshly shelled Schley pecans.

Many months later, wishing to observe the pecan harvest, I went back to Brickyard Point Farms. It was the end of the harvest, but Jim had saved six trees so I could see the whole process of pecan harvesting. I watched him work—from clamping the shaker attachment to the trunk of the tree to bagging the pecans. And then, as if the experience was not reward enough, his wife, Nancy, gave me a bag of her prized roasted pecans.

A member of the walnut family, the pecan is a large, stately, deciduous tree native to the central and southern parts of the United States. Pecan nuts are not true nuts; botanically they are a type of fruit called a drupe. (Likewise, peanuts are not true nuts, but legumes.) Nevertheless, we refer to them as nuts. They are high in protein and antioxidants, and rich in manganese, potassium, calcium, iron, magnesium, zinc, and selenium. And they are delicious.

Marine colonel to pecan farmer

After serving our country as a Marine Corps colonel with twenty-eight years of transience and relocations, my dad transitioned to a permanent home on Lady's Island. He and my mom found this plot of land on the banks of the Coosaw River that had once been part of Brickyard Point Plantation. It hosted a number of mature pecan trees, and Dad adopted the trees as his retirement hobby. Soon he was planting and grafting more pecan trees, and eventually he transformed the place into a pecan farm. My parents delighted in sharing their bounty of pecans, persimmons, pears, and pomegranates with local islanders. After twenty-five years of enjoying life as a pecan farmer, my dad passed away.

Before he died, Dad expressed concerns about who would take care of the trees when he wasn't around. I reassured him that when I retired from the Marine Corps in Quantico, Virginia, Nancy and I would continue the pecan farm. For the next thirteen years, I ventured to Lady's Island to work on the farm each time I was on leave. In 2006, upon my retirement, Nancy and I moved, and I inherited pecan trees that were in dire need of attention and care, along with Dad's tired, broken equipment. With research, some newer equipment, and advice from various USDA extension agencies, I too became a pecan farmer.

It's the hardest work I've ever done, and I'm a marine, so I know hard work. I have always loved a challenge, but that first year on the farm stretched me like never before. In addition to the pecan orchard, we planted more pears, persimmons, pomegranates, and citrus trees—grapefruit, lemons, navel oranges, and satsumas. It took a lot of sweat and a number of years, but the land and trees have recovered and are back in productivity.

Our pecan orchard has more than 300 trees of different varieties. The one's we grow the most are the Schley, Stuart, Desirables, Cape Fear, Frotchers, and Grey Park Giants. Our customers' favorite pecan seems to be the Schley, which has a rich flavor, high oil content, and are easy to crack. Another favorite is the hard-shelled Stuart with its superior meat, which is great for eating raw and cooking. I call the Desirables our prima donna pecan. They are pretty, easy to crack by hand, and produce beautiful large halves of delicious nut meat, but they are the most difficult to grow. The Frotchers are less expensive than the rest simply because they don't look as pretty with their black veins, but they are excellent for cooking.

It's the hardest work I've ever done, and I'm a marine, so I know hard work.

Growing pecans is a year-round job

Pecans are "alternate bearing," meaning they produce well one year and poorly the next. During the productive years, I harvest between 7,000 and 14,000 pounds of pecans from about 300 mature, fruit-bearing trees. During the off years I get anywhere from just 30 pounds to 6,000 pounds.

I'm a one-man band. Because the tasks are spread throughout the year, I can do it all. During the winter months, I rake leaves and prune limbs that broke under the weight of the nuts. I also take soil samples from four or five places on the farm and send them off for analysis. I want to know exactly what my trees need for optimal health. Nitrogen, phosphorous, potassium, and zinc are all important for pecan growth. But, you can fertilize until the cows come home, all to no avail unless you have the right soil pH. Plants can't access the nutrients in the soil if the pH is incorrect. The correct pH for pecans is 6.7.

By the end of February or early March each year, I fertilize the orchard soil. In the producing years, I spread-load a slow-release, high nitrogen fertilizer on a graduated schedule—half in March, a quarter in June, and the last bit in August. I fertilize slightly less in off years. Harvest begins around mid-October, or as soon as the early pecans are ready.

In the Southeast, the soil is great for growing pecan trees, but the high humidity causes a fungus called pecan scab. To combat the effects of humidity, we remove the Spanish moss, prune the limbs to allow more air movement, and unfortunately must also spray a mild fungicide on the foliage. One off year, I chose to forego the fungicidal spray and learned the hard way that it is a necessity. I monitor the health of the trees carefully, and fortunately we don't have pecan weevil or casebearer pests. I don't use pesticides or insecticides, but I will never be an organic pecan grower, as a result of the humidity and pecan scab fungus.

The sex life of pecan trees

Pecans are wind pollinated. Male pecan flowers, arranged in drooping clusters called catkins, are located on the same tree as the female flowers, but in different places. The male and female maturity don't always overlap. The staminate (male) flowers may release pollen before the pistillate (female) flowers are receptive, or the pistil may be receptive before the stamen releases the pollen. There is only a short window when they can self-pollinate, and the timing is iffy and weather dependent. This lack of synchronization on the same tree encourages outcrossing, or cross-pollination with a neighboring pecan tree—a strategy that leads to genetic diversity.

Pecan harvesting

A good pecan tree will produce about 300 pounds of nuts, ripening at different intervals over a six-week period. We harvest from late October through mid-December, working twelve-hour days. When the thick green husk around the nut splits into quarters and turns brown, the tree is ready to drop its nuts. We are on our toes monitoring this carefully, because we are in direct competition with the crows and squirrels. They also know the moment the pecans are ready, and crows will sweep in by the hundreds and decimate our crop.

Over the years, I have gradually improved my equipment and now have the tools of a professional pecan grower. When harvesting, I wait for the morning dew to evaporate. I clean debris from under the tree, back up my tractor with the shaker attachment, and clamp it to the trunk of the tree. A mighty vibration shakes the nuts from the tree. I collect them right away. We think pecans are nuts, but pecans think they are seeds, and they want to grow to be a tree in the worst way. Once they start to germinate, they are no good.

Before I switch from the shaker to the harvester, I use a backpack blower to blow the nuts away from the trunk of the tree and clear a path so the harvester's wheels won't crush any pecans. The harvester sweeps the pecans onto a belt, and a hard mesh conveyor belt turns so the pecans get moved through the machine to a large tank that holds about 500 pounds of nuts. I empty the tank into another truck, so I can continue harvesting pecans shaken from each tree. Using a conveyor belt and fan on our grading machine, we discard the lighter nuts and pour the keepers into mesh bags. We weigh and label each bag and record the information to report to the USDA. We store the nuts in a cool, dry facility until it is time to shell them. We target a four and a half percent moisture rate inside the nut before they are shelled.

The meat of the matter

There is nothing better than a pecan that is cracked and eaten immediately. They are one of the healthiest nuts in the world, and quite delicious. At the farmers market about a decade ago, a woman asked how to shell her pecans. I realized she had a point. It was time for me to take the next step and get some shelling equipment.

The pecan cracker cracks 400 pecans per minute. Then they go into the sheller, where the meat is knocked away from most of the shell. The next step is the aspirator, which sucks up a large portion of the shells. The shells don't go to waste; chefs in Charleston use them to smoke meats. Last in the process is quality control—the pecans get the human touch, and we determine if they are keepers or not.

It is such a thrill to grow something that people really relish. I like to sell my pecans to local folks, so I can see their enjoyment and hear their appreciation. Although I'm a member of Georgia Pecan Growers Association, which is more organized than South Carolina's association, Georgia exports about sixty-five percent of their pecans to China. My wife and I prefer to sell our pecans in three different local venues—here at the farm, through the local food hub GrowFood Carolina, and at farmers markets around Beaufort County. We love going to the farmers markets, and oftentimes we sell out of seventy-five pounds of pecans in less than two hours.

We also sell our other crops—pears, persimmons, pomegranates, and Meyer lemons through Grow-Food Carolina and the farmers markets. Unlike alternate-bearing pecans, fruit produces every year, and provides us with revenue diversification and an earlier market than the pecans.

In the ten years since Nancy and I moved to Brickyard Point Farms, the land and trees have recovered and thrived. I love the hard work. Being a farmer provides us with the same joy that I saw in my dad when he became a pecan farmer. He would be proud of the progress we have made and the continuation of the retirement endeavors that he started many years ago. ❧

Andrea Cooler
Herbalicious

A ndrea's enthusiasm about her microgreen business is contagious. This is a story about seeing a business opportunity, having courage, taking small incremental steps, learning from mistakes, and watching dreams blossom into a profitable business.

Rosemary and serendipity

Everything about my microgreens business, Herbalicious, is a learning process, and my education continues. After three years, I have three employees, no debt, and I'm making a profit. Most importantly, I'm having fun, and I get to be home and outdoors with my five- and eight-year-old kids, who love helping me.

This business venture happened serendipitously. I was waiting tables at a local restaurant, so I could be with the kids during the day, and my husband could be with them at night. I would bring sprigs from my rosemary bush to the chef, and one day he showed me a container of microgreens. He was

purchasing them from California and paying $25 per container. He asked if I could grow microgreens for him.

I didn't even garden. Despite my hardy and flourishing rosemary bush, my houseplants would literally die three weeks after I bought them. Nevertheless, I saw a business opportunity and decided to try it. Fortunately, my mom is a master gardener. She bought me a good grow light and supplies that we set up in my laundry room, where I could grow four trays. In one month, I learned to grow the rainbow mix of greens, and from there it evolved. I started growing more microgreens, selling to more restaurants, and next thing I knew, I was making money and had officially started Herbalicious.

Elliott Shuler
Shuler Peach Company

*I*f I were to choose a favorite fruit, it would have to be a South Carolina peach. Sadly, when I visited Elliott Shuler, it was not yet peach season. The prolific golf-ball-size peaches ripening on the boughs would make me wait until the mid-May farmers market. However, my visit did coincide with the height of strawberry season. Before leaving, Elliott and I stopped by his roadside stand, where he introduced me to his mom and dad, who were tending the store. They gave me a bucket of succulent strawberries for my drive back to Charleston, which made my visit even sweeter!

Son, do not farm!

I was born to be a farmer. Farming is in my blood. I love it, although sometimes I wonder if that's a blessing or a curse. I am a fifth-generation farmer and grew up on this farm. My grandfather and dad were row crop farmers raising corn, soybeans, and wheat on about 1,200 acres, with another 1,000 acres of peaches. They also raised cows and hogs.

The 1980s were the beginning of the end for row crop farmers. A lot of farmers went out of business during those years. My dad hung on and tried to make a go of it for another decade, but by the mid-1990s, he had accrued loads of debt. When I graduated from Clemson University in 1994, my dad's echoing refrain was "Do not farm!"

That year was a bumper crop for corn and beans. However, the sad reality was that even with a bumper crop, the amount of money we made was not enough to dig ourselves out of the deep debt hole.

Cheap food most likely means cheap labor. Farms outside the United States may be paying their laborers less than $1 per hour. When consumers choose to buy cheap food, they are usually supporting farms that pay their laborers a deplorable wage.

We simply were not going to be able to farm our way out of it. It dawned on me then that if a farmer with debt can't survive after an outstanding year like this, then how would he ever be able to make it? My dad ended up selling the whole farm.

I learned early on that farming is not that great financially, so I've always held another job. I've been a wildlife biologist for DNR (Department of Natural Resources) since 1996. I work forty hours a week managing public lands and public hunts. My DNR job always comes first, but I'm fortunate to have thirty days of annual leave, allowing me to schedule time on the farm during the most labor-intensive times.

After my dad sold the farm, my uncle, a retired veterinarian, and some of my cousins were eventually able to buy back most of the land. I purchased about 250 acres from them to farm peaches and strawberries and raise broiler chickens. I recently sold the broiler business, which was under contract with Pilgrim's Pride, and my focus now is on strawberries and peaches.

Succulent fruits

The amount of work planting, pruning, and harvesting strawberries and peaches requires three full-time employees. It is important to me to be able to provide employment year-round, so after the peach harvest, we prune the center of the trees, encouraging new growth to come from the trunk. In the fall, we grow field corn to sell to deer hunters, and during the winter, my employees help my uncle with his cows and farm maintenance.

In October, we hand plant three acres of strawberries, and for the first ten to twelve days provide overhead watering. Strawberry plants must initially be kept wet to get off to a good start. We plant bare roots from Canada, not plugs. If we have a frost, we use row covers to protect them. During the height of berry picking season in the spring, I will have between four and eight workers picking every other day until noon, and thinning peaches the rest of the day. Just as strawberry production is winding down,

the peach harvest begins. I have eighteen acres of peach orchards with nearly 150 trees per acre. I have forty varieties of peaches, staggering their harvests throughout the season. Flavorich is my first variety, ready for the market in mid-May. My last variety of peaches, Fair Time, are harvested through the first week of September.

Our peaches start blooming in March. We fertilize around the base of the trees, and in this humid climate, the blooms require a fungicidal spray or the peaches will rot. Sprays are highly regulated and expensive. Consumers need to pay close attention to the Country of Origin of their fruit, because what's illegal to use here may not be illegal there. It's a good reason to know your farmer! I don't spray if I don't have to. One of the advantages I have is that our orchards are small enough that I can closely watch the weather and pests, and only spray my fields when necessary. Peach trees need to be carefully monitored. Something can always go wrong with them, from diseases, to scale, to an oak root rot, which causes them to die early.

By mid-April, the limbs are laced with so many peaches that the peaches are overcrowded and too heavy for the boughs. We remove lots of peaches from each limb, spacing them about a hand's distance apart. We harvest our peaches, by hand when they are hard enough not to bruise, but at the perfect stage where they will be ripe and ready to eat in a day or two. We start picking peaches at daybreak and pick all day. They are stored in a 34°F cooler.

Shuler Peach Company uses a variety of distribution outlets. We sell our fruit at our roadside stand, at four farmers markets, and through the local food hub, GrowFood Carolina, which then markets them to retailers and restaurants. GrowFood requires that we package them in a produce box, rather than in a half-bushel bucket. Although that packaging takes time and requires labor, the relationship with GrowFood has been a big benefit. They are supportive and flexible, and if I have an extra hundred baskets of peaches or strawberries, they will move them and give me a good price.

Consumers need to pay close attention to the Country of Origin of their fruit, because what's illegal to use here may not be illegal there. It's a good reason to know your farmer!

Cheap food means cheap labor

I am passionate about farming, but this is a business. To be sustainable, the bottom line must work. I have to be able to pay the bank loan at the end of every year. My employees are hardworking skilled laborers, and I don't think anyone working as hard as they do should be making less than $10 to $12 per hour. I wish I could pay them more.

Consumers usually choose their food based on price. I wish they would think more about the people who are behind growing their food. Cheap food most likely means cheap labor. Farms outside the United States may be paying their laborers less than $1 per hour, while I am paying my people a minimum of $10 per hour. When consumers choose to buy cheap food, they are usually supporting farms that pay their laborers a deplorable wage.

I wish consumers understood the full cost of farming. The cost of land, equipment, fungicides and fertilizers, wages for the laborers, packaging, transporting, and marketing—it is all very expensive. We farmers do what we do because we love it. We clearly are not trying to get rich, but we would like to sell our goods for an honorable price. Indeed, it is an honorable career, and I'm proud of the peaches and strawberries we grow. And I'm proud to be back on my family's land carrying on our long history of farming. 🍂

Powell Smith
Clemson University Extension Service

*A*n extension service agent and self-proclaimed agricultural ecologist, Powell is dedicated to helping farmers. I climbed into his truck and accompanied him on his rounds
as he visited farms and farmers. I listened to his conversations with farmers about the weather,
plant diseases, soil improvements, and insects. With ten inches of rain in the forecast, I watched
as Powell advised a farmer on measures to take to protect his fields of almost-ripe strawberries.
And I watched him with an organic farmer as he got down on his knees to attentively look
through his small handheld magnifying glass, scouting for insect pests on kale leaves. Each
farmer's respect and appreciation for Powell's knowledge, insights, and his genuine care and
manner of listening was indisputable. I thoroughly enjoyed my time learning from this articu-
late and thoughtful agricultural philosopher-raconteur.

History and mission
of land-grant universities

Clemson University, like all extension service institutions, came into being when the Morrill Land-Grant
Act, signed by President Lincoln, allowed states to sell
federal lands to raise money to establish agricultural
colleges. In 1862, over half of our population farmed.
The land-grant system's original purpose was to educate the common man, as well as provide informa-

tion to farmers about production, rural living, preservation of food, and community development.

I've always wanted to be a county extension agent. If something went wrong with a crop on my grandparents' farm, they called the county agent. I figured if the county agent was the person my grandparents trusted to help solve a problem, then that was an honorable and meaningful job and something I would like to do. Furthermore, I knew I didn't want to be trapped in a desk job.

At the University of Georgia, I majored in microbiology and had a part-time job in the plant pathology lab. Seeing microbiology applied to plants solidified my decision to go into agriculture. I got a PhD from Clemson University in entomology, and after graduating in the mid-1970s, I got a job as a county extension agent with South Carolina's extension service.

An extension agent is a farm educator. I work primarily on pest and disease management issues. I give farmers information so they can make more informed decisions. I prefer to explain the biological processes to a farmer, rather than give directives. We talk weather, diseases, pest management, soils, and freeze protection. I also mentor and supervise seven other extension service agents, provide in-service trainings and seminars, and teach Integrated Pest Management (IPM).

Managing plant pathologies

Moisture has the strongest influence on plant disease, and the South is humid, so we have our share of challenges. Historically, routine spraying was recommended to combat bacterial or fungal problems. Now, however, by using hi-tech monitoring devices in the field, I can give farmers accurate predictions for when an application of fungicidal spray is required, which eliminates the guesswork and unnecessary spraying and increases efficiency and effectiveness for farmers.

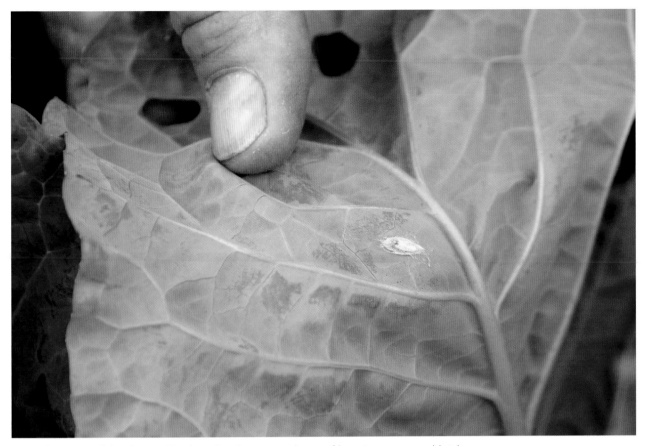

▲ Pupal cocoon of the diamondback moth—the principal pest of brassica crops worldwide.

The extension service also provides resistance profiling for growers of certain fruits. Profiling determines whether a fungicide is effective. A farmer can send a sample to our plant pathologists, who will determine within forty-eight hours if the disease-causing organism is resistant to a battery of common fungicides. If the materials the farmer is using to combat the problem are ineffective, there is no reason to continue allocating money and labor needlessly. It's bad for the farmer's bottom line, and it encourages adaptation and resistance to fungicides by insects.

Through on-farm demonstrations, I provide farmers with information on how to prevent problems by improving their soils. Crop rotation increases soil fertility and recharges the soil's nutrients, but the most important reason for rotating crops is to avoid accumulating populations of pests and diseases that are specific to a crop and remain in the soil.

Integrated Pest Management

The obvious first step in combating a problem is figuring out what the problem is, which is why I always carry my pocket magnifying glass. I show farmers how to use it to scout for pests on crops.

Extension agents used to believe that the way to deal with agricultural pests was with chemical applications. I'm not opposed to using agricultural chemicals—pesticides and fungicides. I think the EPA does a good job to ensure they are relatively safe; nevertheless, we need to minimize the use of chemical inputs. Relatively safe and completely safe are two different things. I'm pragmatic enough to realize that I can't impose my standards on growers, but I do want to lead them and provide them with viable alternatives to chemicals.

The best way to manage insect pests is through the conservation and enhancement of their natural enemies—beneficial insects. This is called Integrated Pest Management (IPM). For example, one of the most problematic pests for cruciferous crops (the brassicas—cauliflower, cabbage, broccoli, Brussels sprouts, kale, etc.) is the diamondback moth, *Diadegma insulari*, also known as the cabbage moth. This moth has a natural insect predator, a parasitic wasp that lays its eggs in the diamondbacks' larvae and kills it.

One problem with pesticides is that they kill both the problematic insects and the beneficial insects. And so the beneficials need to be attracted back to the fields. I encourage farmers to let their brassica fields bolt—go to flower after harvest. The

We need to minimize the use of chemical inputs. Relatively safe and completely safe are two different things. . . . The best way to manage insect pests is through the conservation and enhancement of their natural enemies—beneficial insects.

flowers are a veritable nursery for beneficial insects. Some other attractors for beneficial insects are cilantro, parsley, dill, and carrots. Once they bolt, their blooms are a wonderful food source for parasitic wasps and pollinators.

Despite the well-known effectiveness of IPM, it is a big challenge getting farmers to adopt the procedures, because the effects of IPM are not as immediate as chemicals. Farmers often say, "I used to spray and all these problems would go away, so I must not be spraying enough." However, the problem is those farmers are spraying too much, which leads to insect resistance. Because insects reproduce so frequently, their genes mutate, adapt, and rapidly become resistant to the chemicals used.

Abandonment

Farming is one of the hardest occupations. As an extension agent, in addition to providing technical information, I must also be a listening and empathic ear. A big part of my job is to provide support when farmers have had a disaster and don't know how they are going to make ends meet. The hardest thing I do is work with a grower who has suffered a huge loss—like when their equipment fails the night they need freeze protection, and they lose an entire strawberry or peach crop, or when they must abandon a field for economic reasons.

To be sustainable, farmers need to be able to make more money selling their crop than they put into growing their crop. Inputs like seeds, soil amendments, labor, fuel, equipment, and packaging are costly. When the cost to harvest a crop outweighs its revenue potential, the farmer is faced with the decision to abandon the field because it is no longer an economically sound venture. For example: If the market price for cabbage is $3.00 per box, but the cost of harvesting and getting it to market is $6.50 per box, then the harsh economics will likely lead the farmer to terminate the crop. After all their financial investments and sweat equity, leaving your crop in the field is a very difficult and disheartening decision. Farmers need encouragement and support when dealing with abandonment.

Consumer challenges

Consumers likely never know about farmers having to abandon their fields—due to economics or weather-related events. Nor do consumers, who have come to expect perfect produce, understand the impact of rejecting food with imperfections. Imperfections do not affect food's nutritional value. I wish consumers would understand and accept minor levels of insect damage; it is not threatening from a food safety perspective at all. It is a whole lot healthier and safer to eat a strawberry after a pest has been on it than after a chemical has been applied to it. This education of consumers is just as important as my education of farmers.

My career goal, for over four decades, has been to help farmers solve their agricultural problems and grow their crops more sustainably. The farmer is the star. I am their advocate, advisor, support system, and sounding board. I like remembering those extension agents who helped my grandparents on their farm many years ago, and I hope that I am providing the same beneficial support and help to farmers today. ❧

Ricky Hacker and Matt McIntosh
EVO (Extra Virgin Oven) Pizzeria

*H*aving worked for one of Charleston's most renowned chefs, James Beard Award win-
ner Mike Lata of FIG, these two culinary entrepreneurs and business partners
decided to make the leap into opening their own restaurant—a wood-fired pizzeria using local
ingredients. Wildly successful, they have since opened an artisan bakery and are also creating
artisan chocolates.

From dream to reality

Matt: A restaurant kitchen is a demanding and intense place—mostly controlled chaos—and a chef is
in the midst of all that high pressure. After a few years
working in other chefs' kitchens, Ricky and I decided
to make a go of it with our own business. It's a big
risk; becoming a chef-owner takes lots of guts and
natural instincts. The amount of work and commitment to take the dream of owning our own restaurant and make it a reality started with a huge leap of

faith along with the motivation to provide a culinary
experience that was different and spectacular.

Our dreams started percolating in the kitchen of
FIG, where Ricky and I met in 2003. Originally from
Indiana, I moved to Charleston in 1998 to attend
Johnson & Wales University. I worked at Blossom,
McCrady's, and Normandy Farms, where I was Head
Artisan Baker, before going to FIG. Farmer Celeste
Albers, Chef Mike Lata, and I started the Charleston

▲ Above photo: Matt and Ricky.

Chapter of Slow Food, an international nonprofit, which focuses on regional cuisine and sourcing directly from local farmers.

Ricky: I hail from Maryland, graduated from the Culinary Institute of America, and moved to Charleston in 2003 to become sous chef at FIG. Matt and I cultivated our dream of starting a restaurant during long hours in the kitchen together. With Matt's background in artisan breads and experience with wood-fired ovens, we decided to break out on our own in 2005, incorporating baking, culinary arts, and locally sourced products into our restaurant. That led us to pizza—wood-fired pizza with local ingredients.

We owe a lot to Chef Lata; he taught us well. He is a perfectionist and a great mentor. He was pushing the farm-to-table idea before it became popular. Chef Lata, along with Chefs Glenn Roberts, Frank Lee, and

Sean Brock, are a big reason Charleston holds high status in the restaurant scene. These four chefs are responsible for bringing the focus on local foods and regional cuisine to light on a national level, too.

A mobile pizza cart

Our initial idea was to start with the bricks and mortar, but Matt was twenty-six, I was twenty-three, and we both had recently purchased houses. Since we didn't have the resources for a restaurant, we started small, very small, with a stainless steel wood-fired pizza cart, five by six feet long, that rested on two axles.

Matt: In 2005, in the days before food trucks in Charleston, we debuted EVO Pizzeria at the Charleston Farmers Market. Working next to an 800°F wood-fired oven in Charleston's sultry

We pride ourselves on sourcing from local farmers. We like supporting people within our community and region, we like keeping our dollars local, and we like knowing we have the freshest, most nutritious ingredients.

summer heat was grueling, but people recognized that we were providing something new and different. Our wood-fired oven was throwing off heat, the aroma of our homemade dough and tomato sauce was wafting through the air, and our hand-pulled mozzarella and fresh, local produce were waking up taste buds. We struck on something pretty revolutionary. Something delicious! And we are happy and very grateful that the customers agreed. But we needed to go beyond farmers markets, and started scrambling for catering and special event jobs.

Taming a wild beast

Two years later, in 2007, we opened the brick and mortar home of EVO Pizzeria in the Park Circle neighborhood of North Charleston where we serve wood-fired pizza along with soups, sandwiches, and salads. Everything is made in-house—our mozzarella,

breads, dough, sausage meat, and sauce. Purchasing a couple hundred pounds of curd each week from the same local purveyor provides us with a consistent taste and texture for our homemade mozzarella.

Wood-fired ovens are the rustic way of cooking and provide a complete flavor; however, they are unforgiving, difficult, and can be as unpredictable as a wild beast. Our oven is the real deal, not assisted by gas or electricity. We are baking pizzas at 800°F rather than 400°F, so the cooking time is a super quick two minutes.

In addition to quality ingredients, attaining the best firewood is essential. In the past ten years, we have purchased our firewood from probably twenty different suppliers. The Lowcountry is like a swamp with its steamy, humid climate. Green, damp wood doesn't burn quickly, and can literally shut our whole kitchen operation down. When cooking barbeque, you want the wood to burn slow, low, and smoky.

But with pizza, we need super hard woods like oak, hickory, or pecan that will burn hot. We have a little lean-to out back for storing wood, and we recently started purchasing kiln-dried wood, which is baked at 200°F to remove the moisture. We pay more for it, but it is more consistent, reliable, and provides assurance that the wood is going to burn properly.

More of a good thing

Ricky: After starting the pizzeria, we realized that consumers yearned for artisan breads, so five years later, we opened EVO Craft Bakery. The shop is adjacent to the pizzeria and serves pastries, cookies, and specialty breads. We also sell to local restaurants, retailers, farmers markets, the local food hub, GrowFood Carolina, and to SILO (Sea Islands Local Outlet), the online local food market.

In 2015, we purchased Sweeteeth Chocolate confections. So now we have added hand making small-batch artisan chocolate bars to our repertoire. Sweeteeth is famous for innovative taste combinations, like Sea is for Caramel, which pairs a 65% dark chocolate with burnt caramel and local sea salt. We print our own labels and hand-wrap each chocolate bar. Sweeteeth Chocolates are marketed throughout Charleston at the same venues as our bakery items.

From co-workers, to friends, to partners running a pizza cart together, and finally, to chef-owners of a restaurant, bakery, and signature confectioner, our growth has been a natural progression. But, each new step has required a leap of faith, determination and effort, and we have enjoyed every part of the adventure. It took four years before we felt comfortable enough not to be at the restaurant all day.

Five years after opening, a local chef started working for free on her available weekends. She progressed to part-time, then full-time sous chef, and is now our executive chef. Our general manager started out as a server, was promoted quickly to manager, and has been with us for five years. We have had great luck keeping terrific staff, which is very tough to do in this industry. EVO has about thirty employees; seven or eight are in the kitchen and bakery and the rest are servers. The relationships we have developed with our employees, our customers, and our farmer partners are enduring.

We pride ourselves on sourcing from local farmers and using as many local ingredients as we can. We like supporting people within our community and region, we like keeping our dollars local, and we like knowing we have the freshest, most nutritious ingredients. We work closely with local farmers, visit their farms, and discuss our future needs. The names of our farmer-partners are displayed prominently on a chalkboard over our bar and wood-fired oven. We hope to inspire our customers to get to know their farmers, recognize the quality of good, local ingredients, and buy local foods.

Eleven years ago, with a tiny wood-fired pizza cart, we followed our dreams into farmers markets, hustling for business. One artisan restaurant, bakery, and chocolate confectioner later, we are on the cusp of opening a second EVO Pizzeria restaurant soon. Our dreams, passion, and leaps of faith continue! ❧

Eric McClam
City Roots

ity Roots is a unique and robust enterprise—the first urban farm in South Carolina. Eric and his father, Robbie, worked with the city of Columbia to rewrite the zoning laws so a vacant lot in an industrial zone could be transformed and used for agriculture. Now this once vacant lot is City Roots, an urban farm that successfully grows seasonally diversified, certified-organic field crops year-round. It has three greenhouses of microgreens, one of which is aquaponic and produces tilapia, watercress, and nasturtiums. City Roots uses innovative no-till conservation techniques on the land and creates soil through vermiculture and composting. City Roots has a retail store and events, which provide other revenue streams to augment the crop production. This farm is a community asset and an excellent model for successfully growing food in an urban setting. I'm hopeful this model will be replicated throughout the state and nation.

Architects of an urban farm

Unpredictable events led my life in the most unforeseen direction. After receiving my graduate degree in architecture from Tulane University, I expected to follow my passion directly into that field. Nevertheless, after the economy's 2008 crash, the market was not conducive to hiring architects. Around that time,

Initially, we intended to get an agricultural variance for our urban farm, but realized it would be more forward thinking to work with the city to rewrite their zoning laws so all industrial zones could be used for agricultural purposes.

my parents, both semi-retired professionals, heard an NPR program about an urban farmer in Milwaukee successfully growing food year-round in the heart of the city. It was Will Allen's nonprofit called Growing Power, and his mission is to teach others about sustainable urban food production. Inspired and motivated, my dad journeyed to Milwaukee and spent three months learning about commercial urban agriculture.

Upon his return, Dad was sold on the idea of creating a farm in the city of Columbia, and he commissioned me to design and construct some buildings and help start the farm with him. I expected to stick around for a couple of months, but here I am seven years later. I fell in love with urban food production. I even declined a job offer from the architectural firm I had originally wanted to work for. My passions changed course as I went from architect to urban farmer.

Our first hurdle was finding an appropriate site for an urban farm. My dad, also an architect, had been director of the Columbia Development Corporation, a nonprofit that buys, holds, and resells land for the city. The development corporation owned the site we are on now, but it was zoned industrial. Initially, we intended to get an agricultural variance for our urban farm, but realized it would be more forward thinking to work with the city to rewrite the zoning laws so all industrial zones could be used for agricultural purposes.

The city agreed, and after six months, we leased this nearly three-acre vacant and undeveloped field. My father and I designed and built our main building, modeled on an old tobacco barn like the one my dad worked in as a youth. It serves as our office, retail space, refrigerated storage, and place to wash and pack our produce. The building is naturally ventilated with lots of windows, doors, and a clerestory, which allows the hot summer air to rise, eliminating the need for and expense of air conditioning.

With the infrastructure in place, it was time to get down to farming. We brought in eighty truckloads of highly fertile soil and started growing field crops year-round. Our shoulder season or cool weather crops are turnips, radishes, beets, carrots, lettuces, arugula, kale, collards, bok choy, kohlrabi, and mustard greens. We over-winter with the brassicas—broccoli, cabbages, collards, and kale. In the spring and summer, we grow strawberries, blueberries, and blackberries for our U-Pick, and tomatoes, potatoes, squash, peppers, onions, eggplants, peas, and beans. We also grow and sell cut flowers.

City Roots is both GAP (Good Agricultural Practices) and organic certified. We use micro-drip irrigation to conserve water, and we cover crop to enhance the soil. We received a USDA Natural Resources Conservation Service Conservation Innovation Grant to help us convert to no-till, a farming technique in which the soil is not disturbed by tillage. In the no-till plots, we plant multi-species cover crops, primarily crimson clover and Abruzzi rye. Crimson clover is a legume that adds nitrogen to the soil. Abruzzi rye adds carbon and is allelopathic, which means it suppresses weed growth and hinders germination of other plants. After the cover crops enhance the soil, we roll or mow those crops, leave them on the field, and plant directly through them, which preserves moisture and soil health, and increases yield.

Nutritionally dense microgreens

Microgreens have become our bread and butter crop. Microgreens are the first two leaves, the dicot-cotyledon, that emerge from the seed. The nutritional density stored in the seed is transferred to the first leaves, making them three to five times more nutritious than the full-grown plant.

Growing microgreens is a labor-intensive process. We build the flats, seed them, tamp them down, and cover them to germinate in the dark. When we uncover them, the leaves are yellow and turn green with sunlight. We grow them a few more days, harvest them with sheers, wash, package, and send them out to market.

The organic certification process for microgreens

is the same as it is for field crops. We purchase organic seeds and keep meticulous records. We also work with a soil scientist. Our soil originally came from the city's compost, but now we are vermi-composting, using red wigglers and other earthworms to decompose our vegetable wastes. We add peat moss and vermiculite to the worm castings, screen it, and use it as our nutrient-rich soil mix.

The microgreens we produce are arugula, radish, beet, cilantro, snow pea, sunflower, amaranth, red sorrel, and fennel. Different plants require different microclimates. Fortunately, we have a great greenhouse manager who has figured out the microclimates in each of our three greenhouses—totaling 6,000 square feet of microgreen production.

City Roots is one of the larger microgreen growers in the country. There are many appealing things about growing microgreens—seed to harvest is only about a week, weather isn't an issue in the greenhouse, it's easy to scale production up or down based on demand, and they have a much higher profitability than field crops.

Diversification of revenue streams

Using aquaponics, a system that combines aquaculture and hydroponics, we are raising 1,000 tilapia and growing nasturtiums and watercress. It's a neat, closed-loop symbiotic system. Water is pumped from the bottom of the fish tank to the other end of the greenhouse where we have raised beds in four inches of river rock, an excellent growing medium for the root systems of the plants. The nutrient-rich water trickles over the river rock, the plants uptake the nutrients and filter the water, which trickles back and cascades into the pool, adding oxygen for the fish.

Chefs love our nasturtiums. We make more money selling the nasturtiums and watercress than selling the fish. We sell the tilapia live on ice, because we are not licensed to process them.

City Roots recently added oyster mushrooms to our crop portfolio. The start-up costs are relatively inexpensive, we already have an existing market, and we are getting a good return. We mix mycelium

spawn with wheat straw and stuff it into bags, then we hang them in the fruiting room to colonize and fruit. The same bag can re-fruit for a couple weeks. From spawn to harvest takes about five weeks. Like our microgreens, mushrooms are a year-round product that receive a great price and don't depend on weather.

Dad and I gave a lot of thought about strategies to strengthen the sustainability of our urban farm. We created year-round crop diversity and multiple revenue streams. We use the farm as a multipurpose space and are experimenting with agritourism—the intersection between agriculture and tourism. Bringing visitors to the farm has helped us both financially and with marketing. This year our Mardi Gras event drew around 2,500 visitors, and our Tomato Festival attracted almost 4,000. We rent the farm for private events—weddings and nonprofit fundraisers. Once a month we host a farm-to-table dinner out in the field. We seat about 100 people and provide a four-course dinner paired with wine and beer. The produce is sourced from our farm, and the meat and seafood are sourced from other local purveyors. We partner with an event planner. Multiple revenue streams provide more financial sustainability, enabling us to hire more year-round employees and pay better wages.

City Roots produce is marketed in a variety of ways. We have a retail store here at the farm and a CSA (Community Supported Agriculture) membership of about 100 folks. We sell to more than twenty-five restaurants around Columbia, and sell about ten percent of our overall production to GrowFood Carolina, the food distribution hub in Charleston, which distributes to chefs and retailers in that local market. We also wholesale our microgreens to Atlanta, Hilton Head, Charlotte, and to all thirty-two Whole Foods Markets in this region.

Within five years, City Roots has become a successful and growing urban farm. We've had to lease another five acres at a local school to meet our increased demand. We operate sustainably, are certified organic, and are proving that urban farming can be a viable year-round business. The key is diversification of crops and revenue streams. Although I did not become an architect by profession, I have, along with my dad, become an architect of sustainable, organic urban farming, and I am passionate about this livelihood! ✍

Brian Evans
Halo Greens LLC

I visited Brian on a remote sliver of land at the tip of Wadmalaw Island a couple weeks after a historic twenty-three-inch rain. Although the flooding stranded him on the island, his aquaponic vertical farm suffered no problems. Brian is a young and creative entrepreneur, a designer, builder, chemist, and botanist. He's putting his energy into something important for the future of farming that is transferrable on a larger scale to urban and global settings. His system is innovative with its decreased needs for physical space, water consumption, fertilizer, and labor.

A nutrient rich cycle

I am growing food in a vertical system using aquaponics. Aquaponics is a symbiotic combination of aquaculture—raising aquatic animals in a tank, plus hydroponics—cultivating plants in water. The nutrient-rich water from the aquaculture system is fed to the hydroponic system, where it nourishes the plants and is circulated back to the aquaculture system.

I grow my plants in 100 vertical towers. Each tower is five feet tall with ten plants per tower. This system enables a thousand plants in a growing space that is six feet by forty feet. In typical gardening, that would require at least a tenth of an acre, more than 4,000 square feet.

The convergence of three passions

I'm not from a farming family, so this is all pretty new to me. While serving in the Navy, I developed more of an interest in food and health, and I became very curious about aquaponics. In 2014, after the Navy, I moved to Charleston with a veteran buddy. We both planned on exploring jobs in the food and beverage industry.

Fortunately, my path led me to some amazing people—the nationally renowned chef of FIG, Jason Stanhope, who won the James Beard Award for Best Chef Southeast in 2015; Frasier Block, manager of the Johns Island Farmers Market, who has a heart-felt vision of promoting health and sustainable agriculture through local food; and consumers, who want healthy, fresh, and flavorful products. These relationships inspired me to become a part of the local food movement. I also love chemistry, fish, and plants. I chased those three passions, and they led me to start an aquaponics farming business.

A Kickstarter beginning

In May of 2015, after lots of research on vertical farming and aquaponics, I designed my farm and raised $12,700 through a Kickstarter campaign. Since I am renting this land, and my greenhouse is a temporary structure, I didn't pour cement; instead I leveled the land and built a high tunnel greenhouse using two by fours for the base. The greenhouse has a six-millimeter-thick plastic that is infrared protective with anti-condensation qualities. The transparent material removes ultraviolet rays, but maintains

The main advantage of vertical growing is that the growing towers require a small amount of space to produce a lot of food, and they use eighty percent less water than conventional farming.

the red and blue spectrum that plants need. I worked from dawn to dusk throughout the summer and built this structure with occasional help from some friends, when more than two hands were required.

Unfortunately, my vertical farm will never meet USDA organic standards. The two by fours used for the greenhouse base are directly on the ground with no cement foundation, so I needed to use treated wood. None of my plants come into contact with the soil on the ground, but the use of treated wood nullifies any organic certification. In a way, I feel my operation is even better than organic, because other than minimal supplements and natural sprays, if necessary, to battle pests, the fish are supplying all the nutrients for the plants.

On the aquaponic side

I have a 275-gallon well water tank underground, covered with an insulating tarp to keep the water temperature around 70-80°F, which is the optimum temperature for my fish, and I have a 1,000-gallon fish tank with about 100 fish. Water returned to the fish tank creates a swirling action, which helps move the solid fish waste to the middle of the tank where a pipe with holes sucks water and solids from the bottom. The wastes are transferred to another pipe that supplies this nutrient-rich water to the plants. After cycling through the plants, it returns to the fish as purified water. In this way, the two systems work together, recycling water and nutrients.

For six weeks prior to putting plants or fish in the system, it is critical to establish a bacteria colony to handle the ammonia produced by the fish waste. The bacteria convert the fish waste to plant-available nutrients. I created a bacteria colony in the plantless and fishless system by adding household ammonia every day. Bacteria developed to break down the ammonia. Initially, nitrites appeared on my chemical readings, and then nitrates. It is the nitrates that allow the nutrients to become available for the plants' use. My chemistry and biology classes from years ago helped me understand this part of the process. I test the water daily to determine if I have the proper

pH and micronutrients for optimum plant growth and fish survival.

I feed the fish with an organic feed provided by Aqua-Organic, the only organic fish food available in the United States. I cover my fish tank with a black tarp to prevent algae from growing, because algae, which need sunlight to grow, will compete with the fish for nutrients.

I purchased channel catfish from Southland Fisheries in South Carolina. I'm using a local fish that I knew would thrive in this environment. The most common fish for aquaponic farming are tilapia, but they are not indigenous to our area, and I didn't want a fish that could potentially become an invasive species. Because the fish can't breed in this tank, I will need to replace them eventually. Younger fish are best for aquaponics, because they eat more, swim more, and produce more waste and nutrients for the plants. I purchase fish when they are young so they will easily transplant, adapt, and thrive in this environment. The catfish are currently about five inches long, and in six to eight months they will grow to one and a half pounds. I chose a fish that was edible, and at that size, catfish will be fine for a fish fry.

The hydroponics part

Working symbiotically, the nutrient-rich water from the aquaculture system is fed to the hydroponic system to nourish the plants. Inside each of my vertical plant towers is a matrix media, a flexible and lightweight insert made of recycled water bottles. The media is ninety percent air, providing great aeration and filtration for the nutrient-rich water. Seven to ten gallons of water drip through the towers per hour. If the plant doesn't need the water, it passes through. The matrix media provides extensive biological surfaces for nitrates and other beneficial bacteria. Additionally, I sprinkle wiggler worms on top, which provide more nutrient-rich materials and throw in a vermiculture component to the system.

I grow all my plants from seed, starting them in plug trays. I buy from both Baker's Creek Organic seeds and Johnny's Seeds. It is important to purchase seeds from more than one source and to keep changing the genome. To plant the seedlings in the tower, I pull the matrix media out with a hook, open it, apply a water-absorbing wicking strip, lay the plant's roots on the strip, close it, push it back into the tower, and hang it up.

I've started with easy and well-tested plants, and I'm already seeing success. I planted rainbow chard, lettuce, parsley, lemongrass, oregano, mint, chives, and some varieties of basil. After harvesting, many plants grow back; others I replant, rotating them into the medium of a different tower.

Testing the waters

The main advantage of vertical growing is that the growing towers require a small amount of space to produce a lot of food, and they use eighty percent less water than conventional farming. And, a benefit that I didn't anticipate—I can stand up to farm, rather than hunch over back-breaking rows in a field. I have the system up and running, and it is a very manageable workload.

This is my first season. Halo Greens is a start-up business testing the waters, so to speak, and I am patiently seeing what works best. Much of this is trial and error. But my focus is to grow delicious greens and herbs and to create a successful farming business.

Initially, I am marketing and distributing my greens at the year-round Johns Island Farmers Market. My vertical towers are portable, which allows me to take them to the market so customers can harvest their own greens and herbs. It is a great interactive way to allow people to learn about the food they eat. I've also been talking with chefs around town, and my market research is positive for restaurant sales potential.

The future of farming

I'm a risk taker and an entrepreneur. I have loved researching, designing, and building this self-sustaining aquaponics system from scratch. Seeing it go from a plan on paper to reality has been very satisfying. I'd like to eventually design aquaponics systems for others, as it could be the future of farming. Eighty percent of the farmers in the United States are over sixty years old. I see aquaponics as a way to encourage young people to get involved in farming. I want my system to have a larger impact —to be community strengthening, environmentally friendly, and self-sustaining. To that end, I have a lot more work to do, but the sky is the limit. ❧

Carmen Ketron and Noni Langford
Medical University of South Carolina's Urban Farm

The campus of the Medical University of South Carolina (MUSC), a public institution with Schools of Medicine, Nursing, Dentistry, Graduate Studies, Health Professions, and Pharmacy, spans eighty acres in downtown Charleston. Because many healthcare needs relate to poor diet, university president Ray Greenberg (2000-2013) felt it was important to integrate the built environment with the outdoor environment. His efforts to promote healthy behaviors and eating habits inspired the creation of the MUSC Urban Farm, The Porcher Medicinal Garden, and the MUSC Arboretum.

I wandered into the farm by chance one day, where Noni Langford, the project coordinator at that time, showed me a small paradise within an urban setting. Noni now works full-time designing residential homes, but remains involved with the urban farm in every free moment. Farm educator Carmen Ketron brings expertise and enthusiasm, and welcomes all into this urban sanctuary.

▲ Above photo: Noni.

I have a heartfelt passion for making MUSC's Urban Farm an inviting refuge and sanctuary, because of my experiences with my children, Joe and Maggie, who were both critically and terminally ill at this hospital.

From parking lot to farm

Noni: The MUSC Urban Farm was started in 2013 on what used to be a surface parking lot. Competition for valuable real estate in downtown Charleston is fierce, and this farm on a prime half-acre of space clearly manifested the values of Dr. Greenberg and others at MUSC. Visitors walk through and visually experience the farm's beauty, rub their fingers on fragrant herbs, learn about different crops, and put their hands in the dirt. They make the connection between what we eat and our health.

Beautiful and inviting, this entire medical campus is a Trees Campus USA, a nationally recognized designation by the Arbor Day Foundation for effectively managing college campus trees. Every tree on the grounds is in the process of being recorded and monitored, and most have identification labels. MUSC has twenty-six ornamental flower gardens and multiple fountains. The Porcher Medicinal Garden, in honor of alumnus, professor, and Civil War doctor Francis Peyre Porcher, is one of my favorites. There are over forty medicinal plants each identified with medicinal uses, like digitalis to slow blood flow.

I have a heartfelt passion for making MUSC's Urban Farm an inviting refuge and sanctuary, because of my experiences with my children, Joe and Maggie, who were both critically and terminally ill at this hospital. When you have a loved one who is in the hospital for a very long time, the days revolve around when the doctor is going to make rounds and when the best nurses are on duty. There were many days I never went outdoors, and when I did, I didn't really have anywhere to go to seek peace.

Unfortunately, the MUSC Urban Farm was not operating when my kids were here, but after our time in the hospital, I decided to get my degree in horticulture, work outdoors, and grow things. I ended up back here to help build the garden. It is so meaningful for me to cultivate a restorative space, grow healthy food, and share this farm with patients' families, doctors, students, and others. It is a place to sit in silence, watch the butterflies and bees pollinating flowers, or learn about different crops and how to cook them. It's a living, growing, and reinvigorating place of health.

After the garden was built, we realized it was difficult to push wheelchairs on the mulch between the garden beds. We received a grant from a local foundation to widen the paths, put down a surface that drains well and accommodates wheelchairs, enlarge the patio space under the shady live oak tree, add picnic tables and benches, and invest in some garden trugs. Garden trugs are elevated garden beds designed at an angle so wheelchair-bound people of all ages can access the plants and enjoy gardening too.

We grow a diverse selection of crops, and depending on the season, we have a mix of fruits, vegetables, herbs, and flowers. At the entrance to the garden, there is a kiosk with information describing each item growing at the moment—its nutritional value, how to plant and harvest it at home, and recipes from our Sodexo dining services chefs and nutritionists.

Education and inspiration

Carmen: The MUSC Urban Farm runs year-round, planting and harvesting many varieties of fruits, vegetables, and herbs. MUSC and the Medical Hospital Authority fund the garden jointly, and its operation is overseen by a multi-disciplinary team with personnel from community outreach, marketing, food safety, and nutritional education. I am the only paid farm staff member.

As the farm educator, I handle the educational and team building programs, workshops, and events. I train and coordinate the garden volunteers, who are rewarded for their services in a shared bounty of the farm's harvest. We offer a variety of volunteer programs, which are open to the entire community. We also have trained "farmhand" volunteers, who work when their schedule permits, needing very little direction from me. I oversee all the planting, harvesting, weeding, and Integrated Pest Management.

▲ Carmen.

The farm is designed for hands-on experience, and I provide classes for people who are interested in learning. Our "Weekly Events Calendar" is posted online and here at the kiosk. We usually have three programs a week in our "Work and Learn" sessions. During those programs, I focus on various topics including nutrition, garden pests, organic practices, and planting and harvesting.

The MUSC Urban Farm initiative, "Coupons for Crops" is a rewards program in which hospital department heads and managers recognize outstanding staff. MUSC employees bring their coupon to the garden and choose some herbs, vegetables, or fruit they would like me to harvest for them. It is another nice way to get more people into the garden, let them learn what we do, and provide them with healthy food choices.

Natural and efficient growing practices

The MUSC Urban Farm is not certified organic, but we practice organic principles and use no herbicides or pesticides. We rotate our crops, practice companion planting, and grow flowers to attract pollinators and marigolds to prevent nematodes. Companion planting is a great way to decrease pests. One trick I use is planting rows of garlic, onions, or leeks to create a barrier of tastes and smells that pests don't like. If we have an infestation, the pests will be stopped by this barrier as they try to move across the garden.

I also practice Integrated Pest Management (IPM) and pay close attention to the life cycle of insects and their role in the food web in our garden. If we have a caterpillar problem, what we really have is a parasitic wasp problem—meaning we don't have enough parasitic wasps in the garden to control our caterpillar problem. I let our dill and fennel go to seed to form small flowers that attract parasitic wasps. The wasps lay eggs in the caterpillars, eventually killing the caterpillars. We have ladybugs that eat our aphids, and we also use natural-forming bacteria, called milky spore, to kill aphid larvae. These are natural ways to keep a balanced control. Balance is key when practicing IPM. Not all caterpillars are detrimental to crops. They metamorphose into butterflies and moths, and are important insect pollinators of our food.

If we have a caterpillar problem, what we really have is a parasitic wasp problem—meaning we don't have enough parasitic wasps in the garden to control our caterpillar problem.

A honey bee observation hive was donated to MUSC's Urban Farm by The Bee Cause Project, and we are the first teaching campus in South Carolina to be nationally certified as a BEE CAMPUS USA, designating our campus as pollinator friendly. Bees are often regarded as menacing, but they are major pollinators of crops worldwide, and our food systems are dependent upon them. I keep flowering plants year-round and plant mostly yellow and blue flowering plants—colors that attract bees the most. It is especially important to provide a food source for the bees during the winter, so I let my brassicas go to

seed for them. Honey bees are an important part of our learning program at the farm. We advocate and build public awareness for how critical they are to our food system.

To grow crops most efficiently, I plant companion crops vertically as well as horizontally. I will plant a taller item, like climbing beans, and in the understory, I will plant cilantro, baby squash, lettuce, and beets. The annual herb borage is a companion plant to strawberries. I recently did a trial of strawberry rows with no borage, a little borage, and lots of borage. I found that the more borage, the greater the strawberry yield, as well as a lesser amount of pest

infestation and sunscald. Also, the blue flowers of borage attract the bees, which then visit and pollinate the white flowers of strawberries. We cover crop with edible peas because most other cover crops would proliferate past the garden and into the surrounding manicured landscaping.

Nutrition for the body and soul

In addition to sharing the farm's bounty with volunteers and "Coupon for Crops" employees, MUSC's food service, Sodexo, uses our produce. We can only provide a small quantity, but sometimes they feature our herbs, swiss chard, or other produce in the cafeteria. They put a little sign with the MUSC Urban Farm logo on it, which helps bring awareness to the program. Any leftover harvest is donated to a local food bank. MUSC Urban Farm meets all the Department of Health and Environmental Control requirements.

Oftentimes, I find people standing outside the gates and looking in, but they don't step into the farm assuming it is a research lab. I've started leaving the gates open as a subtle invitation, but we need some welcome signs inviting visitors to wander around, smell the herbs, watch the bees, sit in the shade, and contemplate. Sadly, getting patients out of their hospital rooms and into the farm can be a challenge because they need someone to bring them here. Maybe there will be another volunteer program developed to fill this need.

The mission of the MUSC Urban Farm is to build a healthier community by growing crops and social connections while educating and inspiring people about local, nutritious, and delicious food. We are successfully fulfilling that mission! The farm and its learning opportunities are open to everyone on campus—students, doctors, patients, visitors—and off campus to the greater Charleston community.

I encourage everyone to visit. Come, wander among the rows of vegetables, and find nutrition and sanctuary for the body and soul. ❧

Michael and Lauren Bailey
Veggie Bin

Remember the neighborhood grocery store—the small market on the corner where everyone knew each other and food was harvested from the farm earlier that morning? I am dating myself, but back in the day on the mountain where I grew up, the storeowner farmed and his family ran the store.

The small neighborhood grocery store Veggie Bin is a favorite place to shop in Charleston, because it consistently carries local items—meats, cheeses, eggs, fruits, and vegetables. Husband and wife team Michael and Lauren are co-owners and managers of the family grocery store. They do it all—from placing orders, meeting the farmers with their deliveries, stocking the shelves, maintaining the inventory, and working the register.

Four generations of local

Michael: Although we've recently moved to a new location, Veggie Bin has operated as a retail store for almost fifty years. My great-grandfather started a wholesale business, the John T. Leonard Storage Company in the early 1900s. Located at what is now the historical façade of the Bennett Rice Mill at the Port of Charleston, he shipped rice, flour, sugar, and potatoes up and down the East Coast by boat and later by rail. My grandfather continued the wholesale business, but saw a need in 1976 and opened

Maintaining the relationships with the farming community that my great-grandfather established four generations ago is important to us.

a retail grocery store nearby. My parents ran The Vegetable Bin on East Bay Street until 2005. Three years later Lauren, my brother Will, my cousin Billy Leonard, and I took over.

I started working in the store when I was thirteen and have been working here for the past twenty-four years. Lauren started with us in 2002, when she was a student at the College of Charleston. We have been married now for five years. We moved to this location on Spring Street in 2014.

Maintaining the relationships with the farming community that my great-grandfather established four generations ago is important to us. We like supporting family farms like Freeman Farms on Johns Island. My grandfather was a friend and customer of Mr. Freeman's grandfather. My parents bought produce from his son, Earl, and we keep that relationship with his and several other multi-generation family farms. It is our double mission to support local farmers and provide our customers with a consistent supply of the best fresh, local, and seasonal foods. This mission is beneficial to all.

A neighborhood market

This new location is ideal. It's great being in a residential neighborhood. We've built a customer base quickly, and business is going well. Students from the Medical University of South Carolina and the College of Charleston, neighborhood residents, and many popular restaurants surround us. Most of our clients walk to get their groceries.

We purchase a little more than half of our local products directly from Johns Island farmers. The rest we get from GrowFood Carolina and Limehouse Produce. The sales team from GrowFood calls and tells us what local foods are available each week; we place our order and they deliver. Our Mepkin Abbey oyster and shitake mushrooms come from Limehouse. We make little signs that say LOCAL and mark all local produce with each farm's name.

Veggie Bin stocks as much organic food as we can. Many farmers grow organically, but are not willing to go through the burdensome process of becoming certified. We know each of our farmers and how they farm, and trust in their nurturing care for the health of their soil, water supply, and pollinators.

Right now we have certified organic kale, red kale, collards, mustard greens, and spring onions. In the summertime, we have local blueberries, strawberries, peaches, squashes, cucumbers, tomatoes, and corn. There's nothing like freshly picked corn! During the shoulder months, we carry the brassicas (vegetables like cabbage, Brussels sprouts, and broccoli) along with a variety of hydroponics (tomatoes, cucumbers, and microgreens).

Many of our local foods are available year-round: meats—rabbit, lamb, chicken, beef and pork sausages, ham, and chops; a variety of eggs—duck, chicken, and goose; dairy—milk, butter, cheeses, and yogurt; hydroponic lettuce, tomatoes, cucumbers and microgreens; pastas; and local rice, grits, nuts, canola oil, and sea salt.

We feel it is important to support our local community of farmers by providing them with a market and consistent demand, and we appreciate our clientele, who faithfully support our retail business. Buying locally contributes to relationships and connections that better our community. We love our work and are dedicated to continuing the family business in a city that cares about small family farms and small family retail businesses. ❧

Greg and Monica Tatis &
Pete and Heather Holmes
Charleston Artisan Cheesehouse

I spent eight hours with the Charleston Artisan Cheesehouse team learning about the process of making cheese—from milk delivery to pouring the curds into molds to wrapping, labeling, and packing products for market. Now that I understand the time, care, science, and craft involved in making delicious cheeses, I have a new appreciation and marvel that such culinary delights are not exorbitantly expensive. Every Saturday, depending on which farmers market I attend, I see Greg, Pete, or Heather surrounded by customers, and I delight in the success of their new venture.

Great cheese starts with great farmers

Greg: Hickory Hill Dairy in Edgefield, South Carolina, is a family-owned business that has been in operation for 250 years. They raise Holstein-Jersey cows

▲ Above: Pete, Heather, Monica, and Greg.

that are pasture grazed for eighteen hours per day and produce milk with high fat content. The dairy uses low temperature pasteurization, which heats the milk slowly to 160°F and cools it quickly. That process maintains the healthy enzymes and the desirable characteristics we want for cheesemaking. Charleston Artisan Cheesehouse only uses non-homogenized whole milk from Hickory Hill Dairy.

Our delicious cheeses start with a great dairy farmer's hard work and his well-bred, humanely-raised cows.

Pete: Each day that we make a batch of brie cheese, our milk is delivered in 156 one-gallon containers, a situation that fortunately will change when we move to a better location. As it is, each container must be individually sanitized, opened, poured into the cheese vat, crushed, and taken to a recycling center. Not having the space for a milk tank complicates our production and makes this first step very time consuming. However, before jumping into a larger space and lease commitment, we wanted to see if our business would succeed.

Twelve months ago, when we started Charleston Artisan Cheesehouse, Greg was making one or two batches of brie per month. He started creating unique flavors of brie cheeses, and demand increased to three or four batches per month. Now, we are doing three or four batches per week.

Science, math, and art

Greg: We pour the 156 gallons of milk into this jacketed vat, a huge stainless steel double boiler with hot water flowing through it. This is the only way to heat milk without scalding it. When the milk gets to the desired temperature, I add the first cultures, also known as starters, which ripen the milk by converting milk sugars into lactic acid. Cheese starters consist of lactic bacteria that digest lactose to produce lactic acid. The acid starts the cheesemaking process by forming curds. I incorporate the cultures into the milk by gently moving the milk from the bottom up using a shovel. As artisan cheesemakers, we don't use any mechanical mixers. I let the cultures and milk rest for sixty minutes at a temperature specific for the recipe.

I have a cheese guru in Canada, who has won international awards for her cheesemaking. She provides me with technical advice and the unique French cultures for our cheeses. These cultures give Charleston Artisan Cheesehouse cheeses their distinct character, taste, and texture.

Pete: Although Greg is now a cheesemaker, he previously had an accomplished career as a chef. He was sous chef to Chef Paul Prudhomme for eight years at K-Paul's, first in New York, then in New Orleans.

He returned to New York, opened two Cajun grills, received many awards, and published a cookbook. After moving to Charleston, he became general manager at a brewery-restaurant. The restaurant's owner asked if he would lend his culinary expertise to help his son start a cheese company. After a couple years, the father and son decided to sell the business. At that time, my wife, Heather, and I were moving from New York City, and Greg and his wife, Monica, asked us to partner with them. The four of us purchased the company, and now our business, Charleston Artisan Cheesehouse, has caught fire.

While the milk culture rests for sixty minutes, we each move on to other jobs. Now Greg is working with the mozzarella curds. They have been steeping and softening in hot water and are ready to be pulled and shaped into balls and placed in brine to produce a nice salty flavor. Then we vacuum seal each in plastic wrap. Mozzarella doesn't need to age, so these 200 mozzarella balls will be ready for this Saturday's farmers markets.

Greg: Back to the culture I started an hour ago: It has rested with the rennet, and now I test it for a clean break. Using a horizontal and vertical curd cutter, I cut the curd into squares, and the curds and whey separate. Keeping it at the recipe-specific temperature, I stir it for about twenty minutes to promote the explosion of the whey. Cooking and agitating the curds make them firmer. When the curds reach the precise firmness, we drain the whey and pump it into large barrels, which will be picked up by a local hog farmer. When I stop stirring, the curds settle to the bottom of the vat, and I ladle the curds into Camembert block molds.

Distinct characteristics

Pete: For our brie-Camembert-style cheeses, our yield is approximately one pound of cheese per gallon of milk. We scoop the curds into molds and add flavors. Today, we are mixing black truffles and wild mushrooms in the molds to create a batch we call Wild Boar. Before leaving tonight, we will flip the cheeses so they will drain and be even on both sides. Tomorrow, we will brine them for two hours, dry them for a day, and place them in sealed aging tubs to maintain a stable temperature and humidity. Today's batch of brie-Camembert won't be ready for another six weeks.

In the past year, we have expanded our Camembert-style cheeses using spices from the Charleston Spice Company. When making This Spice Must Flow, we add a chipotle, peperoncino, smoked paprika blend; to French Quarter, we add an herb de Provence mixture. Our flavors are creative. We also make Battery Park, Brittany's Bleu, Dutch Chocolate, and more. We have a semi-firm Chardonnay Wash rind Tomme cheese that we dry-age for six months, wash again in Chardonnay, and age for another two weeks. Similarly, we create an Espresso Wash and Porter Wash.

We began with Camembert-style cheeses and expanded our inventory to include fresh mozzarella, aged farm-fresh cheddar, a cheddar that can be eaten immediately, and a pimento cream cheese called Charleston Caviar.

The process of making each cheese varies. We use cultures from France for all of our cheeses and keep a detailed batch log about everything— temperatures, pH, the time that cultures and rennet are added, how long each process rests, when we cut, pour, flip, and brine, and how long each batch is aged. Carefully documented notes and historical data enable us to both refine our cheesemaking skills and provide specific batch identification. We know the day each cheese was made and where it was distributed. We create our own labels digitally and include the South Carolina DHEC (Department of Health and Environmental Control) required information. We hand-wrap each brie round in a special cheese paper that allows the cheese to breathe, enabling proper rind formation.

Charleston Artisan Cheesehouse is prospering. We sell at twelve farmers markets; to retail stores like Whole Foods, Harris Teeter, and Ted's Butcher Block; and to restaurants like EVO, The Obstinate Daughter, and High Cotton. Our cheeses are also being distributed by wholesalers like Gourmet Foods International, GrowFood Carolina, and Pate Dawson Southern Foods.

Greg: Our delicious cheeses start with a great dairy farmer's hard work and his well-bred, humanely raised cows. We take it from there and apply our creativity and science and mathematical precision to the pH, salinity, and aging of the milk product. In artisan cheesemaking, nothing is mechanized. Everything is done by hand. Our techniques and craft create cheeses with distinct and complex characteristics, and inspire the simple pleasure of eating natural and locally produced foods. ❧

Joey Siconolfi
Frothy Beard Brewing Company

A joie de vivre clearly permeates the bar at the Frothy Beard Brewery. Although I didn't meet Joey's two partners to see if they also sported "staches and beards," the five beard taps led me to assume that they do. These brewmasters' wide range of creativity utilizing locally sourced fruits, vegetables, grains, and even mushrooms results in novel and unique taste experiences. Pictured with Joey are four of their top sellers—Hominy Cream Ale with grits; Horchata Stout with brown rice, cinnamon, vanilla, and cocoa; Andale, a jalapeño and cilantro pale ale; and Modified Neck Breaker, a double IPA with citrus-forward hops and local honey.

Homebrewing to craft brewery

While we were researching whether to get into the brewing business, my partners and I learned that sales of beer and ice cream are not negatively impacted by recessions, depressions, or catastrophic events. That did it; we decided to brew beer. Making a living from craft beer has turned out to be both fun and good fortune. The market is booming, and we have very supportive fans.

There are three partners in Frothy Beard Brewing Company. We met and became friends during our

Our specialty is creating beer from locally grown vegetables, herbs, fruits, and grains. We have had success with watermelon, peaches, lemons, black tea, brown rice, grits, and oyster mushrooms.

late teens and early twenties in the upstate of South Carolina. Despite diverse and seemingly unrelated experience, each of us plays a role that complements the others. Michael worked at the Smithsonian as an entomologist, and he handles the business operations. Steve was an EMS dispatcher. He handles packaging the beer into kegs or twenty-two-ounce bottles. Steve and I are both the brewmasters.

For six years, the three of us homebrewed beers together. We started inviting friends to tasting events. At each party, we'd pair a meal with six different homebrewed beers and send each friend home with a six-pack of the beers from that evening. This is how we built our following—through our friends, which rippled to their friends and more. Our unique creations got such rave reviews that it finally dawned on us to start our own brewery.

Restrictive state laws

When we went into business in March of 2013, there were only four local breweries in Charleston—Palmetto, Coast, Holy City, and Westbrook. At that time, it was illegal for South Carolina breweries to sell beer in-house. We could sell a brewery tour and include a flight, a sampler of beer consisting of four four-ounce pours, but not until the Pint Law passed in June 2013 were we allowed to sell up to three pints per customer at the brewery.

With the passing of the Pint Law, it became advantageous for West Coast breweries to open East Coast plants to save shipping costs and distribute a fresher and higher-quality beer. The Stone Brewery of San Diego was one example, and South Carolina wanted to attract their business. But Stone Brewery was looking for a state that would allow them to create a total brewery experience, one in which they could pair their beer with food. In the summer of 2014, thanks to the persistence and hard work of the South Carolina beer community, a law passed enabling a brewery to sell food along with unlimited beers, like any bar or restaurant, provided the kitchen was approved by the Department of Health and Environmental Control. The Stone Law opened more opportunities for breweries in the state.

Artisan creativity

Frothy Beard's brewing breaks from tradition. Our specialty is creating beer from locally grown vegetables, herbs, fruits, and grains. We have had success with watermelon, peaches, lemons, black tea, brown rice, grits, and oyster mushrooms. Our Oyster Mushroom Stout was a big hit at a local Mushroom Festival, and we created another unusual rice beer for a Rice Festival. Rice beers are typically lagers—light, crisp, and easy to drink, but we wanted to do something different. So we made a dark beer using local, organically grown and milled brown rice from Anson Mills. Our Horchata Stout has brown rice milk, cocoa, cinnamon, and vanilla; it is especially good paired with spicy foods. And our Ginger Pale Ale, using the ginger grown by local farmer John Warren, has a nice fragrant spice. Unfortunately, we can't brew our Ginger Pale Ale year-round, because John's ginger is only available in the fall.

Since we are in the South, we had to make a beer with grits, of course. So we created a Cream Ale using local Geechie Boy Mill grits. This kind of variety and creativity in our brewing wouldn't be possible if we weren't so small. We can easily take risks and try new ideas, because our full batches are only forty-six gallons.

Brewing beer

Typically, we will brew all day, clean up, and then come to the bar to pour beer for our customers.

Brewing takes about three weeks. During the warmer months when the demand for beer is at its peak, we brew a double batch four days a week. Each batch is forty-six gallons. Generally, we are brewing seven varieties of beers, but eventually we will have twenty taps.

We start with filtered Charleston water—beer is ninety-five percent water—to which we add a malted barley and other grains that we've crushed in a rolling mill to access the starch inside. We leave the husk intact to act as a filtering bed when we drain the liquid from the mash. We mix hot water and grain to create the mash, and we must maintain a specific temperature for an hour, at which point we recirculate the liquid in the mash back through itself using the grain bed to filter out the fine particulates. This filtered liquid is called the wort; it's essentially beer that hasn't fermented yet. We pump the wort to the boil kettle while we sparge, or sprinkle, the grain in the mash tun with additional hot water to rinse the remaining sugar from the mash.

Having performed all the calculations to make sure we have the right gravity, we bring the wort to a boil in a fifty-five-gallon pot. We take a gravity reading before and after the boil, and after fermentation. Gravity is a measurement of the density of the liquid. We take this reading to determine how much starch was converted to fermentable sugars. When the wort starts to boil, we add the hops, which bitters and balances the beer, and depending on the variety of hops, provides floral, piney, earthy, stone fruit, or citrus characteristics. During the boil, we remove the grain from the mash tun and save it for a local farmer's livestock feed.

There are more than 200 varieties of hops grown all over the United States. We purchase our hops through a hop broker, the Yakima Chief-Hopunion (YCH HOPS). Because brewers tend to be fickle with their tastes, the YCH HOPS works with their farmers to communicate trends and direct crop planning to meet market demand. This provides some stability and predictability for hops growers.

Day two through fermentation

This next step can take from one to three weeks, depending upon the type of beer. After boiling, the

wort is cooled through a heat exchanger and pushed into a fermenter, where we add the yeast. This is the most critical stage of brewing beer; the temperature and oxygen content must be exactly right for the yeast to do its job.

There are hundreds of different varieties of yeast. We typically use an English strain for most of Frothy Beard's beers, and occasionally a Belgian- or American-style yeast. Different yeasts yield different types of fermentation and different categories of beer. Ales are most common and ferment at a warmer temperature, between 62°F and 72°F. Lagers ferment at 45°F, are raised to 65°F, and then lowered to 35°F. Lagering takes more time, because the yeast is fermenting at a lower temperature and therefore is not as active. Lager yeast is also a bottom fermenting yeast, whereas ale yeasts ferment on the top. Lager is seen less frequently than ale from craft breweries, because it is slower to produce.

After the allotted fermentation time, we transfer the beer into the 35°F cold room, where we crash, or knock the yeast out with the cold. This step clarifies the beer. Then it is pumped into a specialized tank for carbonating. Carbonation generally takes two days, at which point we keg the beer.

Monitoring each stage by taste

Monitoring the beer throughout the entire process is important. We use a computer software program, EKOS Brewery Management out of Charlotte. This system monitors where each brew is along its journey, logging temperatures, times, ingredients, and other important data.

Another very valuable—and fun—way we monitor the beer is by tasting. Each stage gives us a sense of the beer's development and robustness. Tasting provides the most reliable measure of the beer's quality. I taste it and take notes after I do the mash, again after the boil, and after it's been in the fermenter for three, seven, and ten days. I taste it before and after it is carbonated. I also use a hydrometer to measure the density of the sugar. Tasting is a critical part of the monitoring, because after three to seven days, any off flavors would show up. Off flavors could occur if the yeast has been stressed, if we had the wrong temperature, or any of a myriad of things that must be managed precisely throughout the brewing process. If a batch isn't up to our standards, we dump it.

Cans are the preferred packaging and trendier in craft beers. Cans are recyclable, lighter, stronger, don't break, and don't let any light in. The downside is labeling. Each beer can requires a large volume to order, and then we have to find storage space. A canning machine is also more expensive than a bottling machine. Currently, we only package into 1/6 barrel (Bbl) kegs, 1/2 Bbl kegs, and 22-ounce bottles. (A barrel, Bbl, is the standard method for measuring beer.)

Brewing community

Since Frothy Beard Brewery opened three years ago, the number of breweries in Charleston has doubled. You'd think we'd be panicking because of the increased competition, but the brewing industry here is very supportive of one another. If one of us runs out of something, we share. We collaborate well and bring each other customers.

The sense of community extends past the breweries. As a local business receiving such amazing support from local customers, it is important that we give back by supporting and buying local products whenever we can. Frothy Beard is not alone in this initiative. Local breweries are supporting local farmers, local music, and local art through many diverse events and fundraisers that we do for the community.

My partners and I embrace being a small brewery. It's one of our greatest strengths, because it allows us to be creative, experiment, and break free from tradition. Frothy Beard wouldn't be possible without a community that embraces and celebrates small and local. ❧

Woody Collins
Mushroom Forager

A retired commercial fisherman, shrimper, and oysterman, Woody is now a certified mushroom forager. He and his wife, Lynn, tend a large garden, which along with the sea, handsomely provides for them year-round. Woody invited me to join him as he foraged in nearby woods, searching for golden chanterelle (SHAN-tuh-rel) mushrooms.

It was a sultry summer day, but Woody insisted that I wear heavy pants, long sleeves, a hat, and high boots. Before piling into the truck with his foraging friend William, I was dusted down with yellow sulfur to discourage chiggers. I certainly remembered the itch of chiggers—microscopic mites—from my childhood adventures. In their larval stage, they dig a hole in the skin of their host and feed on skin cells. The skin rash itches like crazy. I know, because the sulfur didn't work, and I miserably hosted chiggers for weeks after foraging with Woody and William.

Woody picked a location that would be relatively easy for hunting chanterelle mushrooms. He told me to follow in his footsteps, to watch for well-camouflaged poisonous snakes, and to avoid entanglement in banana spider webs crossing our path at head level. I grew up with brothers, so I don't get the creeps easily, but between venomous snakes and very large spiders at *face-level . . . well, yikes. Post-foraging, I was both relieved and disappointed not to photograph a coiled snake at our feet.*

Chasing chanterelles

If you were a local, I would have to blindfold you. We mushroom pickers are very particular about our special places. By law we are allowed to forage in national and state parks, certain wildlife reserves, public property, and private property with permission. I forage in about thirty different locations. William and I have learned the hard way to pay attention to our location in the forests, to keep an eye on the whereabouts of each other, and to know where we left the truck. It is easy to get seriously disoriented while chasing chanterelles.

I became a mushroom forager about fourteen years ago, but my interests were initially whetted in the late 1940s at the age of five. My grandfather, a Russian immigrant, was an avid forager and took me mushroom picking. I was very young and didn't really understand, but he explained that mushrooms are the fruit of an underground network of symbiotic relationships. They mysteriously appear when conditions are ideal, disperse their spores through wind, animals, and water, and then disappear. I learned there were different types of mushrooms and some were very poisonous. Those early experiences with my grandfather sparked an interest in mushrooms that I have carried all my life.

There are hundreds of different woodland species out here. Today, we're searching for the orange, funnel-shaped chanterelles, but I also keep my eye out for other mushrooms, especially the "chicken of the woods," which can weigh twelve pounds or more.

I don't forage early in the morning, because I want as much sunshine in the forest as possible to improve my sight. There are lots of well-camouflaged copperheads and canebrake rattlesnakes in these woods. I was reaching down for a chanterelle recently and put my hand right on a copperhead. These snakes scare me to death! I made a stick with a metal hook on the end for harvesting chanterelles so I won't repeat that experience. I don't pick as quickly with the stick as I do with my hands, but I feel a lot more comfortable about my safety. I can also wave it in front of my face to fend my way through the thickly woven spider webs. Don't worry about the spiders though; they're large and aggravating, but won't hurt you.

Scattered and camouflaged in the forest litter are batches of mushrooms—flushes of chanterelles. We've hit the mother lode today, but it isn't always as easy as this. Before I put any mushrooms in my basket, I pop the end off to get rid of the dirt. I also check each one. Here's one that is not good. It has a little fungus on its outer tip, and if I put it in the basket, the fungus will spread to the other mushrooms.

A delicious mystery

Chanterelles are the most widely eaten mushrooms in the world. They have been in existence and valued for millennium. In 1991, when Ötzi, the 5,300-year-old iceman preserved in the glacial Ötztal Valley Alps of Austria and Italy, was discovered, he had a small cache of mushrooms at his side.

There are probably twenty different kinds of edible mushrooms in these woods. Chanterelles are plentiful and easy to identify, and chefs love them. William and I normally pick four to six hours per day about four days per week. There doesn't seem to be any relationship between the amount one picks and the amount that may bloom again, but there is evidence that proper harvesting can promote regeneration. Two years ago, I harvested 1,000 pounds of chanterelles; last year I only found half that many.

Some mushrooms can be cultivated—like the oyster and shitake mushrooms that the Trappist monks at Mepkin Abbey grow from spawn. For centuries the Russians, French, Germans, and others have attempted to cultivate chanterelles, to no avail. To date, the chanterelle has eluded scientists and others in their attempts at cultivation.

Chanterelle season runs from May through September in coastal South Carolina. They are extremely weather dependent and somewhat mysterious. They seem to pop up after a large rainstorm followed by very hot weather. I've seen them growing in leaf litter, tall grasses, direct light, dappled light, and in full shade. Although we have successfully picked in this area five times this season, we have also been here looking for them ten other times under conditions that we thought were ideal and have not found one. As mysteriously as they appear, they will vanish in seven days; they just disappear back into the earth.

Decades of symbiosis

Mushrooms are saprophytes. They convert decaying organic matter from the soil into energy. Because they don't photosynthesize or contain chlorophyll, mushrooms produce a different set of nutrients. They are a great source of vitamins C, D, and potassium. They are high in protein, can be eaten as a meat substitute, and are touted to possess anti-carcinogenic qualities. Chanterelles also harbor a natural pesticide with the ability to repel about ninety-five percent of the insects that prey on other mushrooms.

The chanterelle is the fruit of an underground and invisible mycorrhizal relationship with a very old tree, which in South Carolina is normally a live oak tree. (The word mycorrhiza is a combination of two words—mycelium, the underground network of filaments attached to the fungus, and rhizosphere, the soil surrounding the roots of vascular plants.) Not all symbiotic relationships are beneficial to both parties, but in this case the relationship is mutualistic—beneficial to both. A tree must be sixty years old before the fungus colonizes its root system. Then the mycelium and the rhizosphere develop a relationship that grows for twenty more years before the mycorrhiza produces active mushrooms. A magical relationship develops underground over decades before one of these chanterelles appears.

Identification and certification

As recent as July 2014, it was illegal for chefs to purchase foraged mushrooms in South Carolina. When the local food hub GrowFood Carolina started five years ago, manager Sara Clow was shocked to learn that the sale of foraged mushrooms was illegal. In an effort to promote the local food system, GrowFood Carolina, the Coastal Conservation League, and local mycologists worked with Department of Health and Environmental Control (DHEC) to develop a program to legally harvest and sell wild mushrooms in the state.

In August of 2014, the first class of certified foragers graduated with Certified South Carolina Mushroom Identification Permits, which we are required to carry. The permit states which types of mushrooms we are certified to sell. We are also required to keep a journal stating where, what, and when we picked. So if a DHEC investigator were to

Because they don't photosynthesize or contain chlorophyll, mushrooms produce a different set of nutrients. They are a great source of vitamins C, D, and potassium. They are high in protein and can be eaten as a meat substitute.

go into a restaurant and ask where the mushrooms came from, the restaurant has a receipt that provides it with all that information. Additionally, when we sell mushrooms directly to a restaurant or through GrowFood, we have to be on call twenty-four hours per day in the event someone gets sick.

Mushroom identification keys identify if a mushroom is poisonous or safe for consumption. There are a number of indicators that alert foragers if a mushroom is poisonous—if its stem is bulbous on the bottom, if the gills are open, how the gills are attached to the umbrella cap and stalk-like stem, and the smell and color when you break the stem. No one should ever pick a mushroom to eat, unless they really know what they are doing. Less than one percent of mushrooms can kill you, but many can make you very sick. The primary indicator of whether a person has consumed a poisonous mushroom has to do with the length of time between eating it and when sickness occurs. Symptoms may range from dizziness and stomach cramps to hallucinations or death.

The Jack-o-lantern and the false chanterelle are two seriously poisonous look-a-likes that can grow alongside the chanterelles. We know them well. A false chanterelle has the same general color, but it is lighter on the inside and its gills are open, whereas a chanterelle's gills are closed. A person not properly educated can make this mistake. The Jack-o-lantern, the more dangerous of the look-a-likes, is yellow inside and outside, and it exhibits a bioluminescence in the dark.

Culinary delights

After foraging, I immediately shower, keeping an eye out for ticks, and thoroughly scrub down with alcohol for chiggers. Then I record my foraging notes, weigh and box the mushrooms, and deliver them to GrowFood Carolina in Charleston. Upon delivery, GrowFood weighs them again, and when they sell them, they will be weighed one more time, as they will lose a bit of moisture/weight. Chanterelles have a two-week shelf life if kept between 38°F and 42°F,

although they are in such high demand that they are never around for long.

Chanterelles are a choice culinary item, and they must be cooked to reveal their desirable flavor. They are pricy, but chefs know what to do to make them worth the expense.

Like the fruits from our garden and the fruits from the sea, these fruits from the woods are healthy and good for us. Our diet is our choice. So many people fill their bodies with unhealthy stuff, stuff they don't need, stuff that won't fuel them, stuff that is harmful. The analogy I use with my grandchildren is this: "You could put the garden hose in your car's fuel tank and fill it up, and the tank would register full, but you can't go anywhere. You need the right kind of fuel."

The childhood foraging adventures with my grandfather inspire me to forage fifty years later. I get great satisfaction from being in nature, and delight in the challenge of hunting chanterelles. But equally, I love to eat them! I had them with my eggs this morning and with shrimp and grits last night. They are golden delicacies. ❧

Ashlyn Spilis Hochschild
and Abby Tennenbaum
College of Charleston, Office of Sustainability

The College of Charleston (CofC) is an urban campus with an undergraduate enrollment of more than 10,000 students. The school's dining services serve 3,500 meals per day. Imagine the impact it would have on the local economy, local farmers, local land use, and the environment if the food services program at College of Charleston sourced local foods for their daily use. Thanks to the vision and hard work of these young women and their colleagues, relationships have been fostered between Aramark Food Services and the local food hub, GrowFood Carolina. The college has become more sustainable, and GrowFood Carolina has a new institutional customer.

Making CofC sustainable

Ashlyn: The College of Charleston's Office of

▲ Above: Ashlyn and Abby.

Sustainability started in 2011, and I have been a graduate assistant for the program since its inception. I manage the internship program; develop personal and professional programs; plan events, workshops,

Food is such a universally compelling issue. It ties us to every environmental and health issue, to social issues, and to the economy. If we, the College of Charleston, can make a multi-faceted impact by doing business with local food providers and minimizing our waste, we will truly contribute to creating a more sustainable world.

field trips, and conferences; and coordinate the college's Sustainability Week each April.

Twenty-five undergraduate students are working on a host of different sustainability projects, the goal being to empower students to create change through sustainable decisions and actions with respect to food, waste, and transportation. I believe our aspirations are noble and encouraging for the future. Projects include a Sustainable Transportation Initiative with bike sharing, bike safety, and promoting sustainable (not alternative) transportation; a Zero Waste Program that promotes better recycling to achieve zero waste by 2025; a Garden Apprenticeship Program; and a Sustainable Greek Chair Initiative to involve students in fraternities and sororities in our sustainability efforts.

Aspiring for a 100 percent locally sourced dinner

Abby: Aramark is the food corporation that runs everything related to food services for the College of Charleston, from procurement to food waste disposal. The first time I worked with Aramark was during the fall of 2012, when I helped organize a benefit dinner for National Food Day through Green CofC, a sustainability student group on campus.

We decided that National Food Day would be our way to celebrate and highlight the budding local food movement in Charleston. A couple months earlier we met with Sara Clow, general manager of GrowFood Carolina, the food distribution hub for local farmers, and Lisa Turansky, director of Food and Agriculture with the Coastal Conservation League, to discuss procurement of local foods. Initially, we wanted Butcher & Bee to cater the event, because it is a local restaurant owned by a College of Charleston graduate. However, Aramark did not want to contract out the food order and suggested we source the food for the event through a local food distributor

that serves the tri-counties around Charleston, but sources food from around the country. When we looked at that distributor's food availability list, the only local item at that time was Mepkin Abbey mushrooms. One of Aramark's chefs wondered if we could buy from GrowFood Carolina, and so I became the middlewoman, communicating between GrowFood and Aramark.

In the weeks leading up to the event, nerves were high, because I would send GrowFood's availability list to Aramark, and they would send me a draft menu, which would include items that were not sourced locally. Aramark simply wasn't accustomed to making this a priority. And we were adamantly committed to locally sourced food for this event, without compromise. In the end, we were able to work it out.

Our National Food Day event was held October 24, 2012. It was the first ever 100 percent locally sourced and zero waste event the College of Charleston hosted, and it was a big success. The relationships created with Aramark that began that fall continued to progress. The following April, during Sustainability Week 2013, all catered events used locally sourced ingredients.

Waist deep in waste

In the spring of 2013, my internship with the Office of Sustainability focused on the feasibility of the college's dining halls to compost their food waste. Ashlyn and I conducted multiple waste audits, spending many hours elbow-deep in dining hall trash cans and buckets full of other people's food waste, sorting it and measuring how much and what types of food waste were being thrown out. Our persistence and enthusiasm during this project led to a cooperative relationship between students, the Office of Sustainability, and Aramark. Today, all food wastes generated on campus—from dining halls to auxiliary locations and catering events—are being composted.

By the fall of 2013, even more amazing progress was made. Sourcing locally was normalized with Aramark. In the fall of 2013, Green CofC held a benefit dinner in which 100 percent was locally sourced, zero waste was created, and all ticket proceeds went to a local nonprofit. The event was inspiring, and Chef Jason Sisson from Aramark spoke about his excitement working with local and unfamiliar items and his realization of the importance of a local food system.

Ashlyn and I have continued to encourage the GrowFood Carolina-Aramark connection. We learned that sustainable change only happens when we work together. This is a learning process for Aramark, the college, and for us at the Office of Sustainability, and we are all learning together.

The compelling issue of local food

Ashlyn: After working with Abby on the composting program, I became Aramark's Sustainability Intern in addition to my role at the Sustainability Office. I began tracking food purchasing for the dining halls and calculating the percentage of food purchased locally—within 250 miles of the college. Since that first data collection, also the subject of my graduate work, Aramark has continued to improve sourcing and tracking efforts.

GrowFood Carolina was officially approved as a vendor for the college in May 2015, which means that Aramark can now use GrowFood produce and pantry items, not only for catered events, but in the dining halls, too. This semester, Aramark purchased a lot of local, organic blueberries from GrowFood. There's an amazing amount of potential with the new relationship.

Food is such a universally compelling issue. It ties us to every environmental and health issue, to social issues, and to the economy. If we, the College of Charleston, can make a multi-faceted impact by doing business with local food providers and minimizing our waste, we will truly contribute to creating a more sustainable world. ❧

▼ One of many sustainability projects.

Contributors

Abundant Seafood
Mark and Kerry Marhefka
Gechee Dock, 248 Magwood Lane
Mt Pleasant, SC 29464
843-478-5078
abundantseafood@gmail.com
abundantseafood.com

Ambrose Family Farm and
Stono Market & Tomato Shed Café
Pete, Babs, and Barbara Ambrose
842 Main Road
Johns Island, SC 29455
843-559-9999
FAX 843-559-9957
stonofarmmarket.com
ambrosefamilyfarm.com

Anson Mills
Glenn Roberts
1922 C Gervais Street
Columbia, SC 29201
803-467-4122
info@ansonmills.com
ansonmills.com

Black Pearl Farms
David Anderson
1411 Gervais Street, Suite 501
Columbia, SC 29201
803-261-3225
info@blackpearlfarmssc.com
blackpearlfarmssc.com

The Bee Cause
Tami Enright
703-400-4473
tami.enright@gmail.com
thebeecause.org

Brant Family Farm
Don and Susan Brant
3585 Pineland Road
Varnville, SC 29944
843-812-0084
donsusanbrant@gmail.com

Brickyard Point Farms
Jim and Nancy Rathbun
PO Box 249
Port Royal, SC 29935
240 Johnson Landing Road
Lady's Island, SC 29907
farm landline: 843-521-1400
703-915-5208
jim@brickyardpointfarms.com
brickyardpointfarms.com

Bulls Bay Saltworks
Teresa and Rustin Gooden
PO Box 656
McClellanville, SC 29458
843-887-3007
teresa@bullsbaysaltworks.com
bullsbaysaltworks.com

Butcher & Bee
Michael Shemtov
1085 Morrison Drive
Charleston, SC 29403
843-619-0202
info@butcherandbee.com
butcherandbee.com

Carolina Plantation Rice
Campbell Coxe
1515 Mont Clare Road
Darlington, SC 29540
843-393-1812
cpricesale@aol.com
rice@carolinaplantationrice.com
carolinaplantationrice.com

Charleston Artisan Cheesehouse
Heather and Pete Holmes
Greg and Monica Tatis
2457 Ashley River Road, Suite 3
Charleston, SC 29407
843-620-9118
chscheesehouse@charlestoncheesehouse.com
charlestonartisancheesehouse.com

Charleston Collegiate School
Hacker Burr
2024 Academy Road
Johns Island, SC 29455
843-559-5506
charlestoncollegiate.org

Charleston Collegiate School Garden
Kathee Dowis
2024 Academy Road
Johns Island, SC 29455
843-559-5506
kdowis@charlestoncollegiate.org
charlestoncollegiate.org

City Roots
Eric McClam
1005 Airport Boulevard
Columbia, SC 29205
803-254-2302
eric@cityroots.org
cityroots.org

Clemson University Extension Service
Powell Smith
605 W. Main Street, Suite 109
Lexington, SC 29070
893-359-8515
jpsmith@clemson.edu

Clemson's Coastal Research
and Education Center
Merle Shepard, Ph.D.
Brian K. Ward, Ph.D.
2700 Savannah Highway
Charleston, SC 29414
843-402-5389
mshprd@clemson.edu
bw@clemson.edu
clemson.edu/public/coastal/

College of Charleston
Office of Sustainability
Ashlyn Spilis Hochschild
and Abigail Tennenbaum
284-A King Street
Charleston, SC 29424
asphoch@gmail.com
abigailtennenbaum@gmail.com
sustainability.cofc.edu

EVO (Extra Virgin Oven) Pizzeria
Ricky Hacker and Matt McIntosh
1075 East Montague Avenue
North Charleston, SC 29405
843-225-1796
ricky@evopizza.com
matt@evopizza.com
evopizza.com

FIG (Food Is Good) Restaurant
The Ordinary
Mike Lata
eatatfig.com
eattheordinary.com

Frank Lee
#13 26th Ave
Isle of Palm, SC 29451
843-208-0757
defchad2@gmail.com

Fresh Future Farm and Market
Germaine Jenkins
2008 Success Street
North Charleston, SC 29405
PO Box 22194
Charleston, SC 29413
mobile: 843-276-8552
farm store: 843-804-9091
freshfuturefarm@gmail.com
freshfuturefarm.org

Frothy Beard Brewing Company
Joey Siconolfi
1401 Sam Rittenberg Boulevard, Suite One
Charleston, SC 29407
843-872-4201
joey@frothybeard.com
frothybeard.com

Georgia Olive Farms
Kevin Shaw
PO Box 245
Lakeland, GA 31635
229-482-3505
brandi@georgiaolivefarms.com
georgiaolivefarms.com
gaylasgrits.com

The Green Heart Project
Drew Harrison
124 Magnolia Avenue
Charleston, SC 29403
drew@greenheartsc.org
greenheartsc.org

GrowFood Carolina
Sara Clow
990 Morrison Drive
Charleston, SC 29403
Warehouse: 843-727-0091
info@growfoodcarolina.com
growfoodcarolina.com

Herbalicious
Andrea Cooler
Beaufort, SC 22902
843-252-9178
andreacooler@yahoo.com
herbaliciousmicrogreens.com

Hickory Bluff Berry Farm
Walter and Cathy Earley
245 Hickory Bluff Lane
Holly Hill, SC 29059
843-743-8244
hickorybluff@gmail.com
hickorybluffberries.com

High Wire Distilling Co.
Scott Blackwell and Ann Marshall
652 King Street, Suite A
Charleston, SC 29403
843-755-4664
scott@highwiredistilling.com
am@highwiredistilling.com
highwiredistilling.com

Hunter Cattle Company
Del and Debra Ferguson
934 Driggers Road
Brooklet, GA 30415
912-823-BEEF
huntercattle.com

Husk Restaurant
Travis Grimes
76 Queen Street
Charleston, SC 29401
843-577-2500
huskrestaurant.com

Jeremiah Farm
Tim and Casey Price
3853 Platt Road
John's Island, SC 29455
843-276-3115
jeremiahfarmsc@aol.com
jeremiahfarm.com

Johns Island Farmers Market
Frasier Block
Held every Saturday at: 2024 Academy Road
Campus of Charleston Collegiate School
Johns Island, SC 29455
mailing: PO Box 25
Johns Island, SC 29457
johnsislandfarmersmarket@gmail.com
johnsislandfarmersmarket.com

Karalee Nielsen Fallert
Restaurateur and Founder
of the Green Heart Project
217 Huger Street
Charleston, SC 29403
843-478-4141
karalee195@gmail.com
tacoboy.net

Kate and Lindsay Nevin
1630 Meeting Street Road
Charleston, SC 29405
843-853-5557
kate@tswii.com
lindsay@flywaysc.com

Keegan–Filion Farm
Marc Filion
1475 Keegan Drive
Walterboro, SC 29488
843-538-2565
akfilion@yahoo.com
keeganfilionfarm.com

Lady's Island Oysters
Frank Roberts
16 Marsh Oaks Lane
Seabrook, SC 29940
843-473-5018
ladyislandoyster@gmail.com
singleladyoysters.com

Landsdowne Dairy and
Lowcountry Creamery
Josh Brooks
Patrick Myers
Kent Whetsell
info@lowcountrycreamery.com
lowcountrycreamery.com

Lavington Farms
Jimmy Hagood
PO Box 30279
Charleston, SC 29417
843-224-1243
jimmy@fftss.com
foodforthesouthernsoul.com

Livingston's Bulls Bay Seafood
Bill and Kathy Livingston
Jeff Massey
631 Morrison Street
PO Box 70
McClellanville, SC 29458
843-887-3519
livbullbay@aol.com
jeff@bullsbayclams.com
bullsbayseafood.wordpress.com

Lowcountry Local First
Jamee Haley
1630 Meeting Street, Building #2
Charleston, SC 29405
843-801-3390
mobile: 843-224-1243
jamee@lowcountrylocalfirst.org
lowcountrylocalfirst.org

Mepkin Abbey
Father Stan
1098 Mepkin Abbey Road
Moncks Corner, SC 29461
843-761-8509
brstan41@gmail.com
mepkinabbey.org

MUSC Urban Farm
Carmen Ketron and Noni Langford
97 Jonathan Lucas Street, MSC 190
Charleston, SC 29425
843-990-3121
ketron@musc.edu
academicdepartments.musc.edu/ohp/
urban-farm

Old Tyme Bean Company
Josh Johnson
9300 Old State Road
Cameron, SC 29030
803-682-6040
farmerjoshjohnson@yahoo.com

Origin Farm
Lucie Kulze
843-607-6906
lkulze@gmail.com

Sea Island Jerseys
Celeste and George Albers
2463 Leadenwah Drive
Wadmalaw Island, SC 29487
seaislandjerseys@gmail.com

Shuler Peach Company
Elliott Shuler
3627 Vance Road
Holly Hill, SC 29059
803-759-0089
shulerpeachcompany@gmail.com

SILO–Sea Islands Local Outlet
Patrick Kelly
bkpatri@gmail.com
864-344-3113
SILO is under new management:
Walt Raines
SILO-Market, LLC
7A Market #1
Beaufort, SC 29906
843-466-9833
manager@silo-beaufort.com
silo-beaufort.com

Tiger Corner Farms
Boxcar Central
Stefanie Swackhamer
David Flynn
106 W 7th North Street
Summerville, SC 29483
stefanie@tigercornerfarms.com
david.flynn@boxcarcentral.com
tigercornerfarmsmfg.com
boxcarcentrallc.com

Urbie West
191 Seabrook Road
Seabrook, SC 29940
843-592-3535
urbiewest@thegreeneryinc.com

Veggie Bin
Michael and Lauren Bailey
96 Spring Street
Charleston, SC 29403
843-779-0301

Wabi Sabi Farm
Jimmy and Johnna Livingston
685 Anderson Lane
Cordesville, SC 29434
843-312-0856
jlivingston@homesc.com

Williams Muscadine Vineyard & Farm
Cassandra Williams Rush
David A. Williams
21 Gabriel Place
Nesmith, SC 29580
803-397-1859
crushcolumbia@aol.com

Woody Collins
83 Huspah Drive
Seabrook, SC 29940
woodycollins9@gmail.com

Index